# Broken Silences

■

# Broken Silences

## Interviews with Black and White Women Writers

■

EDITED BY

## Shirley M. Jordan

RUTGERS UNIVERSITY PRESS

NEW BRUNSWICK, NEW JERSEY

Library of Congress Cataloging-in-Publication Data

Broken silences : interviews with Black and White women writers /

edited by Shirley M. Jordan.

   p.  cm.

   ISBN 0-8135-1932-2 (cloth)—ISBN 0-8135-1933-0 (pbk.)

   1. Afro-American women authors—20th century—Interviews. 2. Women authors, American—20th

century—Interviews.  3. Afro-American women—Intellectual life. 4. Women—United States—

Intellectual life.  5. Afro-Americans in literature.  6. Race relations in literature.  7. Whites in

literature.  I. Jordan, Shirley Marie.

PS153.N5B665  1993

810.9'9287—dc20

[B]                                            92-28914

                                                    CIP

British Cataloging-in-Publication information available

I dedicate this book

to that chorus of sisterhood,

the women writers who have broken

the silence to celebrate

our differences and embrace

our similarities,

and to women everywhere

who have the courage

to love each other

in spite of everything.

# CONTENTS

■

*The mutual history of black and white women
in this country is a realm so painful, resonant,
and forbidden that it has barely been touched by
writers either of political "science" or of
imaginative literature. Yet until that history is
known, that silence broken, we will all go on
struggling in a state of deprivation and ignorance.*

ADRIENNE RICH


*I would that I could speak of
white womanhood as it will and
should be
when it stands tall in full
equality
But then, womanhood will be womanhood,
void of color and class,
and all necessity for my speaking
thus will be past.*

*White supremacy is your own enemy and mine
so be careful when you talk with me;
remind me not of my slavery;
I know it well.
But rather tell me of your own,
Remember, you have never known me.
You've been seeing me as white supremacy
would have me be.*

BEAH RICHARDS

# PREFACE

■

The history of the relationship between black and white women is a tangle of suspicion, mistrust, resentment, anger, curiosity, and fear that remains submerged in silence, superficial courtesy, and shallow tolerance. Despite these barriers, some women develop rewarding, long-lasting friendships rooted in honesty, mutual respect, genuine acceptance—all necessary ingredients for building the trust that is the foundation for friendship. *Broken Silences* is meant as a forum for black and white women to enter a dialogue concerning their perceptions of each other as individuals and as artists.

Initially, I thought that the two central questions to this volume of interviews would be, Can black and white women be friends and can black and white women authors create "authentic" interpretations of each others' lives in fiction? As I review my work over the past two years, I find the first question too limited. Of course, black and white women can be friends. Numerous examples in history and in current society illustrate that barriers such as race, ethnicity, class, and age can be overcome if both parties genuinely accept each other as equals, though replete with human failings. A sincere desire to know the other opens the gates for dialogue, trust, and possible friendship.

My question, therefore, is no longer whether black and white women can be friends, but why do we perpetuate the silence between us? Why do we allow our shared history to remain buried when understanding how that history has devastated all our lives might help us to comprehend and overcome the racism and sexism so prevalent in America today? And why do we not see that any discriminatory practice causes us all to lose? These questions address the forces that keep the races apart, and until we come to terms with the issues behind them, friendships must remain secondary. Unless we come to terms with the pain, the mistrust, and the misgivings that developed in slave society to keep both groups in their places, that pain and mistrust and all the negative effects of not facing the truth will continue to enslave us. We have already paid an enormous price in loss of hope, in diminished dignity, and in untold suffering because we held our tongues. It is better to speak out, and we will be better for having spoken out.

Some forms of racism and sexism are often so disguised now that upcoming generations will perpetuate them and suffer their consequences without fully understanding their effects or the need for eradicating them. In fact, the less we talk about "the race problem," the more insidious the forms racism will take and the more ingrained they will become on people's hearts, where change is slowest. Speaking to one another allows us to confront the roots of our misperceptions, misconceptions, resentments, and fears. Friendship between black and white women will evolve naturally, but that is not the key concern. Of utmost importance to me is that we genuinely accept one another for who we are, that we respect our differences and celebrate what we have in common. Whether we become friends or not, we still need to grant one another a certain measure of respect just as human beings. That means that I can walk into any store without having a salesclerk stare me down just because I am black, while white customers roam freely. That means that I do not see a blond white woman walking down the street and assume that she does not have a care in the world and that she cannot think for herself. Both images—the untrustworthy black person and the dumb blonde—have historical roots developed to the advantage of some and the disadvantage of others. We must break the silence about why those images were formed and why—often with the complicity of women—they have persisted.

*Broken Silences* is actually the culmination of several ideas that came to a focus even as I conducted these interviews. In graduate school I first became interested in examining how whites were portrayed in black literature. I had read a number of works that explored the image of blacks in white literature, but had seen very little systematic study of the reverse.

At about the same time I had been reading Harriet Wilson's *Our Nig*, published in 1859 and now considered to be the first novel by a black American published in the United States. Questions rose in my mind concerning the voice of the black female character in fiction. The protagonist of *Our Nig* suffers beating after beating at the hands of her cruel mistress. The narrator, however, rarely penetrates the inner consciousness of the protagonist as she reacts to and reflects on her torture. Yet the character still manages to tell her own story. Much of her voice is determined by what the whites, particularly the cruel white mistress, say and do not say. I began to look at other novels in which female slaves were depicted to see on what terms they gave voice to their experiences. It seemed that in most instances black women spoke through their white female counterparts. Depending on the artistic skill and the worldview of the writer, black female slaves were depicted with varying degrees of humanness. Initially, the voices of even black female protagonists, whether in novels by black or white women, were often subordinated to that of white females in order that the black female's story be told at all. Ironically, in Harriet Wilson's novel, it is this subversion of the black voice by the white that empowers the narrator to speak.

These observations led to several literary questions that I filed away for future study, but was able to start examining for a book of literary criticism. Since the black female protagonist, as far as I know, does not exist before 1853 with the publication of William Wells Brown's *Clotelle, or the President's Daughter,* she is not entrapped in the plot expectations of her white counterparts. And for readers at the time, she existed as part of a cultural text only as a vague, ambiguous entity with no humanity or even life outside service to her owners. How then does a novelist, especially a black female, create a "heroine" or protagonist to enter a literary tradition when the very cultural text from which such a heroine is drawn renders her *and her author* voiceless and powerless to change that condition? In other words, how does Wilson, who is marginal to any cultural text her readers might know, locate an entrance for herself and her "heroine"? Exactly which story does she choose to tell? How much control does she grant to the narrator to tell the story? How much to the protagonist if the protagonist and the narrator are not one and the same? What kind of narrator appears to be most effective? How does the author use the literary constructs of her day to tell her story? Does she invent or experiment with new narrative strategies, or does she adhere strictly to convention? Does the white female author use similar strategies to tell the stories of black women's lives? Which specific strategies appear to be most liberating for black female voices? And what role does the audience appear to play in shaping stories of black women's experiences? I expanded this cross-racial study of female writers' creation of black female characters to include as many writers as I could find, from Sherley Anne Williams's *Dessa Rose* to Jo Sinclair's *Changelings* to Lillian Smith's *Strange Fruit* to Fannie Hurst's *Imitation of Life* to Willa Cather's *Sapphira and the Slave Girl* and a host of others, covering nearly 140 years of literary history.

Of course, the same questions that I pose of black and white women authors concerning black female voices in fiction could also be asked of male writers. William Wells Brown's *Clotelle, or the President's Daughter,* the first novel written by a black American, which was published in London in 1853, raises some of the same questions as Carl van Vechten's *Nigger Heaven.* As my research began to take shape, however, I found it necessary to limit my study to how black and white women writers depict female characters with racial identities different from their own. It seemed more useful at this point in the research to limit such a comparative study to cross-racial lines than to complicate interpretations of any findings with consideration of gender differences too.

Besides, it is the silence out of which women's voices, especially black women's voices, emerge that I find most compelling. I also believe that the silence that exists between black and white women concerning their common history, to include their differences and their natural bonds, to be one of the most destructive forces in our communities. Women are unquestionably oppressed, but they can wield enormous power when they are convinced of the truth and act on it. They certainly play a major role in how children are raised and shaped. If we women build on our inner strength, we can make significant strides toward ending oppression for all people. As Adrienne Rich suggests, until we acknowledge that truth about our past and learn from it, we bind ourselves in chains of "deprivation and ignorance." And if we choose those chains, we must accept the responsibility for them.

Another set of research questions that prompted me to examine the relations between black and white women in women's fiction was raised by an experience that was both personal and literary in nature. During the summer following graduate school, I went to live for a time with a newfound white friend and her family in Cincinnati, Ohio, before starting my teaching assignment at the University of Cincinnati that fall. One day my friend brought me a copy of Julia Peterkin's *Scarlet Sister Mary,* a Pulitzer Prize–winning novel. "This book about a black woman's life is so good, you must read it," my friend said. "I don't know the writer, but the book must have been written by a black woman, because a white woman would not have been able to do such a fine job of writing it." How could I have missed this novel? I thought Alice Walker was the first black woman to win the prize for fiction. Could this have been another of those buried treasures we were rediscovering? I couldn't imagine how this oversight could have occurred, but I was certainly just as excited as my friend. The first pages weren't very interesting, but it often takes time for a story to engage the reader so I tried to settle into the pacing of the work. Sometimes we enter an artistic experience so laden with expectations from the praise it has already received that it is difficult to meet the work on its own terms. I needed to separate my friend's voice from the work before me. I, therefore, set the book aside and returned to it fresh and a little more distanced from the echoes of praise and expectation.

Even so, the work did not flow for me. For me, the character simply did not live. I didn't recognize her voice. In fact, I became increasingly more interested in who Julia Peterkin might be than I was in listening to the noises escaping from Scarlet Sister Mary. Did a black woman really write this novel? Perhaps after reading so much Morrison, Walker, Naylor, Marshall, Hurston, Guy, Hunter, Jones, and others I had become a little too sensitive to what I expected to hear in a black female character's voice. Even when a character could not speak directly for herself as in the case of Wilson's protagonist, I had no problem believing that Our Nig was the work of a black woman—a conclusion I came to without having read Henry Louis Gates's long introduction verifying Wilson's authorship. Something rang false about Peterkin's protagonist, and that falseness disturbed me. The action seemed believable enough, but the character seemed cardboard.

I went to the library to look up Julia Peterkin and discovered that she was white. Only then did parts of the puzzle start to fall into place for me. Julia Peterkin did not know Scarlet Sister Mary; she may have known of her, but she had not lived in her world, or, if she had, she certainly had not communicated that to me. She may have employed her, played with her, even visited her home on occasion, but she had never "walked in her shoes."

Was I being fair to this work and this writer? What of my white friend, whom I respected as a person, a thinker, and a scholar and whom I absolutely adored? Was I now saying that white women cannot even recognize unrealistic portraits of black women, much less write realistic ones? Could black women not do the same of white characters? Must the writer only write what she knows first-hand? Could not another black woman have read the book and come to the same conclusion as my friend? Could not a white woman have read the book and thought the same as I? Had I not read novels by black women that were disappointing in some way? Was I simply placing too much of the weight for explaining the difference in our responses on race? These are tough questions, for which I have not worked out satisfactory answers. Of course, I know that writers can and do write moving, realistic portrayals that are far removed from their own racial, gender, class, or age identities. Lillian Smith's *Strange Fruit* is one of the most compelling novels I have read, and all the characters ring true for me—black and white, male and female, young and old, rich and poor—all walk and talk for me. And I have read other novels by white women in which the same is true, so I would never conclude that writers cannot escape the limitations of their own experience. They can go anywhere their imaginations will take them, and they can do an exceedingly fine job of rendering their characters whole, *if* they also accept the responsibility of believing in each character's basic humanity. The writer must also be able to understand and treat difference as a natural part of life rather than as an anomaly in human existence. Difference is as much a part of our humanity as the bonds of experience that connect us.

Out of this experience, I have had to reassess my own expectations of relations with whites. I know my friend to be a good person. I also know that she understands many different kinds of discrimination, racial discrimination included. She has walked through any number of experiences in which I was a victim of racial and sexual discrimination. But that does not mean that I can generalize that she will understand all racial discrimination in the same way or as deeply as I. I believe that it also means that I cannot grasp some aspects of her worldview and life experiences as she does. We, therefore, can read the same book and have totally contrasting responses.

And finally, reading being a very subjective experience, I cannot dismiss the fact that our differing responses may have had more to do with personal preference than with critical judgment. Perhaps because race had been a factor in my high expectations for the book, I saw race as the deciding factor in our responses. After all, the Pulitzer Prize committee had apparently agreed wholeheartedly with my friend; perhaps other blacks felt the same.

It was against this backdrop of research questions and personal experiences that I began to work on a book of literary criticism and on a set of interviews with contemporary writers. As the latter project took shape, I had to devote most of my time to its completion, and I believe that it has sharpened my insights for the book of criticism. I felt that by selecting writers who have either portrayed a female character with a racial identity different from their own or who have depicted black and white women interacting, the work itself would come to focus on the common experiences that shape the creative process and the social and historical factors that have contributed to the "peculiar sisterhood" that has developed between black and white women.

Each interview has two major sections; the first is a set of general questions posed to each author in three basic areas:

1. Relations between black and white women in fiction and in their contemporary social and literary environment
2. The writer's own creative process in general and, if different, in the actual development of fiction in which the character differs from her race (use of written and oral histories, biographies, personal experiences, etc.)
3. The role of audience—editors, readers, critics—in the creative process and the writer's sense of control over her own voice in relation to it

Since one of the concerns of women writers, like that of most working women, is balancing responsibilities to family, career, and self, I also posed a question to address how the authors resolved any such conflict. None of the writers suggested that she would choose career over family, but most seemed to feel that at times the amount of work they produced was affected by the responsibilities of raising children and/or maintaining their marriages. In some instances, promoting newly published works had made enormous demands on their time and artistic energy. Such professional obligations, however, are part of a writer's life.

The second section of the interview focuses on the novel and/or short stories under discussion. Here each writer addresses questions concerning theme, point of view, character, and, to a lesser degree, style. The writer also looks at her particular goals in creating a female character of a different race and the degree to which she feels that she succeeded in developing that desired portrait. Out of that discussion usually arose a number of suggestions regarding limitations of race, if any, in crossing racial boundaries in fiction and the uneasiness that often accompanies such endeavors. Most of the questions focused either on the black or white female character; some of them were also designed to illuminate the work as a whole and to give a sense of the writer's own "search for truth."

Initially, I sent query letters mainly to black writers because I was most familiar with their work. Sherley Anne Williams was the first to respond, and I conducted my first interview in November 1989. In fact, during the early stages of my interviewing process, I found myself playing back Williams's words of encouragement. That interview was also most instructive in that it showed me just how important it is not to enter an interview with preconceived notions, especially those drawn along racial lines. One of the questions I asked each writer is drawn from the data I had collected comparing the number of white women who portray black women in fiction with the number of black women who portray white female characters. I asked each writer to comment on this phenomenon and whether or not she sees this pattern changing in black women's writing. I expected black writers to answer that they would continue to portray primarily black characters. I assumed that since so much of our lives remains unexplored in fiction and so much of the available literature fails to portray the complexity and range of our experiences, there would be very little need to explore other women's experiences except as they elucidate our stories. Williams, however, responded that black women needed to write more works that included whites so that they would have a better sense of how we view them. I was not prepared for that response, and learned from it the pitfalls of preset expectations.

A number of black writers declined to be interviewed. By the time I received those responses, however, I had received several enthusiastic replies from a number of white writers. In fact, from that point on only two other writers declined my invitation, which then presented another dilemma: how to justify a book born of an interest in the development of black women's voices that now included more interviews with white women? Were the voices of black women being drowned out once more by those of their white counterparts? My need to justify or explain who was interviewed, however, faded as my own disappointment subsided. I realized that I could only offer the forum, but I could not force anyone to accept the offer. I also realized that although I valued every interview I completed, my original list of twenty-six writers had been too long for one book.

*Broken Silences*, nevertheless, includes a range of voices representing different age groups, levels of experience, and genres. Most of the writers have Southern roots, even though a few of them now live in other regions of the country. Grace Paley and Rita Williams-Garcia are native New Yorkers and still live there; Joyce Carol Oates lives in New Jersey. Sherley Anne Williams has lived most of her life in California.

Sixteen of the twenty interviews were conducted face-to-face, and three by telephone. Only one (with Joyce Carol Oates) was conducted by mail. She answered, in writing, the general questions posed to all the writers and a set of specific questions related directly to *Because It Is Bitter, and Because It Is My Heart.*

I edited each interview to eliminate redundancy, empty pauses, and false starts, then sent it to the writer for any stylistic changes she might wish to make or any adjustments in content to clarify points or to reflect any changes in her position on a topic. Most writers made only minor stylistic changes, though a few made fairly extensive revisions. I found this process perhaps more time-consuming, but well worth the effort, for sometimes in speaking we do not have time to clarify our position or to phrase our thoughts as we mean for them to be taken. I decided not to permit the limitations of the interview technique to obscure the truth we share.

In doing the research to conduct the interviews, I found a number of interesting observations regarding cross-racial characterizations and stereotypes. In fact, one of the questions I eventually posed to writers was whether there was a role for stereotypes in fiction. Most writers, of course, attempt to circumvent or expose stereotypes; they certainly do not set out to create them. And yet I often felt that characters begin as stereotypes and then gradually attain a depth that renders them complex and whole. Most of us tend to view each other through lenses colored by misinformation, mistaken identities, and the most potent distorter, fear. We do not know one another, and we do not always share of ourselves when we have the opportunity. We, therefore, are likely to continue seeing one another through indifferent or suspicious eyes, if indeed we decide to look at all. Often it is simply easier to look past one another, thus denying any responsibility to respect our shared humanity.

It takes writers of vision and courage to allow the imagination to see images that are truthful because truth is often uncomfortable, unfamiliar, and uncertain. In some of the works by these authors, racial stereotypes dissolve before our very eyes. In others the stereotypes persist, and how could they not? I believe this occurs because our perceptions of one another are so deep-seated that it is difficult to overcome these images even in the imagination. If some black women see white women as victimizers who knowingly or unknowingly conspire in their own enslavement, then that is probably going to be one of the images they create of their white fictional counterparts. A white female character may be portrayed as heartless and cruel or helpless and naive. Depending on that character's role in the work, that is all that she might become. If white women writers see black women as servants, then they are likely to present black characters as long-suffering and nurturant. Such black women characters will not have inner lives or even past lives. They will be seen as springing from some eternal well of towering strength, deeply abiding faith, and enduring hope. Most of the white writers I interviewed speak of at least one servant who worked in their homes or those of their parents. It stands to reason that such characters will appear in their work. It is interesting to note that in a number of instances, even when writers create realistic portraits that defy stereotypes, the qualities associated with that racial stereotype might still remain. In other words, a white character may no longer be the wicked slave mistress, but an unkind, even bigoted, teacher; the black maid may become an innocent black child who nurtures a white schoolmate.

It takes courage to step into an imaginative space different from one's own and fill it with a whole and complex character. I have found the work of such writers both fascinating and courageous. Kaye Gibbons talks about her need to develop friendships with a range of professional black women if she is to explore an even broader spectrum of black women in her work. Both she and Jill McCorkle, native North Carolinians, address the importance of early intervention of schools in integrating young people *before* prejudices become so ingrained that students resist change at all costs. Gibbons also spoke of the influence of Martin Luther King, Jr., on her attitude toward accepting all people.

Both black and white women writers agree that blacks know whites far better than whites know blacks. A few white writers spoke of their concerns in creating a black character, feeling that they could not tell a story from that character's point of view. Black writers, however, feel confident about relating stories from a white protagonist's perspective. Lucille Clifton and Mildred Pitts Walter, for example, note that they know the world of their white characters well.

As members of an oppressed minority who have had to "study" whites all their lives in order to survive in America, the black women writers seemed less apprehensive about the credibility and authenticity of the cross-racial portraits they created. The white authors, however, expressed real uncertainty about their ability to render black characters whole. All seemed pleased with the final product, but some had struggled with questions of believability and verisimilitude during the creative process. The younger writers such as McCorkle and Gibbons were particularly sensitive to how their black characters used and/or did not use language. This same sensitivity is also prominent in Eugenia Price's desire to make her black characters whole. Price's novels, set mainly during the Civil War, are locked into a time period that dictates that realistic female characters be servants. Sherley Anne Williams confronted a similar dilemma in writing *Dessa Rose*, also set during slavery. When I commented that she had developed characters who were able to transcend the limitations of a slave society, she quickly affirmed that she had not humanized the characters, but that in interacting with each other, they had humanized each other. Herein lies the key to life within and outside of fiction: if people genuinely allow each other to be who they are, initial superficialities recede and individuals emerge. As much as characters have a life of their own, they are limited ultimately only by the imagination and the comfort zone of the author. A number of white writers note that because they are unfamiliar with blacks as they interact apart from whites, they tend to portray these characters in the setting they know best—the white household. Consequently, even though it is easier to find black female characters in works by white women, the space these characters occupy is usually the kitchen or some other place in a white home or psyche.

Perhaps because blacks simply have been forced to understand whites better than whites have had to understand blacks, there is more diversity in the kinds of white characters they produce. This is not to say that they necessarily produce less stereotypical characters than their white counterparts, only that their white female characters vary more in terms of occupational and class identity and in their hopes and ambitions.

The question I posed concerning whether or not black women will continue the trend of not creating many white female characters led to a number of insights into understanding why the writers tend to create cross-racial portraits at all. Most white writers seem to feel that black women still have so much unexplored territory that they simply have not ventured out to stories of other women's lives yet, except as they affect their own. They, however, express optimism that this pattern will change. Most of the black women express a similar view but with a different twist. Some assert that they are also not interested in writing about white women, and several emphatically stated that they did not foresee any change in this pattern in their own writing.

In hindsight, I realize that I neglected to pose an equally important question: Why do white women tend to create more black female characters than black women do white female characters, and will this pattern continue? Having originally intended to study black and white character interactions from the perspective of black women, I did not redirect the focus of the question to include the white perspective. I am left, therefore, to speculate why cross-racial characters are more prominent in white women's writing than in black. Both black and white women agree that black women are more interested in writing about their own unexplored stories, but is the opposite true of white women? After all, most white women writers do not include black characters at all, so it is not enough to say that white women have had the opportunity to explore fully all aspects of their lives and therefore have evolved to a point in their writing where they feel the need to explore themselves in relation to other cultures and races.

Again, not being able to do more than speculate, I think several black writers, in responding to other questions, offer some insights into why the pattern may exist. Lucille Clifton, for instance, notes that black women tend to represent qualities that white women are especially drawn to as they define themselves. Williams-Garcia even suggests that white women are looking for themselves in women who are perceived as strong, yet nurturing. If these observations are indeed the case, then they might help to explain the tendency.

Along these same lines, white writers also seemed to find it easier to discuss what they felt black and white women could teach each other about writing and about living. Perhaps their greater ease in responding might be another indication of their *generally* favorable impressions of black women. The black writers often found it difficult to respond to that same question. Yet, despite their misgivings about the women's movement, young black women such as Williams-Garcia, Ansa, and Golden still clearly see the need for black and white women to work together.

Indeed, it was in the writings of authors such as Walter in the young adult field that I saw some of the most provocative images of interracial relations. Young characters usually do not bring as much baggage to such experiences, particularly if they have had an opportunity to interact with people of different races and cultures early on. Walter's *Girl on the Outside*, set in the heat of the integration crisis in Little Rock, Arkansas, places the reader inside the experience of a black girl as she tries to enter a predominately white high school and the white girl who rescues her from the mob. Ironically, the story is not told, as one might expect, from the viewpoint of the black girl, but from that of the white. In fact, that heroic rescue places the white girl "on the outside" of her home and her community for the rest of her life.

Other writers relate similar triumphs and tragedies from the civil rights movement. Shirley Ann Grau wrote a wonderful short story of a little girl who is the only black in an integrated classroom. Her mother is beyond elation, but the child is utterly lost, alone, and miserable. This is an untold side of the struggle to attain equality. Any time a writer commits herself to unearthing the truth and allows her imagination to re-create that truth in stories that speak to the human condition, we all benefit from having shared in that search.

I hope that *Broken Silences* will open the door to more dialogue among all people concerning our shared histories, our common concerns, our dreams, and our general acceptance of the humanity we all share. I have raised only a few of the questions that should concern us, but if even a small part of the overall goal of this book is met, it will mean that we are all more encouraged to break the silence in pursuit of womanhood when "womanhood will be womanhood, void of color and class."

# Acknowledgments

■

First and last, I thank the Holy Spirit, Whose utterance in my life is my life, Whose Comfort is my All in All.

And first in this world I thank for the blessings of sisterhood my sisters, first of whom will always be my mother, Elizabeth Grooms Jordan, who planted charity in my heart early and cultivates it there yet. And I thank my sister, Diann, who as sister and friend, stands by me in all my endeavors.

And I thank those who are sisters in my heart. Thank you, Coleen Monsanto. Our daily walks at dawn with the Master fortified me and gave me strength. Your support helped me drive away all doubt and complaint. Thank you, Glennie Knight Thompson, for being a "big" sister to rely and rest on, and thank you, Coty, for your welcome and your encouragement. Sisterhood is not the same without brotherhood beside it.

And I am especially grateful to the three most important men in my life: my two fathers, Eddie and Willie Jordan, who have always been there for me and who have always believed in me, and my adopted son, Joseph Monsanto, who is my unspeakable joy and my faithful friend.

And I thank my "homegirl" and my anchor, Marilyn Thompson, who gave me a roof over my head when I decided to write full time. I thank too the many other brothers and sisters who have always been there for me. To Joyce Ravid and the rest, I want you to know that there are no small favors.

And I thank Lowanne Jones, whose friendship is stronger than color. That friendship provided the germ for much of the inspiration behind this book.

And I thank for the academic and professional support I have received from a number of important sources: the Hampton University Faculty Research Committee for much-needed funding for research and travel, Susan Lanser of the University of Maryland at

College Park, Clayton Holloway of Hampton University, and Barry Beckham of Beckham House Publishers for his encouragement and advice. And finally, I thank my editor at Rutgers University Press, Leslie Mitchner, for her belief in my project and the patience to guide it to completion.

# BROKEN

# SILENCES

■

# TINA McELROY ANSA

■

*Born in Macon, Georgia, in 1943, Tina McElroy Ansa sets her work in the imaginary world of Mulberry, Georgia. Her first novel,* Baby of the Family *(1990), chronicles the life of Lena MacPherson, a child who is born with a caul over her eyes. From birth, Lena has the spiritual gifts of "seeing" things and communing with ghosts. Ansa believes that writing stories rich in cultural linkages allows African Americans to reclaim and pass on their heritage. Far too often our history has been misrepresented, forgotten, or simply lost. Formerly a journalist for the* Atlanta Constitution/Journal *and later the* Charlotte Observer, *Ansa graduated from Atlanta's Spel-*

*man College, where she returned as visiting writer-in-residence for
the fall of 1990. Currently at work on her second novel, she lives on
St. Simons Island, Georgia. She is married to Jonée Ansa, a photographer at the American Film Institute.*

**JORDAN:** What inspired you to write?

**ANSA:** Since the time that I learned to read, I always wanted to
be a writer. I've been writing since I was a child, when I would
write short stories. In college I was an English major because I
loved reading and writing. I knew that I didn't want to teach, and
I discovered journalism in my junior year. I just thought it was
great. I loved it! I got out of college and was lucky enough to get a
job at the *Atlanta Constitution* as a copy editor. While I was there I
started writing features, and that's when I started writing for a
living. I was always working on a novel and always working on a
short story, but I don't think I was committed to it. I know I wasn't
committed to fiction writing. I didn't have any problem with that.
I quit the *Constitution* in the early eighties, to work on my fiction
supposedly, but I didn't do a whole lot of it. Then I went back
to newspapers in Charlotte, North Carolina, and from there we
moved to Maryland, and I started going into Washington to take
writing workshops. There I started submitting short stories while
I was still free-lancing. Then we moved here [St. Simons Island] in
1984, and I started writing fiction seriously.

A writer friend of mine, Bill, asked me if I were working on
something and I said, "Sure." I had said I had about seventy-five
pages or so, which I didn't. Really I had a short story, "Mamie,"
that turned out to be a chapter in *Baby of the Family*. At the time,
the little girl was going up the street to the beauty shop.

I had submitted the story to some magazines and gotten rejection slips. As I was working on it, I realized that this is more than
a short story; I wanted to know who this little girl was and why.
This little girl was so special that this beautiful woman would pick
her out to talk to. The short story was a flashback in which the
child was an adult. She was having an argument with her husband
and flashed back to this scene.

I was really working on the story and had gone to a workshop in
Macon, Georgia, with John Oliver Killens, who had come back to
Macon for the first time in maybe fifty years except for overnight

trips. There's this program called Writers with Roots in Georgia in which they bring back Georgia writers to talk in colleges, and John Oliver Killens had a residency at Mercer College. I had always grown up hearing about him because my father went to high school with him and they graduated in the same class. So I knew that a black person could be a writer, especially somebody from Macon. He was sort of my mentor without my having met him. I took this short story that I had been working on to the workshop and that's the novel-in-progress that I showed to my friend, Bill. He said he really liked it and that he thought it was good. I knew he was serious about pursuing this, and I needed to go ahead and do it. I also knew that you don't get many offers like this in life. I took about six months from May of 1986 to maybe October. I sent these 180 pages off and got an agent through his agency. Harcourt Brace Jovanovich bought it within a month or month and a half. That's how I came to write *Baby*. It took about two and a half years to write and rewrite it.

**JORDAN:** Were you born with a caul over your eyes like Lena?

**ANSA:** Yes, I was born with a caul over my face, too. When I looked at this child walking up the street to the beauty parlor, I started saying, "Why is this child so special?" and it dawned on me, "She is special because she is born with this caul." It started to make sense when I started to use things that were so much a part of my upbringing, things that were so close that I hadn't examined them. Living here on the island also had something to do with it making sense because people here still talk about dreams and premonitions.

In a way, the more assimilated we become, the more integrated we become, the more we become a little ashamed of these things. We think it makes us sound country and ignorant. When I moved here, I started asking older women, especially women who had been midwives, did they know anything about the caul and what it meant. I started hearing for the first time of giving the child tea made from the caul to "blind" them, as they say, against ghosts. I also started hearing about rituals you have to perform too. I started thinking about how we, black people, had been portrayed in connection with ghosts and the supernatural, especially with the Stepin Fetchit movies and the movies of the thirties and forties. Anytime there would be a black person and a ghost on the screen, the eyes would get big, and the hair would stand up, and it's "Feets don't fail me now." The more I thought about it, the more I could see how whites really have perverted our culture because that wasn't the way I remembered ghosts at all.

I remember my great-grandmother and my great-aunt telling me wonderful stories that I just assumed were part of my family history, and they talked about ghosts in a respectful way. It was beautiful and ancient, not all skewed the way it was on-screen. The way white society is portraying us is wrong. It's a lie. I very much wanted to recapture what I thought was my history and my tradition and my culture and to write about ghosts that were natural, if you know what I mean. The supernatural that is natural and the natural that is supernatural. I wanted to weave it the way that I remembered it.

My great-aunt would tell stories about having funerals in the country and they would be coming back in a big wagon and they might see the deceased walking on the road. Everybody's heard that story, right? It's not about eyes getting big and feet running. It was really quite beautiful and rich and deep. *Baby* grew out of not just my experience but from what I considered everybody's experience who grew up in the South—signs like your nose is itching so somebody's coming or of your palm itching or don't sweep or dust the dirt out the door after dark.

When I started looking at our literature, that's not what I saw reflected in black literature either. I don't see that kind of reverence as much as it should be to reflect our life. And if literature doesn't reflect a people's soul and a people's life, what good is it?

I am also the baby of the family and I remember being pampered and being spoiled and being loved and being sure that I was loved in my community. I was sure that I was loved if I couldn't count on anything else—not just by my immediate family but by my extended family and by the ladies at church, by all kinds of people who cared about me, my schoolteachers. And I very consciously wanted to portray a child where, although she had lots of other problems—everybody has to deal with feeling isolated, feeling like you don't fit in, don't look right, and all the rest, but there was no question about whether she was truly loved and really pampered. Lena is spoiled to the point that she is past pampered, past loved. I had gotten so tired of reading about young black girls who were beaten by their fathers and molested and on and on and on. Don't get me wrong. Of course, that happens. But that's not the only way we were born. To me, it was just as much a perversion to always see black children who are abused. I thought a hundred years from now, somebody who looks back on our literature is going to say, "Why didn't black people just run out in the street and let a big Mack truck run over them?" There was joy, there was laughter and there were inside jokes and storytelling at night and shelling peas on the porch and all the wonderful things that make up the richness of life . . . and I think that it's a lie if we don't present that.

And I don't think it had anything to do with being middle class. It had to do with the richness of culture that I think is often not portrayed. I think we are moving toward that. There has been a bit of criticism lately about what one reviewer in the *Village Voice* called "Black Buppie Writing"—middle-of-the-road writing in which the writers didn't know about white folks and they didn't have racism. This is so ridiculous to me. I don't understand that because I think most black people, especially in the South—I don't know the northern experience so I can't speak about that but I know in the South—people lived their lives for ages without thinking about white people. They didn't have anything to do with you. Of course, they controlled the money for the most part and they controlled the businesses. Those were things you had to deal with, but you didn't sit around talking about what the white man wasn't going to let you do. You knew your mother ran the kitchen, and your father ran the house, and that was the reality of your life. I don't understand this criticism that black people are writing books without having white people in them. This was a black critic who made this observation—as if our books are only valid if white people are the center of the universe. There was a white critic in Atlanta who liked the book and wrote a review of it for a magazine. She said the same thing; she said she just found it hard to believe that integration and the civil rights movement did not come up in my book. Basically when you're saying that, you're saying, "I can't understand where the white folks are." I think writers, black writers especially, have a responsibility to tell the truth. That's the only reason to write; there are all kinds of truth—my truth, your truth—because we all have different experiences. I think we are being really fake if we continue to write the things that are going to sell because white people are interested in reading about themselves through the black experience, through the Native-American experience, through the Hispanic experience, but they still want to read about white people. That's not my job.

**JORDAN:** Do you think black women will start to portray white female protagonists a bit more frequently? Of course, it is easier to find white women who have portrayed black women than the reverse.

**ANSA:** I can't speak for other black writers, but I find black people just infinitely interesting. I never have to write about a white person. I know black people. Although my next novel does not remain in Mulberry, I could stay in Mulberry my whole writing career. There are enough characters, enough stories, enough viewpoints in that one little town to keep me writing. Pivotal characters like Frank Peterson, for instance, do "woman's work." I find women interesting. I would like to think that I could create full, balanced, real characters, whether men or women. As a human being, I hope I can bring that to it. But I think my women are a lot more interesting because I know them so much more. When I was growing up, I remember the men as not being as important. I had brothers; they were bothersome and they were trouble. But they weren't the center of things. The center of the house was the kitchen and the center of the kitchen was my mother and my sisters. That's very subjective, and as a writer, I claim that.

The boys are important to Lena because they love her and they're blood, but in her world, which is "baby of the family," they just aren't that important. As she says, the women have the knowledge in this triumvirate. Her daddy sort of ran things or thought he did. Her mother did all the work, and her grandmother got to do whatever she wanted to. In Lena's world, that's how it worked. Men were important in the sense of what they did, but not in the shaping of things. The people that were of interest to me were the ones I imbued with a lot more interesting qualities, and we get their inner voices and inner life, and they were women. But it was also a conscious decision because that's how Lena's world worked.

**JORDAN:** As I read the novel, I remember thinking how naturally Lena's entire story seemed to unfold. It just seemed very natural that this child could be born with this "special" gift, with which, if she learned to use it well, she could do more help than harm.

**ANSA:** Yes. I know what you mean. For some writers, when the supernatural is mentioned, it's bizarre. It's outside the norm. I think, for instance, Toni Morrison did use the supernatural a lot better in *Song of Solomon* and *Sula*, where it was part of the natural, than in *Beloved*. I knew Sula. I know the characters in *Song of Solomon*. I loved meeting them and I think she did a wonderful job, but I don't know those people in *Beloved*. They don't walk and talk for me. They're not part of the real world. They're part of another world and maybe that was her intention. But I think one of the things about African-American people is that wonderful connection and, quite frankly, Southerners too have that connection. But we're getting away from that point. And when I say Southerners, I mean Native-American Southerners, white Southerners, and black Southerners too. There was that sense of the natural and supernatural as one. For instance, something as everyday as planting a garden was done by the phases of the moon. That's very metaphysical, but there are farmers who would scoff if you told them they were doing something metaphysical. This connection between the natural and supernatural is one of the reasons, I think, Southerners have produced such wonderful literature and are such wonderful storytellers. I always found that just so rich and wonderful to be able to share that in a novel with someone.

**JORDAN:** What have you enjoyed most about the publication of *Baby*?

**ANSA:** There have been two things that have been truly wonderful about the novel coming out. I get touched by the fact that black people love *Baby of the Family*. People say, "I know those people. I'm so pleased to see a little girl who is spoiled and who is loved and a family that is not set on hate and all the rest of it." The family has its problems. Jonah does what he wants to and his actions hurt the whole family and he doesn't really care about it. That's how men lived their lives; they did what they wanted and things were accepted. Women were hurt by that, but they went on. They still had a family. They had dinner to cook; that's how life was.

With the coming out of the book, black women come up to me and share their stories about how their fathers loved them. They tell me how pleased they are to see Lena being loved and having a relationship where she isn't afraid of her father beating her with a broomstick and molesting her. And he isn't all these things that they had read about. So many say, "I haven't been able to tell that story about my father to anybody but my closest friend because I feel so uncomfortable."

I had a college professor in Georgia who told me she was next to the youngest in her family. Her father was dark, and she was the darkest one in her family. She would be teased about it in the community. But her father always let her know she was special, and he would always call her Juice from the saying, "the blacker the berry, the sweeter the juice." That was his favorite name for her. She said they had a ritual every day when he came home in which she would hide behind a chair and whimper. To which her father would reply, "Where's my Juice? Where's my Baby?" And then he'd let her pretend to cry for a while. But he always gave her a big hug. That was such a wonderful story. I have met so many little black girls who are now in their thirties and forties who want to share these wonderful relationships that they had with the black men in their families. The men weren't monsters; they did what they wanted, yes. Even as Jonah thought the whole world revolved around him and did as he wanted, he was not a monster. He still loved his children and he loved Nellie in his own way. He certainly loved his mother.

**JORDAN:** You mentioned another reason you have enjoyed *Baby* coming out.

**ANSA:** The other reason is that black people come to me and say, "I know these people." As a first-time author, I often get questions about the autobiographical nature of the book, but I've really come to understand that question in a certain context. People ask me if the book is autobiographical, not only because they think it is, but because they say they know this family. This family lived in their town or next door to them or they were the folks who had money in the town. So it's not that they think it's not fiction, that I didn't create it, but they're also saying, "This is real to me. This is a reflection of what I know." And I've met wonderful older people. I had a reading at this black bookstore in Los Angeles, and this older man with gray hair came over and said, "This is my mother." It's a wonderful feeling to hear that readers recognize and see the truth in what you're trying to do. It's not everybody's experience, but I don't think anybody is ever trying to write everybody's experience. How can you? It's so varied.

While I was in California, a number of people also came up and said, "It made me homesick for the South." Outside of the South, you can't say things like "I was really happy growing up." I have another friend, a professor in Atlanta, who is from Mississippi, who said that whenever she told people she was from Mississippi, people wanted to send her condolences. She said that she was quite happy growing up. Of course, there were things said about Mississippi that were true and there were things said about Alabama that were true too. But that didn't shape our whole existence. It takes black people out of the realm of humanity when you make them victims. The pivotal experience in their lives was when someone called them "nigger"? I can't believe that. Although at some point we were all probably called that whether it was aloud or whether we were treated that way, that was a formative experience but it wasn't *the* pivotal experience. Women come up to me and tell me stories—like the woman whose father called her Juice—and that was the pivotal experience. She said she always grew up thinking that she was just pretty. The color thing wasn't a problem for her because she was Juice. The pivotal experience was knowing that you could always crawl up in your grandmother's lap no matter what she was doing. *That* was the pivotal experience.

I just don't think we see enough of that in our literature. And I think it's dangerous because it exposes us to people who would give us a job and to college professors who look at us and think, "Oh, this is just this one-dimensional person who is not able to do something," so you're not challenged in college. It affects everything—salesclerks who look at us and assume we want one thing and not another or who think, "What are you doing in this store?" I think women especially of our age who are working in environments that are integrated—and integrated meaning multiethnic—run into this all the time where you have a white woman colleague, for instance, and you all have the same problems that you have to deal with—same boss and if you're married, you still have to go home after you've worked all day. . . . There is a certain level where you have a lot in common. But I think that next step, where you truly share things, is where the problem comes in. And part of that is that image that she has of you and that you have of her—that you don't have something in common.

You had a question on your list concerning the women's movement?

JORDAN: Yes. Do you envision more black women becoming integrated into the women's movement as common concerns such as abortion and child care bring women of all races together?

ANSA: I think it's a very important concern because I don't think those issues of child care and abortion and other things are going to be the things that are going to bring us together in the women's movement. I think that it's images of what we are, because we've always had those things in common. But when you look at the women's movement, it's mostly white and mostly a certain class. I noticed recently on the cover of the *New York Times*

*Magazine.* They did a story about the women's movement: Did it do anything? Did it come of age? The cover photo was all white women. That's what it is! It's that image that we don't belong. It's not that we don't have things in common. We have. We can see that in the friendships we form at work, things that we talk about. But it's the next step where I have to see you as a human being and you have to see me as a human being. And we can't seem to make that step. The same white woman who talks about child care and all those other things will hire a black woman or a Hispanic woman or an Asian woman to take care of her children and pay her a substandard wage and not wonder once, "Well what's this woman's children doing while she's taking care of mine?"

That's the next step that we have to take, and I think that one of the things that keeps us from making that step is literature and television, movies, and theatrical presentations that show us as one-dimensional, always strong, never having concerns, not having an inner life, not having inner thoughts—the kinds of things that make us human.

One of the criticisms I have of that "Black Buppie Writing" review, which I think is just such a bunch of mess, is that it looks at Terry McMillan's *Disappearing Acts*, Marita Golden's *Long Distance Life*, Melvin Dixon's *Trouble the Waters*, and my novel and asks "Where are the white people?" and says "These people just whine." It disturbs me that it was written by a black woman. I find that ridiculous on one level, but also very dangerous. It says something about black people, that we need white people to give us some validity, but we don't allow ourselves to have that inner life. Why can't a black character whine? Why can't a black character, if that's indeed how she sees her existence, whine? That's something that we do: we whine and we become self-focused and all that. Human beings are so complex, varied in all our concerns. And if our literature doesn't reflect that, then we aren't doing our job. We really aren't.

**JORDAN:** Let's continue with the critics. Do you think that critics, especially black ones, have a special role to play in the way black women's lives are read, assessed, and taught?

**ANSA:** Oh sure. I think it's very important. Even though I'm criticizing this reviewer, I think it's very important that she wrote the piece. If that's the way somebody is thinking, then it certainly should be out there where people can read it and folks can say, "Oh,

I never thought about it that way. Let me go back and look at this in a different way." We need all kinds of viewpoints. Even though I don't agree with hers, it certainly should be there. By the same token, I should be able to write a letter saying this is bullshit and express my viewpoint. I think that the problem is that there haven't been enough voices. This is the criticism that white women in the movement make about the canon, saying that it is all male and it's all Western culture and it's all European—Eurocentric—and that they want to get their voices in. I think that's absolutely true, but we need other voices: black male, Hispanic, Asian, black women, gay, lesbian. All of them. I don't even see what the argument is. To me, it's so sane to say we are made up of all kinds of backgrounds and all kinds of viewpoints. Greek mythology and Roman mythology are not the only myths of the world. There's the Asian, the African. Why would I have to make this point? To me, it's so logical. It makes so much sense to include other voices that why would you even have to fight for it. But I guess that's true of all things when you see it so clearly. Why would you have to fight for equality among all people? Why would you have to fight for nondiscrimination? It's right. But that's my viewpoint; that's my truth.

JORDAN: Will things change in terms of the way black and white women view each other?

ANSA: The thing that interests me about the white women, though that's so discouraging, for instance, is to see the picture on the cover of the *New York Times Magazine* with nothing but white women. But I've gone to a number of the women's conventions like SEWSA [Southeast Women Studies Association] where white women will get up and say the only thing of interest in the women's movement is women of color. You see all these white women doing dissertations and doing anthologies on black women. They're getting grants to do work. And I think that's very dangerous. I don't think that they don't have the right to do that, but I just think that the primary voice should come from us and that we should be in there with the voice. It's very disturbing to me that I hear black women graduate students get up and say, "How are we going to do these dissertations? We don't get money to do them. We don't get time off to do these dissertations."

And I think we come in for criticism too. We aren't sharing with each other. We aren't being generous with each other. And it's the truth. It's a difficult thing to say, and nobody likes to criticize family. But we are not being generous with each other in sharing our lives. I think we're so afraid that there's just so much of the pie out there that they're going to give us and Lord if I let somebody else have a little piece of it, what's going to happen to me? And it's a fact of life there are only so many slots. But I think we have to do our part to change that reality. We've got to stop thinking that, "Well, there are only so many slots, and if I let you in, then Oh my God, what is going to happen to me?" I think it's part of a natural reaction to want to protect your own little space and your own little territory, but it's not getting us anywhere. It's like there is a little turnstile and only one can go through at a time and that is not true. As many can go through as people would buy books. And I find black people, white people, Hispanic people hungry for different views. Hungry for them if they're out there. But it's hard.

JORDAN: What specific conditions seem to be in place when black and white women become friends?

ANSA: I think the condition that exists when we become friends is the acknowledgment that we have human conditions in common, that we see the "other" as human beings with the same kinds of human problems and there is that reciprocity. If I need someone to take care of my children, do I think about who is taking care of yours while you're taking care of mine? Whether I have money to take care of mine and you don't isn't what we share. But what we do share is that need: someone to take care of our children. We share that concern of "Okay, it's 3:00 and they're getting off from school and I'm not there to take care of them. Are they okay?" If they are fifteen- and sixteen-year-old girls, are they with some boy right now? Are my girls going to get pregnant? These are the things we share—human kinds of things. It sounds simplistic, but lots of things are simple. What has been missing so often between black and white women is that reciprocity. You see it in the literature. Black women, for instance, are the fulcrum of the household, with white women free to share all their problems. But where is the reciprocity? Is that what you have found in the fiction?

JORDAN: Mostly.

ANSA: You're in the server/served position. White women say all the time, "I never start my morning without sitting down having my talk with Sue. We talk about everything. We share everything."

Well, no, that's not true. What usually happens is you sit down with Sue and share all your problems. Then you get up and go on about your day. I never share mine with you because I don't feel comfortable sharing with you. You don't ask me about what is going on: Where are your children? Are they taken care of? Are you and your husband getting along? You don't talk about how often you all make love. Are you happy with that? But you share all your things with me. You might know how many children I have, but you don't know what's going on with them. You don't know if one is on drugs. You don't know that because you have not asked. You haven't opened up the conversation. So the kind of condition that has to be in place is that reciprocity where I care about you and you care about me. That's not true of the server/served relationship and that's not a friendship. . . . I question relationships where that reciprocity is missing. Some may care about that one black woman who cared for them but if you care about this one black woman and then live your life in a way where you don't think all black people are as human as that black woman, then that reflects your supposed love and respect for this one black woman who loved and raised you.

**JORDAN:** What can black and white women writers teach each other about writing and about living?

**ANSA:** I don't think that black and white women writers can teach each other any more than nonwriters can. All you have is your life and your experiences and your humanity and that's all you have. Because we write, we can put it down on paper and share it with more people. That's the advantage of writing, but I don't think we have any more to share than the woman who takes care of the white child.

**JORDAN:** What kind of role does the black female tend to play in the white woman's novel and what kind of role does the white female tend to play in the black woman's novel?

**ANSA:** I think it's what I have been saying about the roles of the server and the served. Speaking here from personal experience, the white women's experiences are sort of like the men in my novel. They're not central to what I'm writing about. But there is something interesting about the white women in my novel now that you mention them. The white women are the servers of the black women. There's the white clerk in the store, and Grandmama intimidates her. And there are the nuns who are very intimidating in their own way, but they are still serving. We're paying them to serve. Sarah's mother works for a white woman and she brings the clothes there, but she doesn't have a name. And there's a white woman when they come back from the beach, but she is a server too because she works in the store. Isn't that interesting? They're all in peripheral positions, not pivotal to the story. But maybe none of us has moved past that. I'm trying to think of works of fiction in which black and white women are peers.

**JORDAN:** Would you consider Lynne and Meridian from Alice Walker's *Meridian* to be friends? I suppose there's a way in which they are peers, but they aren't really friends. What did you think of *Tar Baby*?

**ANSA:** I didn't like *Tar Baby*. As a matter of fact, you've mentioned the two works that I like least by those two authors. I like *Meridian* least and *Tar Baby* least.

**JORDAN:** There is also a white woman in *The Color Purple*. There is also a "friendship" between a black girl and a white girl in Andrea Lee's *Sarah Phillips*. At the age of twelve, this black girl is sent to a private school where she is the only black. There's also a Jewish girl there who is also on the periphery of the life of the school. I don't know if I'd say it's truly a friendship but they do develop a special relationship because they're both outside the "mainstream" of this all-girls' school. They hang out together and really provide a support system for each other. That's one instance. I can think of some young adult fiction authors where the two are friends as well. They're usually classmates and that's how the friendship develops.

**ANSA:** That's interesting. Traditionally in the South, it's always been said that black and white kids can be friends until they reach a certain age and it stops. That might be a reflection of our society for young adult and children's literature that you can have those kinds of relationships because there's that innocence and freedom that you are allowed, but when you reach a certain age, it stops.

**JORDAN:** That's what's reflected in the fiction. Once you reach high school all kinds of problems arise. When you were drawing the picture of the nuns, were there particular concerns you had about the portrait you wanted to produce?

ANSA: The nuns are probably the strongest images of white women in the novel, and I say in the novel that they weren't really considered white women. Nuns are sort of like butterflies. They're something different, a whole other species. And their being white didn't enter into the schoolchildren's lives as much as that they were figures of authority and they didn't get married and they wore the same clothes and they would say they were married to Christ. So I don't know if they're good examples of white women characters. They're like "other"; white, black, and then other. They could have been black; they could have been Hispanic. Their being white wasn't what shaped their character. Their religious life and the fact that they were teachers and they lived together in a community of women shaped them a lot more.

JORDAN: How do we move beyond the stereotypes and images portrayed so that we get to the reciprocity you speak about?

ANSA: That's the question. I think the more images, the more varied the images that we see, whether they're on television or film, then the better it is for everyone because it just opens us up to the possibilities of differences in people and accepting them. It also opens up the possibility for me to recognize my experience in you or my humanity in you. I'm a big believer in just throwing it all out there. I'm not just for sharing the positive side either; I'm not for censorship. I think it's just very dangerous because then we're talking about choice. You decide what the positive is. I have a lot of faith in humanity. I think you throw it all out there, let them see it, let them decide for themselves.

I think we live so much in fear of sharing ourselves, exposing ourselves, being vulnerable, and you can't do that when you're writing fiction. As a friend of mine says, "You have got to dance naked on the stage." . . . That's when you're really vulnerable. So I think we're going to have to be a lot braver.

JORDAN: Do you think that we do not tend to show as many black and white female relationships in fiction?

ANSA: I think there are more black and white female relationships in the world than we see represented in literature because we are afraid to show them. We are not ashamed of them, but we feel we have to explain more: "Well, she's my friend, but she's okay." We do this when we have a good, good friend who is a white woman if we're talking to a bunch of black women. I'm speaking very subjectively here. I'm talking about how I feel. I feel like I have to say, "Well, she's a white girl, but she's okay." Or "she hasn't had everything given to her on a silver platter; she knows what it is to struggle." We feel like we have to explain these friendships. In fact, I think we're very defensive about those friendships. I don't know if white women feel that way or not. That may be why they don't do it as much. My feeling is that they don't feel as defensive as we do. I don't know.

JORDAN: Probably not. I think if a white woman gets to the point of having a real friendship with a black woman, she seems to have few problems owning up to the friendship regardless of what anybody thinks or says.

ANSA: They see it as a badge. For us, ashamed is too strong a word, but we're a little defensive about it, and that's probably why we don't do it as much. I have white women friends who really come through for me. Jonée has been away these past nine months, and I've been on the road promoting my book. It's really been hard not having someone here I can count on. I have a white woman friend who's always gotten me to the airport whenever I've had to go. She has a family; she has children. She has a job but she has always made sure I've gotten there. That's a friend. I don't think I would write about that, though. I'm trying to be as honest as I can, and I think probably I'm being a little defensive about it. Just now I explained to you why she was a friend. I didn't just say she was a friend.

JORDAN: It's as if we sometimes anticipate that our black female friends might say, "You hang out with *them*?" and before they can even pose the question, you have already explained away any concern for difference and what that difference might typically mean. You can't have a friendship that you have to explain all the time.

ANSA: We all have black female friends who don't fit into the norm either. We don't feel we have to explain them. She's just accepted. If you have, for instance, a professional woman friend—a college instructor—and most of your friends are of that profession or class or whatever, and you have another friend who didn't finish high school and doesn't like to read and doesn't like the theater, you may know in the back of your head that they're wondering, "Well what are *they* doing together?" But you don't feel you have to explain. It's just assumed and taken for granted that she's another black woman, you have things in common. You don't have to explain.

**JORDAN:** That's right. Would you like to comment on what we can do to help our children so that they become familiar with their own family and cultural histories?

**ANSA:** I get this comment a lot when I travel. Young black men and women come up to me and say, "I never heard about the caul and it is so interesting." And I say, "Go home and ask your mama or grandmother. I bet she knows." We aren't sharing our lives. We aren't sharing our histories, our stories. We aren't sitting down telling them stories. When my mother took me to get my first library card, she said, "This is important." It was a real big deal. She let me know that not only were her stories important, but other stories were important too. We aren't doing that with our children. We aren't taking time with them. We aren't telling them stories. We aren't sharing our lives. We aren't sharing our pain with them. I knew when I was growing up that things were hard, that money didn't grow on trees, for instance. "I had to work all day for this money." Or "I bought those encyclopedias. You go in there and look it up." My parents didn't hide things from me. I think we have wanted to assimilate and protect our children so much—and it's a natural instinct. I'm not criticizing it—but I just think it has worked against us not to let our children know, "Hey, this is the world. You are going to meet people who don't like you because of this, this, this. Life is hard. The world doesn't owe you a living." All these things we need to share with our children. We can be held responsible for that.

**JORDAN:** I'm afraid so!

**ANSA:** Who else? Show them that we have an inner life. I remember when I was growing up, my parents and relatives would say, "Put that book down and go out and play," but I was also allowed to have an inner life, to make up games and to have imaginary friends. A box was a clubhouse. A car. It was everything I

wanted it to be. And I don't think we allow our children to do that
simply because it's harder. It's easier to sit a kid in front of a television or a Nintendo game rather than say, "Let me cut up this old
dress for you and you use these rags for that." It takes time for that.
I understand that the world is a lot different than it was forty years
ago. People had a lot more time for sitting around and talking. The
world is really different. We are all busy. But I think we're going to
have to say, "Well, this is important to us." If our children aren't
important to us, then what is?

**JORDAN:** Otherwise you get students who really know so little
about their own histories and who sincerely want to know who
Malcolm the Tenth is.

**ANSA:** Yes! But the thing that is encouraging is the students
who come up and say that they don't know anything about these
stories, but they are interested in them. I think that that mad rush
to assimilate, a natural instinct to make things easier because it's
easier to go along, has hurt us.

**JORDAN:** And, of course, we don't want the children to remember the pain.

**ANSA:** But in keeping out all that pain, we're keeping out the
other things too.

**JORDAN:** We forget about all that though. What, if any, responsibility do readers have in allowing the story to come to life? What
is the reader's responsibility in the creative process?

**ANSA:** To be open to things. I think that's all an author asks of
his or her readers is that they be open to possibilities, of not assuming, "Oh, this is a black story, so this is how it is." "Oh, these are
black characters and this is what they are thinking." In getting
back to what we were saying about full-dimensional characters,
it's the writer's responsibility to make the story come alive and to
be real for the reader. And it is certainly the reader's responsibility
to be open to it; to say, "I've never met a person like this before,
but this is interesting."

**JORDAN:** Did you feel pressure from your editor or anticipated readers to portray a particular kind of character or to treat a particular set of themes in writing *Baby of the Family?*

ANSA: You have to shut all that out and focus on the story. You know your characters better than anybody else. So you have the responsibility to shut it out. But I do think you come under all kinds of pressures, especially black women. Black writers, not just women, are pressured to portray characters the way that their editors, who are usually white women or white men, think that they should be. I had problems with editors not being able to "get" Lena. They didn't. "Well, what is this? She's spoiled; why is she so special?" And I would say, "Gosh, she's the baby of the family. Her parents have money; her grandmother spoiled her too." Then I said, "Well, you have to bring something to a character too. You're a human being in this world. You grew up whether it was in a family or in an orphanage; you have to bring your own collective history, your society's history so when you read, for instance, you know, 'Oh, this little girl is spoiled rotten.' You've got to know what that means even if you may not have experienced it!" When some white people come to a black character who is spoiled, it is like a brick wall. Wham!

JORDAN: They aren't poor though.

ANSA: Absolutely. The family has money; money is not a problem with this family. They have other problems, but money isn't one of them. There was a problem from my editor with the fact that the mother wore Joy perfume, a problem with the fact that she even knew about it. Yes, there are all kinds of pressures to make these people what your editor or publisher sees, and that is the responsibility that we were just talking about. The reader has to be open to the possibilities of things outside of their experiences, outside of their prejudices, outside of how they see things.

JORDAN: Are there ever uses for stereotypes in fiction—perhaps to introduce a character or to point out the danger of such attitudes?

ANSA: I don't think so. Stereotypes by their very definition are not real people. Now there are people who fit people's stereotypes, but that's not what they [writers] are doing. You're writing characters. I don't think anybody should write stereotypes; I'll go that far. I don't think anybody should sit down to write a stereotype because that means it is not a real person. That goes against what you're trying to do. But there certainly are people that fit all kinds of stereotypes and that's the difference, I think.

JORDAN: Do you think that ambiguity is a device that black women use in relationships with white women?

ANSA: My goodness, yes! We go back to the question of the server and the served. It's been used forever. You go back to slavery and see how we used the spirituals to talk about going over Jordan and Moses freeing the Hebrews. That's all ambiguity. That's part of any oppressed/oppressor relationship. It's a worthy device. It's a dangerous device, too, because when you're trying to step past that relationship of oppressed/oppressor, server/served, then that ambiguity keeps you from knowing each other and keeps you from having that reciprocity. It's very useful in one situation and very dangerous in another. It's like men and women in the workplace, for instance. Many women have found it useful to present themselves as "Oh Lord, I don't know what I'm doing here. Please help me"–type people. And that may work real well at one point, but when you want to be taken as a serious person who's capable and able to do things, it works against you. It's the same kind of ambiguity. Any time you get away from honesty, you can also get into real dangerous situations. Ambiguity is useful, but also dangerous.

JORDAN: Jonah intrigued me a lot. What do I say about this man?

ANSA: I like your response: What do I say about this man? Interesting people evoke that kind of response. They're not all one thing, one-sided. Most people aren't like that. I don't know anybody who's all one way or the other even if all I know about that person is negative. There's all that other stuff too: their own family life and their own past. There's so much about people. I think so often about this statistic that I cannot get out of my head that twenty percent of all women eighteen and older have been sexually abused. That means if there are five women in this room, one of them has probably been abused. What are we all dealing with? What are we holding in? What things have happened in our lives to make us whatever way we are? Bitter. Mean. Hateful. Too giving.

Or promiscuous. We're all just so complex and I think our responsibility as writers is to try to get as much of that as we can into a character or into 250 pages when you have five or six or seven characters walking through those pages and you only have so many lines to get them in. I think that is our task.

I don't mean to cut you off, but I'm real pleased when you say you don't know about this man, because that's the truth. Jonah is certainly like that. I don't think it's bogus or fake to have a character who has a great many character flaws, and Jonah does, and he also has these shining characteristics—things you just want to hug him for or things that you feel sorry for him about.

**JORDAN:** Was there some deliberate ambiguity about Lena telling the Sister about Cynthia's mother? Has a voice spoken or is it Lena, but she can't figure out which, or does it matter?

**ANSA:** I think it matters, but I think it matters in the sense of what the reader thinks and what the reader brings to it. I could tell you all kind of possibilities, but you know all those. When you become a certain age, you do feel torn with your friends. You want to love them and you want to get them in trouble. You want to have favor with people in authority and you want to be accepted by your peers. There's a lot of ambiguity. That's one of the things that surrounds Lena's being given a lot of gifts in life. But I hope that one of the points of the novel is that no matter how many gifts you are given, there's a lot of responsibility that goes with gifts. Just because you're given gifts doesn't exempt you from the pain of life and from life's troubles. And part of Lena's pain and part of the gift of being given this veil is that she is different. And being different is very difficult, especially given the age where she is. She wants to fit in and she is different.

Her mother not going through with this ritual causes the ambiguity in her life. She doesn't know. She doesn't know whether a person is a ghost or not. She doesn't know whether this ghost is going to be good to her or scare her. She doesn't know whether the voices that come out of her mouth are hers or what. She doesn't know if she is crazy or not. She could be just psychotic. She could be schizophrenic. We hear about multiple personalities. There are a lot of possibilities, and I hope I did leave all those possibilities open just the way they are in life. It's up to the reader as far as I'm concerned, and I hope the reader brings enough curiosity to my character that they would think about that and wonder and come to their own conclusions.

**JORDAN:** It struck me that after Lena "told on" her friend that her friends then started to remember these "strange" incidents. I had been thinking along the same lines as Lena that she was different on the inside, but not really on the outside since no one outside the family had mentioned these differences. After that scene with the nun, I realized they had known all along or seen little things but had not said anything about them to Lena.

**ANSA:** That's probably true. Your little friends in school know you probably better than anyone else outside your family. You spend eight hours a day with them and then you talk on the phone after school and you play together on Saturday. I think they probably know you as well as anybody in your life. But when someone is your friend, I think they overlook a lot of things and they don't examine. The other thing is that Lena is cute, she's smart, and she fits in so well otherwise. She doesn't have money problems. She doesn't have problems with the nuns simply because she is smart and her parents give money to the school. But that doesn't do it. There are still things that come up that make your life difficult and that's what life is about. And at that age, children are very vicious. Margaret Atwood wrote about it in *Cat's Eye*, especially at that age of puberty where if you don't fit in, then just get out of here. Don't draw attention to yourself and don't go outside the norm. We can be very vicious with each other. I've seen it on the playground.

**JORDAN:** I thought that it was very interesting that in death Miss Lizzie could advise Lena in a way that didn't work as well when she was alive.

**ANSA:** Well, I think it's very much part of our tradition of African-American culture to look to the ancestors, of having some links after death, that everything isn't what we see here from birth to death; that isn't the whole world. There's something outside of that. There's wisdom outside of our day-to-day reality. There's knowledge we can't have on this plane. It's very African, Afrocentric—having a connection with the ancestors and the ancestors always being able to help us, even more so after they die because then they have a connection with that whole history of knowledge that we don't have—that whole continuum of knowledge that we can't have because we're so tied to this plane and our feet are so tied to the earth. Miss Lizzie was an irritating woman, but she was a wise woman, even when she was on this earth. But you're right. She didn't know. She thought she knew; she thought she hadn't cut herself off from the old ways. She thought she was keeping tradition. She thought she was so much smarter than Nellie who only believed in modern stuff and who was so disgusted with all that old-timey superstitious stuff. She didn't know how much she didn't know until she died. I think that's very much part of our tradition and our culture. When I was growing up, I remember hearing people say, "So and So came back to me in my dreams last night and told me where to find my such and such." It's very much a part of our culture.

JORDAN: Do you see residuals from older tales and myths in contemporary black folk experiences, our stories?

ANSA: I think so. I think writers think about that a lot, and I think that's why it shows up more in writing than it does in everyday conversation. I don't think you can think about your life, think about where you are on this earth without thinking about your history and what your parents and grandparents told you. All they told you were those folktales. Animal tales. Animals talking about being smart. John the Conqueror and all those stories. They're all a part of our life. I think the dangerous part is just what we were talking about. At one point it was passed down orally. Whether you ever wrote or not you still knew about it. You didn't have to go to a book for it. But now we aren't passing it down orally from one generation to the other, and it's getting so that the only place we do know about it is in books. And now we have this whole generation of illiterates or semiliterates; they don't read, so where are they going to find out? It's a big concern. All of that was a part of my story. It was a very conscious effort on my part to imbue my story with those kinds of images and legends because I think they should be kept alive.

JORDAN: Are the MacPhersons on the fringes of two classes? They're middle class, but they aren't really.

ANSA: Well, I think class is a word that black people use with some trepidation. I think that we don't even like that word. I don't. I was just treating myself to rereading *Their Eyes Were Watching God*, and they tell Janie, "You've classed yourself off." That's something we bristle at. That was a criticism when people would say, "Oh, you think you're of a different class." I think that's a word that we don't like. The MacPhersons are middle class simply because they have money. They're middle class not because they send their children to private school. There are a lot of poor children in the school. You pay what you're able to pay, so that doesn't really "class them off." They're middle class, but the stories that they tell and the way they make their money—gambling and liquor—are probably low class to some people. The fact that Nellie buys only the best clothes and the best material to make clothes and the kind of perfume she wears makes her middle class. There are a lot of ways of looking at class in black America. We could be middle class, but our parents could have been illiterate, subsistence farmers. Someone would say that's lower class. But that's part of your life too, so does that mean you're in a different class from your parents? That can't be. I think that there aren't those sharp divisions in black families that sociologists would like to say that there are. One of the things I was thinking about was an article on middle-class women who have babies with low birth weight just like some lower-class women. Was it nutrition? The article went on to ask if that meant that there were residuals of nutritious socioeconomic decisions women make. It just shows that you're never that far away from whatever class you were brought up in or your grandparents were brought up in.

One of the things that my family used to do every summer was to make a trip back to the family farm. We grew up in Macon, which was considered a town, but my grandfather was from Wrightsville, Georgia, and his family were farmers in that area. There was Uncle Sunshine and he had a mule, and we were just thrilled with that. They had a well and all of that. We're never far from that.

One of the things that we, as black people, used to do was to make a conscious effort not to "class ourselves off," not to forget that we came from these farmers or from people who may not have made it through grammar school or high school. I hope that's true of the MacPhersons—that no matter how much money they have, they still shell peas on the porch and drink liquor. They make their living off liquor and working-class people. Nellie doesn't "class herself off" from the folks. When she's working at the "place," she fries fish and she gets hot and sweaty and all the rest. I don't know whether we're moving away from that, but I know in the era in which this was written—the fifties and early sixties—"classing yourself off" was not something that you really wanted because that was something you would get criticized for. I think that's true of the community in which I grew up. You could only live in the black community or out in the country. Just because you had more money, just because you were a schoolteacher could mean you might be living next door to someone who worked at the pulp mill. Your house might be a little better because you might be able to get your house painted and the people next door maybe couldn't. Or you could grow grass when they didn't have grass or grow flowers. Those were the kind of distinctions you'd make, but you were all living out in that community.

As I think back on that, it must have been difficult for people who were struggling every day to live next door to someone who got in their car and went off to an air-conditioned building as a schoolteacher or whatever. I think there was probably a lot of resentment too.

**JORDAN:** Lena does have a special girlfriend, Sarah. There's one scene in particular in which Sarah and Lena are "playing" or experimenting with their bodies when Sarah's mother rather harshly reprimands both girls and sends Lena home. Thus ends the friendship.

**ANSA:** Well, this family is having a hard time eating. They have a lot of children. The mother works—gets part-time work. The father stands on the corner waiting for these trucks. It was day labor, and basically, you got on the truck if they needed you to work that day. And if they didn't, what did you do? It was a very hand-to-mouth kind of existence. And to see this little girl show up to play with your little girl when she is dirty and doesn't have pretty clothes and this other little girl shows up all shiny and clean and her hair all combed with bows in her hair with pretty handmade dresses on every day caused a lot of resentment. The mother comes home; all she wants to do is read her newspaper and she finds these two little girls being sexually experimental. But it is also that she finds this little girl in her clean dress. Her family doesn't ever have to worry about anything; they've got money and they're the big folks in town. I think it's natural that she would be that angry. I think it also shows the interactions in those kind of neighborhoods in small towns where people making different amounts of money, different "classes"—middle, lower, upper, lower middle—all lived together. There was the neighborhood store and you all went there when you needed a loaf of bread. And most likely, you all went to the same church. I don't think there were those strict levels we see now.

**JORDAN:** Or would like to think there are. My last question is: What do you do when writing pulls you in one direction and other responsibilities pull you in other directions?

**ANSA:** I tell you the truth. When I'm writing and getting something done, I probably ignore it. Your kitchen always needs cleaning. Your bath needs cleaning. You have letters to get in the mail and family responsibilities—I don't have children. There are things you cannot ignore but I know that you make decisions about what can be ignored and what can't be. The world doesn't have to end if your house is filthy. It just won't, not if you're using that time to write. And I think when the Spirit really is moving and the story is really flowing, you have a commitment to that story as well as you have a commitment to cook dinner. Cooking dinner is not a good example if you have small children because you have to do that. But if you have teenagers, you have to make that decision to say, "Mama works for a living. What she does is write. You can get in there and make yourself a peanut butter sandwich or if you go to the store and get everything together, you can say, "You're a big enough child now to do that. If you need clothes, we have a washing machine. You need to know how to run that." Now that is a responsibility too on your part. We keep coming back to how busy we are. It takes time to teach a child how to run a washing machine and how not to put the reds in with the whites. It's hard. I don't know how people do it with children. I'll be honest but I guess they do what everybody else does. They make decisions and they make priorities. If my child needs me right now, then that's a priority I have to do, but she can't need me twenty-four hours a day. I need some time for work. I think it's very much a matter of commitment because once you make the commitment, things come more easily. You've said, "This is what I'm going to do. Now how am I going to do it?" I was talking to my editor, Elizabeth, at Harcourt Brace Jovanovich. I say "was" my editor because she's no longer there. She's always concerned about whether I'm writing, whether I'm getting anything done and I told her, "Jonée is coming home." When I was writing this book, Jonée did everything. I cooked, but he worked to bring money in the house. He took phone calls. He did everything, which helped me greatly. I couldn't have done it in the same way. However, by doing that, he had to put his career on hold. The focus of the whole household was *Baby of the Family*. Everything revolved around it. And, of course, I was as happy as a little lark. That's fine with me. Let me be the focus. However, now that he's gone to the American Film Institute and he's going to be traveling more and hopefully making films, then the focus is shifting. Now when the focus shifts, that just means that I will never have it as good as I had it before, but by the same token, my having had it so well meant he had to sacrifice and I don't want anyone to have to sacrifice. In your heart, you don't want anyone to have to sacrifice. But truly you don't care who has to sacrifice as long as you get your work done. As I was telling Elizabeth all this, she said, "Well, Tina, you just don't stop writing." I said, "Oh no. That's not even an issue of me not writing. But we are going to have to decide how we're going to do this." And that is it. Once you make a commitment, you have to decide how to do it and that's different for everybody. Life changes. It's always a change. Never the same.

# ALICE CHILDRESS

■

*Alice Childress was born in Charleston, South Carolina, in 1921, but was raised and educated in Harlem, New York. She performed on and off Broadway with the Negro Theatre from 1941 to 1952. She has written a number of prize-winning plays that are performed by professional and amateur theater companies across the United States, including* Gold Through Trees, Trouble in Mind, Wine in the Wilderness, Sea Island Song, *and* Gullah.

*Her work has been met with hostility, resistance, and critical ac-*

*claim. When her play* Wedding Band, *which portrays an interracial relationship in South Carolina during World War I, was televised in 1973 by ABC, some affiliate stations refused to carry it.*
*Even her novel,* A Hero Ain't Nothing But a Sandwich, *was pulled from the shelves of a library in Savannah, Georgia, in 1973. Yet, her screenplay based on that novel received the Virgin Islands Film Festival Award for Best Screenplay in 1977. She has received numerous other awards for her work, perhaps foremost among them the first Paul Robeson Award from the Black Filmmakers Hall of Fame.*

JORDAN: What can black and white women teach each other about living and about writing?

CHILDRESS: For one thing we can teach each other the differences in our experiences rather than struggling all the time to say, "It's the same." We can ask each other, "What's different about us?" Of course, I think there are blacks who are overeager to say, "I don't know anything about any black/white differences. I never ran into racism myself. I came from the 'Midwest' and never knew anything about racism until I came 'here.'" I ask, "Where is that place?" I don't believe there is a place like that. All of us have heard, felt, and seen racism, but many do not wish to see it. It's too painful. Denial is comforting. They want to say, "Everybody loves me. They're all crazy about me." In my play *Wedding Band*, a black woman, Fanny, tells another: "Don't make it hard for me with your attitude. Whites like me. When I walk down the street, they say, 'There she goes'—Fanny Johnson, representing her people in an *approved* manner." What Fanny is saying is "I'm inferior to whites." And their acceptance makes it possible for her to function on a lower level. Something about her is reassuring to a racist. They feel Fanny "knows" her place and is happy in it.
But in relation to the question you asked, I say that it is important and healthy to say how we are different. I wouldn't tell a woman of another race or culture, "Oh, there's no difference. I'm just like you. Whatever you experience, I experience the same thing." That's almost dismissing her when she's trying to share her differences. Arrogance enters when we don't care to hear her differences by saying, "I've had it hard too." It's telling the other person

that her particular pain is unimportant, and this is what I think frequently happens between black and white women.

Not only would I be saying that your experience is unimportant when I don't care to hear your particular problems, but I'm saying that you have no special problems. If whites got jobs in the five and dime when they didn't hire black people, it's because no black person was allowed to work there, but we were able to shovel the candy and put it in a bag. Everybody in the United States could shovel candy and put it in the bag. But Jim Crow hiring policy definitely made differences based upon race. Banning blacks from working in the five and dime was done to make legal differences between blacks and whites.

And now they tell us, "Work hard and think positive and you can achieve anything." However, if they advertise one job and five hundred people apply, the one they hire is used to prove that if you were as good or better, you would have had the job. There was only one job and 499 were not hired. There is no way that we can believe that the other 499 were not good. They only wanted one. The one hired might have been the best but if you had five hundred people all thinking positive, only one was going to get it. Then they may say, "That's the one who thought the most positive."

I think we're almost mesmerized by that kind of thinking of try harder, shovel harder, smile more. It's mind conditioning, and it hurts us the most, but it hurts white women because I think some have been trained to think that if a black woman can do her job—can do what she does—just as well or better, that lowers the position. But if two white women go for the same job and one white woman gets it, the loser feels it was just chance or limited opportunity. She doesn't feel "I'm considered inferior to that other white woman who got it." But too many feel a particular insult when a black woman gets a job over her. And this attitude is too rife in American society.

African Americans are the only people in America where it was against the law for us to speak a native language. Frenchmen didn't have that. Germans didn't have that. People from all over the world can speak to each other in their own language, legally. They actually passed laws so that we couldn't speak Mandingo or any other African tongue because they wouldn't know what we were saying and they thought that we were going to plot to get free. We're the only people who were forbidden by law to go into an American public library. We were the only Americans who paid full fare and were not allowed to sit where we wanted on public transportation. We couldn't get into any industry when unions shut us out. We couldn't join the unions for a long time. They don't want to make up for that. They held people back for 350 years and grumble about offering any chance to make up for lost time.

**JORDAN:** What's the difference between the white woman's liberation as a woman and the black woman's liberation?

**CHILDRESS:** The white woman has had to fight for the right to work. The black woman has always been working. She almost had to fight not to. She worked "for free" first in slavery, and she worked for substandard wages and positions after Emancipation. We must understand our differences. The white woman's husband didn't want her to go out to work and that was a good way to keep her subject. Then she put up a good fight to vote but she complained that her black male servant could vote and she could not. She was more offended by this than the white male right to vote. Harriet Tubman and Sojourner Truth spoke out for the rights of all people. Look at Sojourner Truth's speech, "Ain't I a Woman?" She wasn't invited to the suffragist meeting as a speaker. Neither was Harriet Tubman. They used to attend the meetings and talk from the floor. Now they are quoting them as if they were invited as speakers. They spoke from the audience.

Most white women don't care to say they were part of the slave system. They were. There were some who spoke publicly against slavery. They don't write many stories about them. The whites who took our part are mostly absent in history because taking the right position eliminated them from being praised. There was a British actress, Fannie Kemble, who married an American plantation owner, Pierce. Her friends in England asked her why she would marry a slave owner: "Do you know what slavery is? We gave up slavery a long time ago." She said, "He is such a good person and says he is so good to his people on his Georgia plantation. If it weren't for him, they wouldn't eat."

When she arrived here and landed in Georgia, the slave women came down to the boat to meet her. They were glad to hear he was now married and they came to ask her to intercede for them. Their complaints: He wouldn't give them time off for childbirth. They held up their clothes and showed unhealed whipping scars on their bodies. Fanny Kemble was horrified. She complained to her husband and the overseers. Later, after they had two children, her husband went to court and got custody of them because of Fanny's position on slavery. She went back to England, but was not allowed to take her daughters. She said when she first arrived she had seen light-skinned slave children running around and she asked her husband where they came from because there were no other white men there. He said that white salesmen and travelers came through at times. She thought, "Some of them looked like him." He sold some of the slave children to other planters so they wouldn't embarrass him. This would make a fine film. I know a white woman who's been trying to get it done for the last twenty-five years. No one will pick up on it.

And then another thing that sometimes happened was that white women gave birth to black babies. Some of their husbands went away for two years. If a baby was born black, they gave it to a slave woman to raise as her own. If she was from an upper-class family, they gave it to a black woman. Of course, the husband might sell the child and the slave guardian—four hundred miles away. These secrets and different experiences keep black and white women apart in discussing themselves. She didn't do it, so why is she defensive? Why couldn't she say, "That's horrible that these things happened and slavery was a terrible institution. People suffered under it." Instead she says, "Can you prove that?" She goes to the defense of the slaveholder too often, I think. If you say, "I'm going to be superior to you no matter what you say," she acts as if her listening to you makes her kind and understanding. The answer to that is, "Well, I don't think we have anything to say. Your mind is made up and there is no dialogue." Plus we don't even enter the dialogue to ask who is superior and who is inferior. We all have a right to be here.

All too many white women, working underneath a black woman, ask themselves "Why am I working underneath *her*?" And some say, "I'll do it, I'll work under you," but they want special credit for that. They say, "I work for a black woman. A black woman is my boss. I accept her." What does she mean that she accepts her as her boss? It's supposed to be the other way around—the boss accepts the employee. Don't think that there aren't white women with white supremacist feelings.

**JORDAN:** In spite of the arrogance that you sometimes see in white women and their subtle condescension, can black and white women be friends?

**CHILDRESS:** Yes. I have white friends, but they cannot lead me on racial things. They may be able to lead me on something else, but they require too much patience and silence about my particular misery. They tend to silence us too much: "It takes time. Look at how much further we are." But particular things are on our backs. Some of our people have quietly died due to racism. I can get along with just about anyone. I think the greatest barrier between black and white women is racial; if it were class, the white women in your economic class could possibly be your good friends. White women do not really identify with us.

There are black and white people who have guarded friendships. You share much with them but not all of it. For instance, if some racial mistreatment made you very angry, you don't call them up. You call your black friends because if you call the white friends, they will say, "Wait, wait, wait. Maybe that's not what they meant" even before you get deeper into the conversation. You, of course, know damn well what was meant. Maybe, even if you are wrong, her first thing as a friend could be, "Oh I'm sorry you had to go through that. That was awful. How did it happen? I hope he didn't mean that." But you seem to present a threat as an angry or hurt black woman, so they tell you, "Wait, wait." Her job is to calm you down, not for your good, although she'll tell you, "Why upset yourself about him? That's ignorant." That's another thing we've heard all our lives, mostly from our own people: "Pay it no mind. That's just ignorance." Well, ignorance is something to mind. It can get you killed.

JORDAN: Do you think that ultimately it's the image that we have of one another that keeps us from being friends?

CHILDRESS: Their fate is different than ours too. There are a lot of good white people who have done a lot of good things. The Quakers worked hard to make life better. Say that you have a white woman who knows the house next door is for rent and she tries to get a black family in her all-white neighborhood. Before she knows it, someone may try to burn her house. Relatives will tell her, "You don't care about your children? You would let your children get hurt or die trying to do this? Your husband is going to lose his job." Her fate is such that maybe she would have to drop her plan for improvement of race relations. And it can happen to a black woman as well. I'm talking about the rigidity of some people who feel, "Look we can't do this all at once. I can't move you next door without my house being burned." She will not say, "I can't help you." Maybe she can't. Sometimes people cannot help you. Not if they have a baby in the home and someone says "I'm going to burn down your house." It's not that the person is weak. I can understand that. But she doesn't want to say, "I'm afraid." She says instead, "That's not good for you."

But there are a few people who have the better relationship, and they may be challenged on that even by someone in their own race. Whites are so challenged more than blacks. A black person who can't stand white people will still say, "She has been good to you. I can say that." But whites will be more puzzled by it and will ask things like, "Oh, does she take care of your family?" even when you say, "No, I like her, we're friends."

Then there are those who will say, "We just love her so. She took care of my cousin, she took care of my uncle." This one white man was a good sport about his story. He said, "I was raised by a black woman who now lives in a nursing home. My mother never had time for me, but she did. She was so good to me." He was proving a point to me. He said, "I loved her more than my own mother. I was that close to her." He's a grown, middle-aged man telling me all this. I asked, "Do you have a will?" He said, "Yes." I asked, "Would you leave your money to your mother or to that woman who raised you?" He said, "Oh Alice, go on." She was kind to him and he enjoyed her kindness, but he did NOT put her above his people. He would leave his money to his mother, not to her. That's fine, but don't say he loved her more.

**JORDAN:** You mentioned that the white women in *Rainbow Jordan* and in *A Short Walk* are based on actual persons.

**CHILDRESS:** Yes, Rachel, the Quaker woman, in *Rainbow Jordan*, is based on a woman I know who is now ninety-six years old. May in *A Short Walk* was a friend of my mother. They were people who did not feel racist . . . or had overcome such feelings.

**JORDAN:** Do you envision black women becoming more integrated into the women's movement as common concerns such as child care and abortion bring women of all races closer?

**CHILDRESS:** I think they've done that. Black women have been the most militant women in America. I don't call it integration when you're invited to say a word here or there. I was invited to a planning meeting some white women were giving on women's rights. I noticed no other black women were present and I asked about it. They said, "We're trying. That's why we invited you." They were saying it's theirs. That's all right; something can be somebody's and they invite someone in to be a part of it. I asked, "Well, where is it going to be?" I figured they wanted me to bring some black women into it. They said, "It's going to be at such and such a place." I asked, "How many people?" and they said, "Oh, the number's set. We're not going to have over three hundred." I asked, "Well, why am I here?" They had decided everything. What was my place on the planning committee? In other words, they were telling me, "We've made all the plans." We can no longer be integrated into strange territory. It has to be ours too. They have to be willing to share it, not give it up but share it. The question is: Am I a part of this? Am I here to share leadership? I've served on councils where they had one black at a time. At the next election, I'd be off and another on, so that they could then say, "We've had a black one every year." But there were never enough of us to matter when a vote was cast.

I no longer like the word "integration," but if you could simplify it and say we will be a full and equal part of the women's movement, I think that would attract a lot of black women. I don't belong to NOW [National Organization for Women]. I don't object to it. It's a good idea but they don't seem to have enough interest in black issues. There are some issues that are particularly black and they feel everything else that is not particularly black is more important. They figure we can all join hands on things that are not particularly black; it's for anybody. But we are all particularly somebody with very particular needs. It's like belonging to an organization, inviting Japanese women, but advising them not to bring up Japanese things. If you can fit in with us, you're welcome. Let the outsiders worry about being integrated. How can we achieve that?

JORDAN: When you look at young children and teenagers who often do not know their own family histories and do not have or know the words to voice their experiences or what they see, what kinds of things ought to be done to help them gain control over their own voices, to appreciate their stories and their personal histories?

CHILDRESS: I think we should teach histories and we should observe and celebrate commonly recognized American holidays in more creative ways. How about Thanksgiving? What do we have to be thankful for? We were enslaved then, so we shouldn't just have a turkey and talk about Puritans. We need to talk about being thankful for Harriet Tubman, Nat Turner, and being thankful for all who brought us out of bondage. We ought to remember those who came here for religious reasons—the Puritans—then put people in stocks and harassed so many who did not share their beliefs. We must remind people of the past and present human condition. We should also have memorials that would be educational. Easter is resurrection, the rising-again for Christians. It is the blooming of spring after winter passes . . . and we should think of that when we feel defeated or when we are down and people say that nothing else good can happen. The stone still rolls away, new grass grows green, and we still rise above it all together. We need to give an honorary roll call by calling the names of those people who gave their lives for this country, even in slavery. I think that black churches as well as schools have a great role to play in teaching children. Only by recognizing and respecting ourselves can we respect others.

**JORDAN:** Is there ever a role or function for a stereotype in fiction? Perhaps to introduce the reader to a character or to expose the danger of such attitudes?

**CHILDRESS:** I wouldn't say there is no role for a stereotype. I think the role for anything in literature is to lead us to some point or some important conclusion. The question is, why is that person a so-called stereotype? Do we know how to recognize a disguised stereotype, someone all dressed up, looking fine, and speaking fine nonsense with everyone applauding them and handing out awards? We see that frequently today where disguised stereotypes are dressed in finer clothes. If we can't tell it's a stereotype and it is, we can be influenced in dangerous ways. Old-fashioned stereotypes were easily identifiable. They were not easily understood because white people were the first to wear blackface as comedians, partially to make fun of black people but also because it was against the law for blacks and whites to act on the stage together. Whites played all the black parts by blackening their faces. When blacks could get on the stage, they also blacked their faces. For Bert Williams, a magnificent actor, that was the only way he could get on the stage. He had to do a caricature of himself. Today we assume nothing is wrong, but I think stereotypes are more disguised now so we are easily confused.

**JORDAN:** Was storytelling a part of your growing-up experience? If so, how has it affected your writing?

**CHILDRESS:** Yes. I listened to stories told by my grandmother and her friends. I also read a lot. But I mostly liked sitting around listening and going to Wednesday night testimonials in church. Every Wednesday night, people went to church and gave personal experiences. They got up after song and prayer . . . one might relate something like this: "My brother was in jail. My mother was in the hospital sick unto death." It was almost a chorus of others responding. "I got down on my knees, but I got up in the morning. Something told me to go downtown . . ." They were explaining how they worked their way out of a rough situation.

Another might say, "My daughter has a chance to go away to college and she is going to need a suitcase." Someone would say, "I'll do that." Then she might continue, "and she got to have a winter coat." Someone else would say, "I'm here, it's all right." The student was outfitted and a suitcase provided. We have lost a lot of our caring.

**JORDAN:** Have you ever felt pressure from your publisher and/or editor or audience to portray a particular kind of character or to treat a particular set of themes, or have you remained free of such pressures?

**CHILDRESS:** Oh, you get pressure. Everyone gets pressure and if you ignore it or pay it no mind, they squirm loose from you or try to get it changed themselves or interfere with it in some way or let you alone. It's not so much that they disagree with you. The commercial world is very smart. They know the place from whence rejection will come. If you show your work to that place where finance will be provided—they know what they're doing. Discrimination, racism, prejudice is not what is called a loose cannon. It's a well-organized thing. They'll say "Don't you think maybe you can do without this?" But that is your main point. You think, "I'll give in on this and give in on that and save this one to go straight on down the middle to the heart of my subject." That's the one they'll find on page 52. Never think they're so dumb they don't see it. We share that with sisters of any race—and some brothers too.

# LUCILLE CLIFTON

■

*Lucille Clifton has written nearly ten volumes of poetry and at least twenty books for children. Born in 1938 in Buffalo, New York, she began writing stories as a child. Haki Madhubuti writes that "at the base of her work is concern for the black family, especially the destruction of its youth."*

*The* New York Times *cited Clifton's first book of poetry,* Good Times: Poems *(1969), as one of the best books of 1969. She published her first children's book,* The Black BC's, *the following year. Her books of poetry include* An Ordinary Woman *(1974),* Two-

Headed Woman *(1980), and* Next: New Poems *(1987), among others. Her extensive list of children's books includes the* Everett Anderson *series,* The Boy Who Didn't Believe in Spring *(1973),* The Times They Used to Be *(1974),* Amifika *(1977), and* My Friend Jacob *(1980).* Sonora Beautiful *(1981), the focus of this interview, is one of the few works by an African-American female writer that features a white protagonist whose story is not related through the eyes of a black person.*

*Clifton has received numerous honors and awards including Poet Laureate of the State of Maryland, 1979–1982; and a Coretta Scott King Award for* Everett Anderson's Goodbye *in 1984. She has received two grants from the National Endowment for the Arts and holds honorary degrees from the University of Maryland and Towson State University. She is currently a professor of English at St. Mary's College of Maryland.*

**JORDAN:** What specific conditions seem to be in place when black and white women become friends?

**CLIFTON:** Well, that's an interesting one. Let me preface this by saying that I've only written the one book [*Sonora Beautiful*] with a white female character. I do have friends who are white women and the ones that I consider really my friends are people who respect me not only for my likenesses to them but for things that are not like them. They are the women whom I don't have to "get white" for or be any image except be myself. I can be exactly who I am. Sometimes it takes a little time to know if that's possible. But when it is, you know. You can be yourself with them, which doesn't mean they're perfect people either. Perhaps they're not liberals in the broad definition but I think with any friendship, it's the person who allows you to feel free to be yourself and who respects your similarities and your differences who is truly a friend.

**JORDAN:** Does class keep black and white women apart more?

**CLIFTON:** Sometimes, but I think class keeps black women apart from each other too. And white women apart from each other too. I think seeing beyond class, seeing beyond a lot of things, recognizing class but not allowing it to be a barrier, is important. I think that both black and white women are guilty of not recognizing class for what it is. But then we don't always begin and end in the same class. I always say I wasn't born on the hill. I'm on the hill now, but if I forget that I was not born there, then I'm in trouble, because I might fall off it. I'm around a lot of different classes. It's amazing to me that I tend to be. There are people in all of the classes around whom I feel comfortable because I don't see their lives as very different from my own at one time or another. I think people allow things like that [class] to get in the way.

**JORDAN:** So you definitely would believe that a white employer and a black maid could certainly become friends if they didn't allow things like class to get in the way?

**CLIFTON:** If they allowed themselves to, yes. Now I think in things like that though, one of them will think they're friends and the other one won't. In that kind of situation I've seen a lot of white employers like that, but you ask a black person if this is your friend and she'll say no. That happens all the time where because the other person did not hit them, they think they're friends. [*Laughs*] Oftentimes white people who are of a higher class think that just because you have not hollered "black power" in their face, you must be a friend. They think of it as a much more superficial thing. I'm not talking about that kind of thing when it comes to talking about my friends.

**JORDAN:** I've often been in situations where I wonder if the black about whom a white woman is speaking would also respond that this white woman is indeed the "friend" that she believes herself to be.

**CLIFTON:** I think that often she [the black woman] would not say that they are friends. I think with a lot of these people who say they are friends, ask them when they are alone what they think and see what they think. And I think often the person who is considered to be of the higher class will be mistaken about it. I have two friends that I'm thinking of. One of them would be considered in her younger years of a lower class than the other one, but they are both people who have gone against a lot of things and are sort of classless in a lot of ways and, me, too, and so I think we recognize that in each other and the things that we do that are class-based sometimes we can laugh about because we can recognize the roots as being class rather than in something intrinsic to our character and personality.

JORDAN: When a white woman "mistakes" or misperceives a black woman as being a friend, why do you think that happens?

CLIFTON: I think that because they would like to believe that sometimes—I'm really talking off the top of my head here—then they do believe it. It makes them feel good about themselves for one thing. A lot of people like to have a black friend. It's nice. [Laughs] It's true. And they can then have you in front of the others. It gives them a good feeling about themselves. But also I think there is a tendency not to recognize how complicated and subtle black people can be. We are considered simple people. But everybody I know, myself included, is much more complex than that; there are many more layers than that. And then also there are people in this country that are hungry for friendship, hungry for something, and if you tap into that, sometimes they hold on because they are hungry for some connection to something outside themselves. That's true of a lot of people.

JORDAN: And I think, for instance, the black maid would present herself as listening regardless whether or not she was. What matters is that she is perceived as listening.

CLIFTON: In a lot of cases the black maid has made a life of understanding others. The white employer has not. And so the black maid does *appear* to be more understanding, more forgiving, more tolerant. The other woman can recognize in that something positive, but she hasn't had to do that. We have had to do that. We've had to pay attention to other people. You had better. They've [white employers] sometimes not found it necessary to be as attentive, as understanding.

JORDAN: Do you think that in fiction in which white female employers are portrayed with their black maids that ambiguity is a major device, among others, that black women use in relating to white women?

CLIFTON: Probably. I think it's a very complicated thing because here are two women who've seen each other as enemies on more than one level in more than one way as females, as racially, so it's race and gender working against each other in a lot of ways. Certainly from our earliest time on this shore, black women and white women have been in competition in a lot of ways. Both recognize that. There is that complication, and then there is the ambiguity of females who traditionally in this country have not been socialized to be comrades. Traditionally, females in this culture—males have been socialized to bond—have been socialized to get males, to see each other as competition to get males for favors rather than as comrades and so there is also that working, I think. But it is changing. But there are a lot of levels of ambiguity and because the black woman is something of an enigma to others, to lots of others, it is ambiguous for a white woman as well, who may see things in a black woman that she would perceive as friendship or enmity when it's not that at all.

**JORDAN:** In looking more specifically at the novels, what role does the black female tend to play in white women's novels and what role does the white female tend to play in black women's novels?

**CLIFTON:** I don't know if I really know that question well enough. I have a feeling though that black women for white women writers symbolize a kind of exotic "otherness." And that is sometimes close to the noble savage idea, which is very common in American literature: the primitive still in touch with her animal nature who will lead us out of this high-tech, sophisticated thing to our baser selves. I'm not sure that's a compliment. [*Laughs*] Of course, I don't think black women novelists think of white women as the sophisticated, high-tech creature to which we aspire either. [*Laughs again*]

**JORDAN:** Is there ever a use for a stereotype in fiction—perhaps to introduce a character to the reader or to expose the danger of such attitudes?

**CLIFTON:** I think that if it is done well, yes. But there's always the danger that the stereotype will not be recognized as stereotype, and that's what happens. There're all kinds of possibilities but one has to be so careful to remember that when one writes a book that it will be read not only by like-minded folk, but it's out there for everybody, and like-minded folk are probably not the media and interpeters so you're in deep trouble really because it will be construed in a way that's not intended.

JORDAN: As you were drawing the character of Sonora, were there particular concerns that you had about the portrait you wanted to produce and what do you think of it?

CLIFTON: Well, she is a child, a young person, and in hearing the words I wanted her to say, I thought that those attitudes and words were typical of a certain class of persons—a person who has a parent who is a writer—and that's more generally true of white people of that milieu in which she finds herself. Now it was based on my kids so it's clearly not true for just white people. But it's more generally seen. It's sort of a halfway, New York attitude, and so I thought, "Well, this is a white kid." Now when I realized that, I actually called two friends to say, "Guess what? I'm writing this children's book. Everybody's white. What do you think?" One of my friends, Sharon Bell Mathis, said, "Why not you? Ezra Jack Keats can write about his characters, and they're black and he's white. Surely you can do this." I have forgotten who else I called, but they said, "Go on ahead. Write on." And so I did. And truly why not? I know Sonora better than Ezra Jack Keats knew Peter, his character. I had no question that I could do this because I have paid close attention so I didn't doubt that I could make a true-seeming girl. I've seen a million of these kids, and I've paid them attention. I believe that people can write what they want to. I'm very anticensorship, but I think they have to take the responsibility for what happens after that. I feel almost sure that not a lot of white authors can know black characters as well as I know white ones. This might be changing. But when they write something about what my kids might do, I don't know if they know my kids well enough at home. Even if they are teachers at school, they know kids at school. That's a different kid from the kid at home. It's just the nature of our experience on this continent that we have known these kids better. We have suckled these children. Not a lot of white people have suckled black kids. I don't know why they haven't. It's just one of those things. [*She laughs.*] It's possible to do cross-culturally.

Still, there are those who write irrespective of color or culture. There's this writer, Paul Goble, an Englishman, white, who writes about Native Americans. He writes some of the best books about them written for children. Byrd Baylor, a white woman, writes about Native Americans. Perfectly wonderful. Respectful, loving portraits, but they are rare.

JORDAN: What do you think makes for the difference?

CLIFTON: I think that you have to first of all realize that there is a culture to respect. I taught a course on American women writers at the college where I'm teaching now. I taught it because I noticed that my students there—primarily white middle class—didn't have the faintest clue about anything. I had them read all kinds of things. I showed them *The Autobiography of Miss Jane Pittman*. I presented them with a lot of women—American women of different kinds—and they were to write reactions periodically, and one of the girls wrote, "I don't even need this course as far as I'm concerned." Now she was trying to tell me how unprejudiced she was: "Black people are just white people with terrific tans." Now I understand that as not hostile, but I said, "No honey, no! No, I'm not." But they would write out of that idea that we're just like white people with a darker color. My whole history denies that. Don't trivialize my history. It's the same idea that people have when they say they're color blind. A lot of teachers tell me that. That's trivializing a hundred years. It isn't that we're all the same, so it's okay. It's that we're different and it's okay.

JORDAN: That's the tough part.

CLIFTON: That's the hard part. The fact is that I'm a black woman who's gone through quite a number of changes in fifty-four years, and my friend, Maude, has gone through some changes in her years and they're different changes, and we've seen things from different sides of the fence a lot. But we like each other. It's okay. She doesn't want me to be Maude and I don't want her to be Lucille. It's not possible. But I accept hers and she accepts mine. It's not like I've got to get like her for her to like me. There's something sinister about that idea which I think is very prevalent nowadays—that you have to be like me in order for me to appreciate you; that's a very sinister idea.

JORDAN: That's what a lot of kids feel particularly when they are on predominantly white campuses.

**CLIFTON:** Oh yes.

**JORDAN:** They're already trying to figure out who they are and then in the process they somehow buy this notion of assimilation at all cost, or maybe they've been brought up to think that if they really want to assimilate, they have to be white.

**CLIFTON:** And the white kids don't make it any easier because they get annoyed when . . . I'm the only black female on my campus and they [the students] come to me with all kinds of problems and foolishness. One thing white kids say is, "The black kids all eat together."

**JORDAN:** They always say that.

**CLIFTON:** And what I try to say is, "You had a hundred years to eat together." There's this kid who wears this t-shirt that says on the front, "Free South Africa," and the back says, "It's a black thing. You wouldn't understand." Well, this child is not a revolutionary. She's just kind of loud; she's great. The cutest thing. Well, the white kids were going to die. "Oh Lucille, how are we going to make it if she wears this t-shirt? It just puts us off. We can't have it. We'll never have dialogue if she wears this shirt." And I sat down and we had a little forum about it and I said, "You mean to tell me, when I get up I have to figure out if my clothes are going to get on your nerves? It's too much." "We understand, we understand South Africa. It's a human problem." I said, "Be that as it may. If we go to South Africa, they're not going to pick me up because I'm human. They are going to pick me up because I'm black. That is just a fact. Now the fact that you don't fully understand doesn't mean that you don't understand. It means you cannot have the same understanding I do. You see, that's the either/or thing. But, of course, you can have some understanding. My friend, Cathy, doesn't understand the kinds of things that I have gone through in my life, but she does understand that I have gone through some things. And that can be enough. That can be as much as she can do. I appreciate that.

**JORDAN:** It's interesting listening to you because I think that sometimes when I've been in situations where I started to get to know white men and women, I sometimes wanted them to understand fully.

**CLIFTON:** I don't think they can. But if they make the effort, if they make the valiant try because little, tiny things they wouldn't know anything about . . . little, tiny things in particular. And that's the trade-off whereas their life is something you know more about than they know about yours. That's just a fact. But there's a trade-off with anything. What we as black people understand about each other is our possibilities. We know that we might get knocked down at any time wherever we are. All of us—me and Harry Belafonte—can go into a certain place and if they don't know him, we're both going to be cussed out. That's the big thing that we have—our possibility about which they can't begin to understand how that feels. But if they make a try at it, that's a brave thing.

**JORDAN:** Yes, it is, even if there is some denying of the truth.

**CLIFTON:** Yes. Sure, sure. We have people who deny our history. I have a book that's called *The Times They Used to Be,* and it has illustrations and the people look like black people. I got a lot of letters from black people. Most of the letters from people who didn't like the illustrations were from black people who said: "Those black people are ugly. You shouldn't have those people in there. They got big, ugly noses." I don't get it. We buy into these definitions. Black people also sent me letters about the language because they don't wish to sound ignorant in front of white people. Well, we don't sound ignorant. *They* say we sound ignorant. That does not make it so. That's my thing about definitions. I don't care what *he* says, *he's wrong!* I'm not going to tailor what I know to be so and the richness and beauty of our casual language because some fellow in Dubuque, Iowa, might think that makes me ignorant. He's wrong. That's just the way it is. We have to be more self-defined and recognize bravery and recognize foolishness in ourselves as well because we can be right simple, but so can everybody else. We got a right to be simple too.

**JORDAN:** To what extent do you use sources such as histories, biographies, and autobiographies to create and/or develop characters?

**CLIFTON:** I use my personal experiences and the life that I have lived, which has been a lot of things. I have a very varied, I suppose, interesting life. It hasn't been lived on one level. It hasn't been lived in one world at all. It's been lived in lots of places in lots of ways and I use it all and I respond to the life that comes before me. I'm very big on learning and I have learned from my own experiences—learned to watch people to see how they act and to try to see beneath. I want them to see beyond me, the superficial me, and I want to see beyond that too.

JORDAN: With Sonora, you heard the voice and you knew the language.

CLIFTON: Yes, I knew the language. The language is different across the country. Black people don't speak the same way or use the same vocabulary, and none of us speak the same way all the time. And when I heard this language, it seemed to me that this language was more white language and would be better understood that way.

JORDAN: White women have often written novels with black female protagonists or main characters, but the reverse happens less often. Would you comment on this phenomenon? Do you think this pattern will remain the same, or will black women begin to portray white women a bit more frequently?

CLIFTON: Well, I think the reason for that is what I was saying earlier about what black women symbolize to white women. I don't know if white women symbolize anything to us particularly. We have not needed that kind of symbol, and I think they have more. They have been protected and stuff. We *wish* we could be. [*Laughs*] We're trying to get protection right now!

JORDAN: What can black and white women teach each other about writing and about living, or what can we learn from each other?

CLIFTON: [*Pause*] Let's see, what can white women teach me? Let me think about what Cathy, my good friend, has taught me. Let's see. I truly believe they haven't taught me. I truly believe I've taught them a heck of a lot more than they have taught me. I think it's the nature of what has been our relationship. I think that we can take to them something about buying definitions because they have been defined by others as well, and they have bought it, and it's been a disservice to them, and I think they're beginning to see that. We can learn something about what not to do. This is true.

We can learn something about not becoming caricatures of ourselves and not allowing ourselves to be imitation males and about not getting caught up in a lot of foolishness.

**JORDAN:** But, of course, we already know that.

**CLIFTON:** Oh yes. We undervalue what we know.

**JORDAN:** Do you envision black women becoming more integrated into the women's movement, if you think there is one, as common concerns such as child care and abortion bring women of all races closer?

**CLIFTON:** I think there's a women's movement that is redefining itself, and it is beginning to understand how it has been elitist to a strong degree. It is beginning to understand that it isn't necessary that they have to run it and they have to set the agenda. I think that it takes longer than one lifetime, and I think the women's movement might also be something that has to be like race—has to be reinvented every morning because a new generation of women are coming along with their experiences and expectations and have to be reeducated to be vigilant. I think there are different agendas for black women and white women. If we accept that, and if they accept that we can be people who work together, sure. I don't buy into men as enemy. I was married too long and have two sons and had a father and some men are less interesting than others, but contrary to what a lot of people say, I have been more messed over because of race than I have because of gender. I have heard women say that the opposite is true, but it's not true for me. I've always enjoyed being female and not felt myself put upon because of it. If I were put upon, I always believed it was for race. I believe in the women's movement. I know there are things that need to be addressed but I think black women have to address our own agendas, not address an agenda that is decided for us. And the same is probably true of white women and that's okay. It's not like, "I can't write it, I can't be in it. Let's forget it." If that happens, we've got other problems: growing up.

**JORDAN:** How should the agendas differ?

**CLIFTON:** Well, let's see. White women want to get off those pedestals, right? We want to quit cleaning them and they want to get off them. I have a poem, "Something to My Daughters," that starts: "Remember some of our sisters who put down the bucket are looking for us to pick it up." And I think that's true. If we are all going to "sister" together as female in our varying ways, there's more than one way to be female just like there's more than one way to be everything else. We all have to accept our varying ways, and I think that includes doing something about homophobia because I know people who don't want to be associated with the women's movement because somebody might think they're gay. Well, people think all kinds of stuff. Who cares? If we are sisters, we are sisters whoever we sleep with and you know who you are.

# ELLEN DOUGLAS

■

PHOTO BY EMILY HAXTON

*"Ellen Douglas" is the pen name of Josephine Ayres, who was born in Natchez, Mississippi, in 1921, and spent her childhood in Mississippi, Louisiana, and Arkansas. She currently lives in Jackson, Mississippi, where she continues to write. Her first novel,* A Family's Affairs, *won the Houghton Mifflin Fellowship in 1961. The* New York Times *named it one of the five best novels of 1962. In 1963 Houghton Mifflin published her first collection of short stories,* Black Cloud, White Cloud. *It too was named by the* New York Times *as one of the five best works of fiction for that year. Ten years*

*later, her novel* Apostles of Light *was a National Book Award final-ist, and nearly a decade later,* A Lifetime Burning *won a Missis-sippi Institute of Arts and Letters Award in 1982. She has written two other novels,* Can't Quit You Baby *(1988) and* The Rock Cried Out *(1979).* The Rock Cried Out *won a Mississippi Institute of Arts and Letters Award. Her short story "On the Lake" was included in the O. Henry collection of best stories of the year in 1962.*

*Ellen Douglas has been a writer-in-residence at the University of Mississippi for almost ten years. She has also served as a visiting professor at the University of Virginia and as the Welty Professor at Milsaps College. In addition, she conducts workshops, lectures, and readings throughout the country.*

**JORDAN:** What specific conditions seem to be in place when black and white women become friends?

**DOUGLAS:** For me, we're covering a long span of time, and conditions that have changed radically over the years since I first began to know black women, really as a child. I knew two or three black women whom I admired very much and who were strong women—that would have been in the twenties and early thirties. Except maybe in a few places like New York, Chicago, maybe, there was no way for a white woman to know a black except in the kitchen or in the laundry room. There would have been those cir-cumstances in the thirties and forties and even up to the fifties. Although in the fifties, I worked on a couple of community projects where there was a more equal give-and-take situation. But then, of course, everything changed radically in the sixties and the cir-cumstances under which black and white women, particularly younger black and white women, came to know each other were very different even in the South. Black women were involved in the civil rights movement, and so were white women. There were Head Start programs in the South, and liberal and radical white women were working in Head Start. To a certain extent I saw black women in those years but I'm not really very active in community projects. I'm a voter and active politically in some ways, but I don't take much part in campaigns. But my friends who were more political made close friends with some black women working on mainly politics and education and community projects. A certain kind of white woman made good friends among black women.

JORDAN: You're not going to say what kind?

DOUGLAS: [*Laughs*] Well, my friends. I have a good friend who is working in Congressman Espy's office in Washington, and she's a white woman friend. She's very active in Democratic politics over the years and has made close friends among her colleagues. So there are those two very, very distinct, disparate worlds and I don't have much experience [in the world of politics]. I have some experience practically speaking, but I don't have the kind of gut experience that enables me to write about that second world—those women [those politically inclined]—many of them are considerably younger than I am, and I don't come to that as readily as I do to the relationships that start in the kitchen. And then too, what those earlier relationships have to make them attractive for a writer is all the ambiguities and the varied hatreds and all the ignorance—whether deliberate or feigned—of each other. All that's very useful to a writer of fiction. I'm sure it would be true that there would be ambiguities in the second set of relationships too.

JORDAN: Probably so. If the situation isn't one in which there is true give-and-take anyway, then does race matter in terms of the women really becoming friends?

DOUGLAS: I don't think it's possible unless there's true give-and-take, but I think in some of those old relationships there was sometimes true give-and-take. When I read black women writers, the hostility toward all white people is so much the basis of the energy of the books that it makes me very much aware [of it] in personal relations. I may sometimes think there's more give-and-take than there is, because we're all so polite to each other. We're all *very* polite.

JORDAN: That's right. We may kill each other being very polite. [*Laughter*] Is there no in-between?

DOUGLAS: That's a lot to think about. I've been thinking about it for forty years.

JORDAN: I guess as long as we struggle with the questions and are aware of them, then maybe that's all we can do sometimes.

DOUGLAS: Yes. Bear witness.

JORDAN: What kind of role does the black female play in white women's novels? What kind of role does the white female play in the black woman's novel?

DOUGLAS: I don't think I can answer that very intelligently other than to go back to the sorting out of the two kinds of relationships. I can speak about my own novels. I think both white and black women novelists—as far as that is concerned men, too—and I tend to use what they see and what I have seen is the strength of black women. The characters one is drawn to and puts in books have that resilence. That's what I see white women writers using a lot.

JORDAN: I think so.

DOUGLAS: It seems to me that is true. I've read some Toni Morrison and I've read some Alice Walker and I've read some Toni Cade Bambara, these are the main black novelists that I've read, and it seems to me—I'm not sure about Alice Walker because it's been a long time since I've read any of her work—but with the other two there's usually a tendency to write about white people in an abstract way. The writer's purpose is not to deal with white characters, and white people are almost all the enemy so that there's not nearly as much variation in character even like in *Beloved* where the white woman saves the baby's life and really saves the woman's life too. She's not a character in the sense of being a personality. She's more like a function of that book. You know what I'm talking about? And I think that black women tend to do that with white characters in general.

JORDAN: You don't really get to know those characters?

DOUGLAS: Right. In the view of the novelist, the whole system has been so destructive that it's only her own people that she's concerned about whom we see as character. The rest is all the system. That may be too broad of a generalization but it's sometimes true anyway.

JORDAN: You have so many black female characters that we could talk about.

**DOUGLAS:** Yes, I do. I've been lucky. You do draw your characters from your life. You do. You have to. You start out from the real world and transform everything. And I've been lucky. I've known some interesting black women.

**JORDAN:** To what extent do you use sources, such as histories, biographies, or autobiographies, when you are developing a black female character, or do they come mainly from your imagination or own experience?

**DOUGLAS:** More from a combination of imagination and my knowledge of black characters. But occasionally a random reading of something will strike me. For example, when it first came out, I read the autobiography of Nate Shaw—*All God's Dangers*—and it was just such an extraordinary book. It just struck me so, and I used the voice and the character of Nate Shaw in the creation of the character Noah—the old man in *The Rock Cried Out*. I haven't run across anything like that that I've been able to put directly to use with female characters so mainly it's been the transformation of people—real people.

**JORDAN:** But you don't read autobiographies and things of that nature?

**DOUGLAS:** Not deliberately. Not for the purpose of building a character. I might do something like this. If I were going to try to put a woman like the mayor of Myersville, Juanita Blackwell, if I were going to try and put somebody like that in a book, I would go and see her and talk with her and ask her a lot of questions—if she would see me and I'm sure she would because she's very generous with her time. But I haven't done that because I haven't tried to do that kind of character. So it would depend on whether I knew someone I felt I could trust to understand what I was doing. For example, if I were going to put a doctor in a novel, I might spend a lot of time talking to a doctor just to hear the way a doctor talks and particularly, for example, the way he talks to himself, because I think if you have a technical profession, you talk to yourself in a little bit different way. So I would do that if I were going to build that kind of character.

**JORDAN:** Was there a lot of storytelling in your family as you were growing up?

**DOUGLAS:** Yes. Yes. I was fortunate to have two grandmothers who lived into their nineties. I knew them until I was in my thirties and I had access to huge amounts of material about their lives. And one of them loved to talk and to tell stories and the other wrote stories. She wrote children's stories and put us in them.

**JORDAN:** Is that part of what inspired you to start writing?

**DOUGLAS:** Yes. Yes.

**JORDAN:** It just seems to me that you must have heard a lot of stories for a long time and were very familiar with the art of storytelling.

**DOUGLAS:** That's just something you acquire almost unconsciously.

**JORDAN:** Your narrators clued me in. There's a way that they know how to tell a story and sometimes they seem especially confident about their ability to do so.

**DOUGLAS:** Sometimes I mean for a story to be formed in the way that an artwork is formed. The old man who is based on Nate Shaw is a storyteller, and he very often uses the structure of a biblical story, then moves it forward to say something that happened to his grandfather. Then all of a sudden you realize you are hearing the story of Abraham and Sarah. I knew an old man who used to do that. I could have never thought of that by myself.

**JORDAN:** Let's focus on some of the black female characters in some of your works and how they came to take shape in the various works. Perhaps we should begin with *Can't Quit You Baby.*

**DOUGLAS:** In a way, I'll be talking about how the book took shape, because that's governed by the way I knew Tweet. What I started out with was a character. I mean a live person, although she was dead by the time I started the book. But I had known a woman over a period of fifteen years or so who had Tweet's voice. That's Matilda Griffin talking and she told hair-raising stories— very often to embarrass the white person who was listening. She could assess who she could say what to and how uncomfortable she could make someone before she had to quit. And she told me that story about moving to town pretty much like the one in the book. I had—give or take—a half-dozen stories; I had more than I needed and I made up a couple of them. At first I was thinking about a collection of stories that Tweet would tell—and then I thought about it. I realized I had to decide what the circumstances were for her telling the stories and who she was going to be telling them to. It seemed to me it would be difficult, if not impossible, to have her in her own house telling those stories to black people because I hadn't heard that, and it would be very hard for me to imagine accurately; so I decided she had better be telling them to a white woman, and obviously the white woman is the woman in the kitchen, though I didn't particularly want her to be telling them to me. I made up a woman for her to be telling the stories to. Then I realized what I was doing was not putting together a collection of short stories but beginning to shape a novel. I got more and more interested in the development of a white character and the play between the black woman and the white woman. Having known a good many white ladies who, if not literally deaf, are deaf to what they don't want to hear, I decided I would try to make Cornelia that kind of woman and then bring her to the point where she had to hear and act through the agency of Tweet's forcing her to look at the world. So that's how the book evolved.

I actually went over to that woman's house [Matilda Griffin's] the day Martin Luther King died and we stood there and looked at each other just the way it is in the book. I made up the story with the stepfather. I had a good time with that. She did have an old grandfather though, who had been a veteran of the Union forces and had a federal pension. And then it went on from there.

With Carrie Lee in "I Just Love Carrie Lee," I set myself a kind of task. I wanted to see if I could make the narrator tell stories about her life, which she thought put her in a flattering light, but which really revealed her as selfish and self-centered, as a sad character. Again you start from the real world. I've known people who seem certain they're saying one thing, when in fact they are saying something else.

JORDAN: What do you think of your black female characters once you've produced them? Do you like them and are you attracted to them? For instance, do you find yourself sympathetic toward Tweet?

DOUGLAS: Oh very, very sympathetic to Tweet, but to Cornelia too. Both of them. I think when you're working with material like that—it's all very well to be sympathetic, but somehow you have to draw the sting of sentimentality. It's so easy to fall over into a sentimental version of those people. To give Tweet the toughness and ruthlessness that she has was essential or she would have just been a blob of dough, and by the same token it was necessary to give Cornelia the elopement—the business of the rebellion against her mother—or she would have been a pasteboard character. I'm always conscious that it's easy to fall into clichés, clichés in writing about black people.

JORDAN: Was it easier to portray one character than another?

DOUGLAS: Lots of time what gives you trouble is the fault of the book—making the book work rather than whether it's easier to portray one character than another. I had a terrible time putting *The Rock Cried Out* together. It has a complicated plot, and a lot goes on, but it wasn't the characters I had problems with. It was giving the book the form I wanted. With *Can't Quit You Baby*, I knew what I wanted to do with Tweet from the beginning. It was just a matter of doing it. I had more trouble in putting Cornelia together than I did with putting Tweet together.

JORDAN: Is there ever a use for a stereotype—perhaps to introduce a character or to point out the danger of such attitudes?

DOUGLAS: I hope not. I think the most minor character needs to have an individual voice and not be a stereotype. I hope that I can do that.

JORDAN: The next question concerns the narrative voice in *Can't Quit You Baby.*

DOUGLAS: I had a good time writing that book. The other thing involved was that I set out to try and make it a kind of fairy-tale book. There's the Rapunzel story, and there's the story of the villainous stepfather, so that when you say that the narrator shapes that story—like art stories—it's true and it's one of the things that I wanted to make work in that book.

JORDAN: Well, you just answered my next question on narrative voice. Sometimes I am just as intrigued by the voice of the narrator as I am by the voice of the character. I get caught up in the narrator commenting on something very directly—sometimes telling the reader, "Now pay attention to this."

DOUGLAS: I had the problem in that book—it is just true that ever since Flaubert and Henry James, we're supposed to vanish from our books. [*Laughs*] We're just not supposed to be there. And I have a strong feeling about the difficulty of telling the truth, the difficulty of telling a story that is true, however much of it is fiction. That difficulty comes in part from the fact that I lie to myself. Everybody lies to himself. And so at every point in writing a book you have the temptation to make the easy decision—to make a decision that won't make you uncomfortable as a writer or as a person, to justify yourself. After all, I'm not up in the clouds. I'm a sixty-eight-year-old Southern white woman who has lived in this world and seen injustice and been a party to injustice, party to blindness, party to deafness all my life, and the temptation of the writer, it seems to me, is to gloss over what's unpleasant, not to tell the truth. To fool oneself into thinking that you've told the truth. Using the narrative voice as I did in *Can't Quit You Baby* was really a device to say to the reader, "Look, this is a hazard you face when you read my book. It's not a book by an abstract creature out there floating on a cloud. It's not abstract; it's a book by a person who has axes to grind and has a hard time trying not to grind them." That seems to me to be integral to that book. Not always all books but that book.

JORDAN: When you're trying to be honest with yourself in the writing, could you be honest in knowing that you're about to lie and then just be comfortable with that?

DOUGLAS: But if you're going to be honest in a book, the reader has to know that—not just you. The reader has to recognize what that tension is between the writer and the material. In this book, it seems to me, the reader needed to know the tension between the writer and the material. And that's why I used that device. I would stop every now and then and say, "Wait, listen to me. I'm here." And as a matter of fact, my editor was dubious about that device, but I thought it would have destroyed the book if I had done it any other way.

JORDAN: I will return to a question about editors later, but for now I'd like to know what do you perceive Cornelia having to offer Tweet besides a job? I'm trying to get at what is the core of the friendship for Tweet, who must know that Cornelia is not listening to her most of the time. But it doesn't matter, because there is still something that brings her to that house every day besides the paycheck.

DOUGLAS: Maybe that's a flaw in the book. Maybe she doesn't offer enough. She's genuinely fond of Tweet. There are two or three scenes in which I try to dramatize that: the business of the scene when the old man dies and, of course, the Martin Luther King scene when she goes down to help. She offers very little, very little, but it's also true in all situations or in most situations like that that not much is offered, and it would be untrue to the situation for her to offer much more and for her to offer as much as she does is unusual. It's a good job for Tweet—to be in a household where people are kind and courteous and pay her wages every week. That is not so easy to find, so that to some degree it's self-interest. To some degree it's the recognition of a genuinely kind character and to some degree it's a limited friendship.

JORDAN: I ask that question because I can see what Tweet offers to Cornelia, so I can see why she would be drawn to her—I thought it was realistic, but I was trying to figure out what makes a woman like Tweet talk so openly with a Cornelia—maybe not "make," because she is clearly there by choice, because if she didn't enjoy it, she's the kind of person who would be someplace else. She understands enough about Cornelia and likes this woman enough to come. And then Cornelia's mother . . .

DOUGLAS: Oh she's bad, isn't she? [Laughs] That's another fairy-tale character. That whole structure of the elopement is really a Rapunzel story. She's bad, the old witch.

JORDAN: The scene in which she whips Cornelia is a tearjerker. I cried.

DOUGLAS: Did you?

JORDAN: Yes! That was awful to do that to that little girl and to not seem to have a clue as to how badly she had hurt her, not only physically but emotionally too. Is her mother's influence—I know she's not the only major factor in shaping Cornelia's personality, but she's got to be one of the big ones—a major reason she chooses not to hear?

DOUGLAS: I think I intended that Cornelia's total commitment to the man who rescued her and her total commitment to her children would be played off against that. She would be consciously or unconsciously saying to herself, "I'll never have a life like I had. I'll never let my children have a life like I had." And she says I think at one point to John that she did not love her mother the way she should have, and she can only love him and the children and it seems sometimes they're the only people she can love. And I think that comes out of the emotional deprivation of her childhood. It's a miracle that she can love anybody.

JORDAN: That's for sure after that mother.

DOUGLAS: I had a good time making that character. I love that dream.

JORDAN: Well, she was truly a witch, and I was just happy Cornelia left her home. As the novel begins, why does Tweet now feel the need to tell Cornelia her story? Is it really needing to tell Cornelia, or just her need to tell her story at this point in her life?

DOUGLAS: I think it's a need that I've seen over and over again not just in black women but in black men too, to look the white person in the eye and tell a story that'll make them think again and again. To tell a story about your life that forces a white person to see you in all your complexity, in all your difficulty. I've seen that.

JORDAN: By the end of the novel, Cornelia seems to have done more growing than Tweet. Tweet seems to have a strong sense of herself already. Would you comment on this growth that both characters to some degree undergo?

DOUGLAS: Yes, I think that Tweet came to accept Cornelia. In a very limited sense you might say Tweet grew in her capacity to accept this woman as her friend. Most of her growth has taken place prior to that. If she hadn't been growing all her life, she'd be dead. The major transformation seems to me with Cornelia. Of her coming out of her Snow White sleep and recognizing what the real world is like and accepting it. She needs to have things neatly laid out and to have clear-cut answers about everything. But Tweet has taught her as the record says, "I love you Baby, but I hate your low-down ways." [*Laughs*]

JORDAN: Now to "I Just Love Carrie Lee." Does the white woman understand Carrie Lee or feel the need to?

**DOUGLAS:** No, I don't think so. I don't think she ever could. What she says at the end is, "Carrie Lee is the only thing I got left of my own" as if she owns her—not loves her, but owns her.

**JORDAN:** Well, is Carrie Lee truly "one of the family" as she says?

**DOUGLAS:** No, I think Carrie Lee would have had a very ironic view of that.

**JORDAN:** Is it possible for this white woman to change?

**DOUGLAS:** Yes. I think it's possible to change. It's possible but not likely, but possible, always possible.

**JORDAN:** White women have often written novels with black female protagonists. But the reverse happens less often. Could you comment on this phenomenon? Do you think this pattern will remain the same, or will black women start portraying white female protagonists a bit more frequently?

**DOUGLAS:** I would think that the whole genre of novels by black writers not only will change but is changing. I was thinking before you came about what sort of experience you could compare the experience of black people to, as it's being expressed by novelists—that is the experience of deprivation and of all that we know is true of what went on in the South and not just in the South but in the whole country. And I was thinking about the Holocaust and thinking, too, not just about the Holocaust but the whole of Jewish life as has been expressed by someone like Isaac Bashevis Singer or Saul Bellow. There is a writer who has written about being in a concentration camp, and he was in a concentration camp—Primo Levi, an Italian; he's really a good writer. In one of these [true] stories, a father dies of starvation practically before his son's eyes. The boy is sixteen years old and the picture of him when he is released is the picture of a skeleton. But Levi writes with an extraordinary detachment about all of that. I'm not saying that he minimizes it, but he writes with a detachment and objectivity about man's inhumanity to man that's amazing, and more powerful for being objective. And it seems to me that as black women explore the black experience and the connections between black and white people, they'll move toward that objectivity and detachment. It seems to me that over the last few years there's been so much hatred, so much frustration to express, and it's obvious that you've got to get that out. Writers are just beginning to write about the Vietnam War with objectivity and detachment. It's as if you've got to get some distance first.

**JORDAN:** What can black and white women teach each other about living and writing?

**DOUGLAS:** I don't know if we can teach each other anything except to be humane and to be direct and to see each as human beings. That's about living. About writing—I don't know if I can teach anybody anything about writing. I have a hard enough time teaching myself. But just to read each other's works and keep an open mind—that's the main thing.

**JORDAN:** Do you envision black women becoming more integrated into the women's movement as common concerns such as child care and abortion bring women of all races closer?

**DOUGLAS:** I hope so and I think so. And I think in the next few years the women's movement is going to be considerably more active than it's been over the last few years. There are so many issues that we need to address, and they're issues that are the same for all women. They're not color related except in the sense that poverty is color related. I think there are issues that black and white women ought to be able to look at together.

**JORDAN:** When you look at young children and teenagers who often do not know their own family histories and do not have or know the words to voice their experiences or what they see, what kinds of things do you think ought to be done to help them gain control over their own voices to appreciate their stories and their personal histories?

**DOUGLAS:** That's something that really concerns me. It seems to me that not just for black kids, but for white kids too it's more and more true. The reason that people sat around and told each other stories was because they had nothing else to do. A winter evening, a summer afternoon—that's the only way you had to entertain yourself. I think it's essential for parents to give their children a link to their familial past and of the community they live in if it's humanly possible. I don't know exactly how to encourage that. For many more black kids than white kids the past, the period of the civil rights movement, was so difficult. So many risks were taken and life was so hazardous that what parents try to do is protect their children from that. They don't tell them about it because they don't want them to be scared. They don't want them to be scared to be themselves. I go to a black studies class that I occasionally sit in on in Oxford, and the kids up there have never heard of Medgar Evers, they've never heard of Emmett Till. They don't necessarily know who Henry Aaron is, and I think in part it's because the parents are trying to protect them from those frightening times. And the parents don't want to think about those times anymore either. But I think that's wrong. That's why I think it's important to have black studies in colleges and universities. If they're not getting those stories at home—white kids need to be getting them too—then they need to be getting them somewhere, and school is the only place they have.

JORDAN: I teach in a black college and I see these same kinds of concerns all the time. And it's too bad that in some ways in trying to protect the children from painful circumstances the parents are in a way not preparing them for the same set of circumstances that may come up in different forms.

DOUGLAS: Right. Right.

JORDAN: Have you ever felt pressure from your publisher and/ or audience to portray a particular kind of character or to treat a particular set of themes?

DOUGLAS: I've never felt any pressure of that kind.

JORDAN: What responsibility, if any, does the reader have in the creative process?

DOUGLAS: Just to read with an active imagination and to be receptive and to put your attention on the work and try to see what the writer wants you to see.

JORDAN: Have you always been disciplined in your writing?

DOUGLAS: No. When I'm working I try to sit down every day and work awhile. I go through long periods when I'm dry and nothing comes. And then I think of other things to do and do them to avoid writing. And, of course, when I wrote my first three books, I had young children at home, so there were a lot of interruptions.

**JORDAN:** When writing pulls you in one direction and other responsibilities pull you in another, how do you resolve the conflict?

**DOUGLAS:** Of course now I live mostly alone. My grandson is just here temporarily. But when I had young children at home, I had a husband who thought it was a good thing for me to write and made it possible for me to spend time writing and was encouraging and supportive. I think for a woman particularly that's essential—maybe not essential but extremely helpful; and the truth of the matter is I had a black cook, so I didn't have the whole responsibility of the household. When the children went off to school, I could go into my study and go to work. I can write a book in a few years if I can spend as much as two–three hours a day on it and if you have that much free time, you can do everything else. Working on this book, I'll be teaching in the fall. I spend two and a half days in Oxford every week. The other four days I can work on the book for at least half a day every day so it works out pretty well.

**JORDAN:** I liked reading the afterword to *Black Cloud, White Cloud*. It's so poetic to end it by saying change does not change. What did it feel like to go back and read the stories?

**DOUGLAS:** Well, I was scared to death. I hadn't really read the whole book in twenty or twenty-five years. And I thought, "It's going to be so dated and maybe I'm going to hate it." I was pleasantly surprised to find that it really still spoke to the issues that concerned me when I wrote it. I didn't feel like it was dated. I was glad.

# KAYE GIBBONS

■

*Kaye Gibbons was born in 1960 in rural Nash County in eastern North Carolina. She studied at North Carolina State University and the University of North Carolina at Chapel Hill.*

*Her first novel,* Ellen Foster *(1987), was widely and enthusiastically reviewed throughout the United States and Europe and won the Sue Kaufman Prize for First Fiction from the American Academy and Institute of Arts and Letters and was accorded a spe-*

*cial citation by the Ernest Hemingway Foundation.* Ellen Foster
*was also chosen by the American Library Association as one of the*
*Best Books for Young Adults in 1987.*

*Her second novel,* A Virtuous Woman *(1989), also received wide*
*praise from reviewers and widespread international publication.*

*In 1989 the National Endowment for the Arts awarded Gibbons*
*a fellowship to write a third novel,* A Cure for Dreams, *which was*
*published in the spring of 1991. For her work-in-progress, she re-*
*ceived the Pen/Revson Foundation Fellowship. She is writer-in-resi-*
*dence at the library of North Carolina State University. She and her*
*husband, Michael, a landscape architect, and their three children,*
*Mary, Leslie, and Louise, live in Raleigh, North Carolina.*

**JORDAN:** What specific conditions seem to be in place when
black and white women become friends? For instance, does class
seem to matter more than race in the forming of such friendships?
Is it easier perhaps for two middle-class women to become friends?

**GIBBONS:** I think in talking about black and white women in
the South you almost have to draw a line between black and white
women in rural areas and in urban areas. I think that discrimination in real estate and in the job market in urban areas is the biggest barrier, although that is breaking down. Women meet other
women through their jobs but also through living together, and I
think that in urban areas if we can't live together then we can't be
together. There is so much reluctance to go into a black area to a
gathering or cookout or to a white area to a Sunday afternoon
cookout. But I think that in a rural area, it's much easier because
historically black and white women have lived along beside each
other. Although that relationship in the South has generally been
the domination of the white woman over the black woman with the
black woman being the employee, still friendships were formed. I
know that for both of my grandmothers, the black women who
worked for them were their confidantes and could be counted on
as friends. On both ends of the relationship, the black women and
the white women, both considered themselves primarily involved
in an economic situation but they also knew that they were involved in a friendship. I think that one condition that is in place is
where people live, and I think that is a much stronger condition

than preconceived notions of class and race that we get off television. I can watch *Eyes on the Prize* all I want to but when I go out on my street, when people are out on the sidewalks on a Saturday afternoon pruning the trees, if I don't see both white and black people, what good is that show to me? It changes my heart but I don't have any place to practice it. All it has been is an intellectual exercise, and I think that conquering prejudice is a spiritual and emotional exercise, and the only way that can be done is by seeing and being with people of color.

**JORDAN:** So you believe that blacks and whites must have the opportunity to actually participate in activities together to get to know each other?

**GIBBONS:** Right. And I think that sending children to school is not enough. If it were enough, then 1954 would have taken care of Bensonhurst. Integrating the schools has not been enough. I think as was shown in Chicago in 1964 when the Southern Christian Leadership Conference went in and tried to make headway into real estate discrimination, that's difficult. Very difficult.

**JORDAN:** What kind of role does the black female play in white women's novels? What kind of role does the white female play in the black woman's novel?

**GIBBONS:** My reading over the past ten years has been limited to historical and scientific nonfiction and Southern novels. Sometimes I've branched out when someone has handed me a book and said, "You should read this." Understandably, I've not run across this in the nonfiction but when I have noticed it in Southern fiction as in the stories of Peter Taylor or with Eudora Welty or the older generation of Southern writers or with Faulkner, I've seen repeatedly the role of the stoic, strong, somewhat manipulative, but still good black woman and the quiet white woman who is dependent on her. I noticed when I wrote *A Virtuous Woman* that this came through in a big way with the maid. She is in charge of the household, but she lets the white woman believe she is in charge. But everybody knows that the white woman can't boil water without burning it. That's also true in my own past, in my own history, so via fiction and my personal experience I have this ready-made black woman for me, and in order to get beyond that I have to increase my circle of black female friends to the point that I am close enough to bank vice-presidents who happen to be black females so that I can understand their experience enough to write about it.

And I think that it is better for a white woman—and this may sound bad—writing with truth and validity and through knowing and through a personal knowledge than to write about a black woman she's read about in the paper because she won't know this character. She won't know this woman. And I think it's a mark of white superiority—this tradition in the South of this superiority or the tradition everywhere—that white women writers feel like they know black women and know their experience but that's certainly not true. But I think on the other hand . . . I've not read a novel written by a black writer with a white female protagonist because I think that maybe an author like Toni Morrison—she is sharp enough to recognize that one writes what one knows and she does a beautiful job of that. She does not exploit the stereotype of the modern white female—whatever that is. As far as I'm concerned, the modern white female is beginning to look like a very unattractive creature. I read in the paper the other day in the Want Ads of a woman in a very good part of town who advertised that she was looking for a substitute mother to care for a newborn baby starting in July, which I assume is when she delivers. I wanted to call up and say "I'll take the job," and then go over there and bark at her. In some ways I read between the lines, and I see her wanting a strong and caring older black woman to care for her baby so that she can go to work and make her BMW payments, and I've had enough of hearing about that. She should just drive a Toyota and look after her child herself.

JORDAN: As you were drawing the character of the black female—here I am speaking of Starletta but feel free to comment on the maid in *A Virtuous Woman* as well—were there particular concerns you had about the portrait you wanted to produce? In other words, how was this figure born? What do you think of her?

GIBBONS: I have with me a copy of the Winter 1986 *Carolina Quarterly* in which I wrote a poem in 1986 before I wrote *Ellen Foster*. It's a poem called "June Bug" written from the point of view of a small girl named June Bug, whom I later named Starletta. It's written from the point of view of Ellen Foster talking about June Bug—i.e., Starletta, and the poem is reproduced in *Ellen Foster* in the funeral scene when she looks up into the audience and sees

Starletta squirming. In the poem she says: "Starletta has orange teeth; she plaits her hair for . . . ." The child in the poem is just expressing her admiration and love for June Bug and also a great deal of longing to be like her and have this freedom to express the elemental and primal nature that her own alcoholic father and sickly mother thwart in her. She can't be a child but Starletta can be a child and she does. She acts out. So Ellen Foster looks at that and longs to be that way, but she can't be that way because she's too busy trying to make sure her own needs are met. She's a perfect child of an alcoholic but because June Bug's or Starletta's parents look after her she can do things that a ten-year-old is supposed to do. She can suck her face in and draw what she can from the red clay. And when Ellen Foster tries to do this, she gets slapped, so the core of the book started from this relationship between a white child and a black child. And when I started to write the book—that isn't all that I wanted it to be about—I wanted that to be a part. I didn't know exactly what I wanted the book to be about but I wanted to hear this Ellen Foster's voice so I didn't start with a list of notions about class and race in the South and then create characters to go through these motions. It started with characters. It started with the concrete, and if the concrete notions rose and fed on themselves, then they became the personification of abstract ideals like "Do unto others as you would have them do unto you." "You can't depend on your white family to look out for you. They can have a knife in their hands." Because I don't trust books that start out about an idea—they always sound stilted and they read to me like sociological treatises and not good stories. I started with two little girls and I let them have the idea rather than let them be mouthpieces for my ideas about the way the world should work.

**JORDAN:** Ellen Foster's voice sounds so real. Was it difficult to get inside her head?

**GIBBONS:** Once she started talking, the problem at the end of the day was leaving her voice. I listened and wrote. Because *Ellen Foster* was the first novel and had been incubating for twenty-five years, it just so happened that the structure and organization—all those craft elements of the novel came simultaneously right along with the voice. The voice was never out of control, but with the third novel that I'm finishing right now, the woman sounds like an adult Ellen Foster, and the voice in the previous draft was out of control. It was wild, and what I've had to do is go back and calm her down and put this woman in order.

**JORDAN:** So the editing process is where you are more involved in helping the character to control her own voice?

**GIBBONS:** That's right. She sounded like she was on a manic swing. She was sitting in a room talking to herself; she sounded very disjointed. Now I've had to go back and tell her "You may know what you're talking about but we don't. So just calm down."

**JORDAN:** How long did it take you to write *Ellen Foster* then?

**GIBBONS:** I'm a little embarrassed to say—I always am. It only took about six–eight weeks because the voice was so strong and the voice edited itself. And I was silly enough to think that would happen again. So when I started writing the second book and it did not happen, I became very depressed and discouraged and said, "Well, so much f⸱⸱ writing books. I'll waitress or something." I have no marketable skills so I was in quite a fix but my editor, Louis Rubin, talked to me and explained that I wasn't a one-trick pony but that art and craft have to be. We can't take craft for granted so the voice may be clear and wonderful and good, but we have to use that other side of our brain to edit.

**JORDAN:** For the most part you don't have a problem getting out of the way of the characters and just letting them speak?

**GIBBONS:** No. All three books are told from first-person point of view. I spent a long time beating myself up because I was not writing in the omniscient voice, and I started to believe that I couldn't write in the omniscient voice, and I started writing my own bad reviews. I began writing things like "when will she graduate beyond this first person," like what I'm doing is easy. The omniscient voice is hard, but I also think that that was my own inability to give myself a break. There is also a Southern History Collection in Chapel Hill of interviews collected in the South of both black and white people talking in 1939 by the Federal Writers' Project. I read those—a lot of them—this sounds phony but I said "The human voice is art." The human voice is just as artistic as is that omniscient narrator's voice in *Love in the Time of Cholera*. There's no difference in the level of artistry. In the preface to a volume of this collection, W. T. Couch, a regional director, said, "With all our talk of democracy, it seems not inappropriate to me to let the people speak for themselves." And I said, "Right on! That's wonderful!" and it was just the encouragement I needed to sit down and once again let a Southern woman tell her own story.

**JORDAN:** One of my questions for you had been whether or not you had considered using omniscient or limited omniscient narration because first person worked so well in the novel.

**GIBBONS:** Never in the first one. Sometimes in the second one. But the omniscient narrator didn't work in the third one—it just didn't work. It's just lately come upon me that if it doesn't fit, don't force it. I'll start to read novels that fall apart on page two, and I realize that the author has had a notion before he or she started writing of who should tell a story and they have to let the person tell the story come hell or high water. And in the background, a minor character is bursting at the seams to tell the story. And I have just lately let that character come forward and speak. It's like having someone standing on a stage and usually in the second and third book they were white men and they were strong—and they were stoic like Andy Griffith and they were standing center stage talking the story. And it was boring because their language was ordinary and in the background—in the chorus there was a woman—a real woman with a rich, metaphorical, allegorical bent to her language who could tell the story so much more beautifully, and I've had to yank this Andy Griffith character away from the microphone and push the woman up there and say, "Now you tell it." And constantly every day when I sit down to write I give this woman courage to tell the story because she started out as a milk-toast character. She listened behind the walls when her husband talked nasty about her to his friends and now I've gotten rid of him. I killed him off very early. And she just tells the story the way she wants to and I like her so much more.

**JORDAN:** My next question has to do with to what extent do you use sources, such as histories, biographies, or autobiographies, when you are developing a black female character?

**GIBBONS:** With the first two, I didn't at all. With the third, I wasn't planning to, and I wasn't at all until I stumbled on a book of midwife stories from Georgia, and I stumbled on these interviews.

What I gleaned from these sources more than anything were some anecdotes that I put in here, and it wove into this narration—like the man who drinks forty-two cups of coffee on a dare or the young man who overdoses on BC and Stanback powders and his lips turn blue. I got that out of there and medical journals too. I got the language. In this book there's so much bizarre language in it that has been rescued from pre–World War II South. After World War II so many people left the rural area and moved to town, moved to Raleigh, and they left that traditional language behind to die out. It was like an excavation process. For example, in one interview a woman talks the whole interview about menopause but she never says menopause. She says, "when nature left me." And then having a baby out of wedlock, the woman says she has the baby "behind Jesus's back." And there's the story of the old woman who traded guinea eggs for fish hooks. Or the man who was "polite as a basket of chips." Isn't that wonderful? I more or less luxuriated in this language, and I wrote everything down and I plastered my office walls with them. The first draft looked like I wrote the story just to keep all this stuff but by the third and fourth drafts these metaphorical speech patterns had worked themselves into the story so they don't seem showcased. And I expect the copy editor to flag lots of these things, and I'll have to say no. I'll have to make a case for using "fellowshipped" as a verb or calling the story of the family moving so often to beat the rent and the small daughter having fits for the "setting out" man. They called the landlord the "setting out" man because he would come to set them out and so the girl Florence would fake seizures. Or the story of Kate and King Solomon Sims from Florida. He was a disreputable man who married a young black woman. And she birthed twins, and he left her and went back to Florida. And she just mourns for him. He comes back and abuses her again and then runs off again to New York City and she says—and they named the babies after their home states of Florida and Georgia—and she says "King Solomon Sim never give me nothing but Florida and Georgia but how I do love him is untelling." You should look for this book. It's called *Folks Do Get Born*, and the editor is Marie Campbell. It's wonderful; she edited it right before World War II.

**JORDAN:** I will do that. White women have often written novels with black female protagonists. But the reverse happens less often. Would you comment on this phenomenon? Do you think this pattern will remain the same or will black women start portraying white female protagonists a bit more frequently?

**GIBBONS:** I think back on the history of published novels by black American women. I think in the recent past, I see Toni Morrison, I see Alice Walker, rise up, and when I think of the publication of black female novelists before this time, Zora Neale Hurston rises up to me. And I've read these women's novels, and they do have the black protagonist and I think the underground well—the rich mine or lore of stories by black women—has just so recently been tapped and these women have just so recently been able to earn recognition by a publishing community dominated by white male New Yorkers that they have exploited the black experience and the black story. There is certainly enough for these women to use. If I were a black female novelist, I would look first to my own experience and to my story, and I think that there is so much there with African tradition. I'm thinking back on the turn-of-the-century poet James Weldon Johnson; he was just a poet until he tapped into African history and African symbols and African rhythms. So if I were a black female novelist, I think I'd have enough to write about using these traditions twenty-four hours a day, seven days a week. If I had so much beautiful background material, I don't know that I would go searching for another protagonist. I really would not see the point, and I think that it's important for young black readers to read novels that portray black families in a positive light. The *Cosby Show* can't be the only family that's portrayed in America, and I think that by reading stories written by black women with black families that are intact all children can learn that there's more to the black experience than what they see via Dan Rather. So I'm not so sure for this point in time that it's so necessary for a writer to portray a white lead.

But I think that it's more important that white women learn to portray black women as characters who are not just acting as maids, quiet confidantes, the way I have portrayed black women in my fiction because that's all I know. And as I develop more black friends, I will be able to see the experience and know the experience through something more than the literature of Paula Giddings. And I'll be able to portray—not in a more positive light— I've tried to portray black women in a positive light because the black women I've known have been positive—almost saviors of me. They were. They saved me as a child. I'm not quite sure but I think that black female writers should not go out and artificially construct a white female protagonist for the sake of having a white female protagonist because that would come across as phony and contrived if it's not a character constructed out of experience, out of knowing. But I'm perfectly satisfied right now with the work that Toni Morrison is doing. She's really phenomenal.

JORDAN: Yes, she is. You answered part of my next question, which is what can black and white women teach each other about writing and about living?

GIBBONS: We have to teach each other about living first, by living and interacting. And I think out of the living will come the driving force for the writing. I certainly was taught some things by reading *Beloved*, but in some ways that reinforced to me the sadness that I already suspected and really that I already knew deep down was there. After *Beloved*, you can never go back—you can't go back in the history of black literature. I think that book propelled the whole tradition forward and it moved up the agenda. I've not read *Temple of My Familiar*, but I have that and it's on my summer list. And I'm probably a little shaky about reading it. I mean it's something that you just know is going to be a big experience that you circle it and stalk it and figure out the best way to approach it. And also what *Beloved* did was encourage me to learn about the Civil War and to learn the facts that I had tried not to learn. I went and got Shelby Foote's three-volume history of the Civil War to do that, but I think that until people are really living together and doing life together and until people are out on the streets together that not as much will be learned as could be learned.

JORDAN: Do you envision black women becoming more integrated into the women's movement as common concerns such as child care and abortion bring women of all races closer?

GIBBONS: I think certainly the women's movement is perceived as a white woman's movement. One of the reasons being Betty Friedan, Gloria Steinem, and Bella Abzug—all white women, but also there's Barbara Jordan. But when I think of those women as being positive forces in the women's movement in the sixties and seventies my tally is three white women and one black being the team. And certainly when I was reading *Ms.* magazine, it was almost for, by, and about white women. To some extent black women were included but I think that has to change, and I think that black women will be involved. I think of the woman who is leading the tenants' management movement and travels about from public housing project to housing project—I can't remember her name—empowering people to take charge of public housing. Certainly, women like this that you don't see on the *MacNeil/Lehrer Report* arguing the fine points of the women's movement, but they're there. They're out in the streets; they're doing work. And I would hope that white males don't perceive the women's movement in relation to black women as something that white women are doing for black women because that would be horrible, and I think that's crippling to issues like child care. It has to be either something black and white women are doing for each other or with each other. There has to be a parity. I asked my husband the other night if he thought the world was in sorrier shape than it had ever been in and he seems to think that because we are getting so much more information about it than we used to that . . . but I don't know. It's depressing to me. Here in North Carolina where I live has the highest infant mortality rate and that was just published yesterday. That's depressing, but we're building roads, we're building a baseball stadium, I say with irony. We're going to see that baseball team, and we're going to have that new children's museum built. [*Pauses*] That's despicable.

**JORDAN:** Well, when you look at young children and teenagers who often do not know their own family histories and do not have or know the words to tell their experiences or what they see, what kinds of things do you think ought to be done to help them gain control over their own voices?

**GIBBONS:** Let me address that from a first-person point of view because I recognize that with my own children. My husband's family is small and lives in New York. They're all up in either the Bronx or Queens. We see them three times a year. It's nice to see them, but we don't see a lot of them. They tell family stories; they tell stories my husband's never heard; and when they see me coming, they know that they're going to be asked to tell about the time that Uncle Ed threw urine out the window and they know I'm going to ask them to tell about the time Uncle Ed cooked stew on the porch and the time that Uncle Ed took the taxicab from Cork to Galway, Ireland. I don't get the feeling that they had been telling these stories until someone got up there who wanted to use them in a book. I had come from a large extended family, but I have not had much communication with them. We've been feuding for years, and then I realized the other day that my five-year-old did not realize that I had parents. They're dead, but I suppose that maybe she thought I was hatched, and she was surprised to learn that I had a brother. She vaguely remembers going to visit a sister. She has no concept that I have aunts, uncles, or cousins, and when I told her this, she was thrilled. She wanted to go meet them. How could I tell my child, "Well, we had a big falling-out years ago so I'm going to deny you your history because I have so much pride?" So I'm almost at the point—not quite—that I'm going to just suck it up and reenter the larger family group because it is very important. There are so many families literally cut off from families through death, through distance, that they have no way of assimilating family history into their present-day experience. But I do. I have a big family thirty miles from here so I need to swallow my pride and go back, and I just sense the emptiness. I grew up in this huge family—forty cousins—and we didn't grow up telling stories. There was no overt storytelling tradition. We didn't sit around a pot-bellied stove, and my grandfather didn't spin yarns. Now I sort of laugh; they have storytelling festivals and people go and use it vicariously because they don't have the chance to live the stories. I think it's more important that my children live and create stories than to go to the state capitals and sit on the lawn and listen to stories by a man who has read them or listen to a woman telling Zora Neale Hurston stories. It's so much more important and significant that they help create them so I've got to do that. That's on my list. As soon as I finish this book, I'm going to reenter the social group of the family.

JORDAN: Do you see literary critics, particularly black ones, having a special role in shaping how the stories of black women's lives are read, assessed, and taught?

GIBBONS: Well, if the writers read the literary critics and use the criticism as editing, that's tragic. And I have too much confidence in the women. I don't think the sharp cookies will let this happen. I think that if a young black female writer lacks confidence—well, if she sits down to write a book, that implies so much confidence, and I think that implies enough confidence to disregard what is said. I used to think of literary critics with a big L and a big C, and I referred to them as "The Critic," but recently I've come to see them as professors trying to get tenure or people who are getting paid to write a review and—oh this sounds so ugly, but they seem to be people who either like the sound of their own voice, or people really trying to make a contribution to the corpus and history of fine literary criticism in the United States, and I think the latter is the minority. For example, I read—and they blew this up and put it on a poster for *A Virtuous Woman*—a review of *A Virtuous Woman* that called it "a small masterpiece." My head just got so big, and I was very proud of it, and then I met the person who said that, and she was a wonderful woman but she was not a trained critic. She was a receptionist in the Features department of this newspaper who had written the review to make extra money. I'm sure other people who read it said, "Ah the critic says," but it was just a human being. It was just somebody writing this review, so I would hope that someone wanting to write a book about her own experience as a black woman growing up in the United States would not read articles about Toni Morrison's work or Alice Walker's work thinking "Will they like this" or "I have to sound like that." Good writers that I know don't do that. The bad writers that I know do it all the time. Their writing is more or less a corollary to their reviews, and that's bad.

**JORDAN:** Now I would like to ask just a few questions on the novel *Ellen Foster* in particular. It would be easy for Ellen Foster to become a racist like her father and to share the narrow-mindedness of her aunt or her grandmother, but she doesn't. What allows Ellen to be so different from her family? Does the legacy of her mother's compassion influence her to see beyond the surface, or is it simply circumstances that allow Ellen to grow and change?

**GIBBONS:** Well, I think she does start as a young racist mimicking what she hears at home. You never hear the mother say anything like that, and later we find out that the mother and Mavis have been good friends, so it's safe to assume that the mother was not a racist. But the father is. And we are what we eat. We are what we hear, and so naturally Ellen Foster starts out parodying racist slogans like "I won't eat after a black person. I won't drink after a black person," without ever giving it any thought. When I saw *Seven Days at Bensonhurst* or when you look at footage of the children at Selma and Chicago, you see children out there saying, "Nigger, go home." And they don't know; they might as well be saying $E = mc^2$. They're words that have been put into their mouths, and that's why I think that intervention at a very young age is important before the words burn a hole in the child's mind. With Ellen Foster, Starletta came along before the words were burned into her psyche and before she started acting out those racist slogans that she had been taught by her father. I think that she went to Starletta's family and used them first as a refuge. When she first starts going, she wouldn't sleep under the covers. She thinks something, I suppose, might crawl on her. I never figured out what she thought would physically happen to her in the bed that a black person had slept in. But I can remember as a child my father parroted to me all the bigotry that he'd grown up with and on and on. And I can remember having those feelings, but Martin Luther King and black friends intervened into my life before they were burned into the front of my head. And the same thing happens here. At first she just uses and embraces Starletta's family as support or as a refuge, and then she realizes that by being there nothing has happened to her and that she's safer there than she is at home, and I think at that point she starts to think of racism as an intellectual problem and once she gets it in her mind that it's illogical, then she can start to feel it because Ellen Foster isn't a child who feels first and then thinks. She is a child who thinks first and then feels because that is the survival instinct. She had to examine the situation and then the feeling came.

JORDAN: Do you think that Starletta knows Ellen Foster as well as Ellen seems to know Starletta?

GIBBONS: I'm not sure. I think that Starletta is the perfect child because she doesn't seem to care. She just literally doesn't think about it. Ellen Foster is just grooving on the thought that Starletta might be amazed by the towels with the S's on them, and I think Starletta just went into the bathroom and pulled any one off the rack and probably got it real dirty and left it on the floor. But that was okay. She didn't need to reciprocate. Ellen Foster just needed to get it out of her system. She needed to act on her new and good impulses. I liked Starletta a great deal, and I got to the end of the book and realized she hadn't talked. She had done lots of stuff, and I had enjoyed the sight of her but she didn't talk. I think I put off having her talk until I got to the end of the book and I said, "Kaye, you've got to say why this girl has not said a word and I said, well she stutters and doesn't like to talk." I took care of that real quickly.

JORDAN: I found the ending especially moving. I felt a great deal of growing tension because I was afraid that Starletta wouldn't understand that it was so important for her to come to Ellen's house. I couldn't be satisfied until I got to the end and knew for myself that she actually was going to show up and in fact did.

GIBBONS: Ellen made sure she did. She had the sack at school with the personal hygiene in it. That was important to me that she came. And I don't feel like I handled it. I feel like Starletta handled it, and Starletta handled it just right. I watched what she did and got my cue from her and wrote it down. So it couldn't help but be right. Starletta was going to do what came naturally to her. Learning that as a writer requires a great leap of faith, and it's like delegating responsibility, and I had to learn to delegate responsibility for my story to my characters and not feel this urge to be in control all the time. It's like the president of a large corporation who's always going to the warehouse to make sure the right widgets are in a box. He has to trust that the people on the line put the right number of widgets in there, and I had to trust Starletta.

JORDAN: Well, I felt that Ellen Foster was finally happy. She had a family, and I just wanted to make sure she also still had her friend Starletta.

GIBBONS: You hear the saying that someone who is at peace with herself and has a peaceful mind can slip off to sleep without having to read or without tranquilizers or without having a drink. You see people who can just fall asleep like children and when Starletta went to sleep, I thought here's a girl who is so at peace and this feels so natural to her that she can fall asleep. But I could see in my mind's eye that there was Ellen Foster just grooving on the fact that this has all come to fruition.

JORDAN: Was it easier to portray one character than another? The father? The grandmother? Ellen Foster versus Starletta? Or did they all seem to come naturally?

GIBBONS: Well, the grandmother was hard for me because I disliked her so much that I didn't want to bless her with any humanity at all. So I had to constantly say, "She's a human being." There has to be a motive. She can't just be a sinister type. She has to have some degree of humanity. I hated her to the point that I couldn't let her show it. I had to let Mavis. Mavis told it. Mavis got me off the hook. She did a beautiful job of releasing me from the responsibility of humanizing the grandmother.

**JORDAN:** Have you ever felt pressure from your publisher or audience to portray a particular kind of character or to treat a particular set of themes, or have you remained free from such concerns?

**GIBBONS:** Well no. The only thing I get from my editor who is Louis Rubin, the undisputed godfather of literature in the South, is that I strive for excellence. I know that sounds like something they say during the Olympics; it sounds so phony. With *A Virtuous Woman*, the manuscript was ready to go into production, and he sent it back to me and he said, "there is no reason why we shouldn't try to make this the best it can be." I forget the part but he said, "This is a weak link. Why don't we see what we can do with this to strengthen it and bring it up to the level of the rest of the book?" I had had it with writing the book by then; I was about nine and a half months pregnant. I wanted no part of it, but he was right. There was no point in putting something out that I didn't think was the absolute best that I could do. So I've not been forced to write a particular story but I've been forced to tell my particular story the best I can.

**JORDAN:** Are there ever uses for stereotypes in fiction? Perhaps to introduce a character or advance the plot?

**GIBBONS:** If I were going to write about an elderly black male, I am going to start with a stereotype because that's all I know. My personal experience has not exactly been overrun with elderly black males; I'm going to start with a stereotype, and the stereotype will probably be my idea of what the man would look like, talk like, be, and I would probably get that from Katherine Porter's fiction or Peter Taylor's fiction or William Faulkner's fiction. And this stereotype is probably going to be of a kind, benevolent, wise man. He probably will know folk medicine, folkways, and he'll probably know slave stories passed down to him from his parents. So that's where I would start but in writing about it and in writing and rewriting, by the time I got to page two hundred this will have grown, and he will have started talking for himself and telling me things and surprising me and so he would have—I hope and this is always the hope that the stereotype will explode—and he will become a true individual and a person. I feel that I get to know characters after writing the same story forty or fifty times. I finally know the people. I think it's just dangerous when I get to the end of a book and the stereotypes are still stereotypes. They've not taken on a life of their own. That's always the goal.

**JORDAN:** Do you ever think about the role that readers have, if any, in the creative process?

**GIBBONS:** Yes. I can only speak for readers who have read what I have written. My idea of an ideal reader is someone who has the ability to take a kernel of information about a character and extrapolate and build and make that character grow within her own imagination. And I don't want people who have read my work to get my book, go out on the deck, put up their feet and say, "Okay, Kaye Gibbons, do it," because otherwise they can just march off to genre fiction like historical romance or something where everything is done. I guess I count on people more. I count on my readers to see with me, to hear with me. I count on my readers to enjoy language as much as I do, and if they don't enjoy language as much as I do, they can go off and read books that depend heavily on clichés, and there are plenty of *those* floating around. I speak at a lot of universities, and I seem to have some readers tell me the only books they've read this year are my books and Danielle Steele, which is a dubious honor but I'll take it. And then I had one girl who wrote me and said that she had just read *Ellen Foster* and Ibsen. That's okay too. I'll take it. I want it to be a learning process but I don't want readers to be concerned with how to be better people or how to love one another. I want them to learn and grow through language. And with the third book, I hope that the older readers—particularly older readers in the South—can read that and say, "I had not heard anybody talk like this in fifty years." That would mean a great deal to me because I spent so much time trying to rescue the language.

**JORDAN:** Finally, when your writing is pulling you along a particular path and other responsibilities other than writing are pulling you in other directions, how do you resolve the conflict?

**GIBBONS:** I don't. I used to try to resolve it. I have three children. My husband is at home with them. We're all at home. And some days you have to take the car in to have the carburetor cleaned out, or there are days when Louise has an ear infection and she's screaming, or there are days when I need to get the tomatoes mulched, or there are days when I've had publicity commitments. I used to try and resolve it and to find a way to be at peace with it but all I ended up doing was just stuffing it and sucking it up. I was still miserable, so I think what I do is I just recognize the conflict and whine and complain about it to my husband. My husband has been good about it. He listens. I complain to my friends that I'm pulled in so many different directions. And I go to an adult children of alcoholics meeting every week, and I complain and complain to these people, and it goes both ways. I complain my domestic responsibilities are pulling me one way when I'm really getting my stride or some days I complain that the novel is pulling me when I really would rather waste time in the kiddie pool. That's happening now as it gets hotter. Because I'm not very good at making peace with things, I've given up. I don't do it. I just don't suffer in silence. I complain and I feel better. You know there's always another day.

# Marita Golden

■

*Marita Golden reversed the usual order of things by publishing her autobiography,* Migrations of the Heart *(1983), before completing her first novel,* A Woman's Place, *in 1986. Born April 28, 1950, in Washington, D.C., Golden began her writing career as a journalist with a master's degree in journalism from Columbia University. Of her writing, Golden states, "I use and need journalism to explore the external world, to make sense of it. I use and need fiction to give significance to and to come to terms with the internal world of my own particular fears, fantasies, and dreams, and to weave all of that into the texture of the outer, tangible world. I write essentially to complete myself and to give my vision a significance that the world generally seeks to deny."*

*Golden's second novel,* Long Distance Life, *was published in 1990 and, most recently, her third novel,* And Do Remember Me, *was published in the winter of 1992.*

*Formerly an associate producer at WNET-Channel 13, New York, Golden has also taught at the University of Lagos in Nigeria, Roxbury Community College, and Emerson College. She presently teaches at George Mason University in Fairfax, Virginia, and lives in Washington, D.C., with her son.*

**JORDAN:** What specific conditions seem to be in place when black and white women become friends?

**GOLDEN:** I think probably in the last twenty years various political movements have certainly brought black women and white women closer. There were some white women who were involved in the civil rights movement and then the feminist movement even though it kind of splintered off into a black women's movement and a white women's movement. You can find some very intense, meaningful friendships between black and white women who were united by the political fight against racism and sexism. I think a lot of times you have white women who in an effort to throw off a personal and cultural heritage of racism have in the course of that struggle inevitably come to know black people, come to bond with black women. So I think the political arena has been one realm, and the professional realm another, with the post-affirmative-action generation of blacks moving into the white professional corporate world, which has brought us into contact with whites. And white women just as blacks reach a ceiling even though our ceiling is much lower than theirs. They reach a ceiling too, so that I think our moving into their universe and then the struggle against racism would be two reasons for it.

**JORDAN:** What kind of role does the black female play in white women's novels? What kind of role does the white female play in the black woman's novel? What strategies do the authors use to develop the character's voice to make her "real"?

**GOLDEN:** When white women have portrayed black women, there are certain archetypal roles black women and even black men tend to play in fiction and dramas by white people. One, of course, is the nurturer. The tower of strength figure, the black woman who nurtures when the white family fails to understand and nurture. We see this in Carson McCullers's *The Member of the*

*Wedding;* the cook plays that role. In *Gone with the Wind,* the black female character plays that role. It's a little ambivalent because, on the one hand, it is a very limiting role that is simply an extension of the black female servant, except she is a psychological servant. It is also a role that is a testimony to the endurance of our humanity and the absence of certain humanistic skills in bourgeois white families. In it is found a certain measure of truth in that we as a people have played that role in our families. We've played that role with white people. It was how we survived.

**JORDAN:** Do you think that black women servants and their white "mistresses" or employers can also become truly friends?

**GOLDEN:** Well that's a very problematic question. I remember when I went to see *Driving Miss Daisy* with a friend who is from the South. At the end of it, I was just outraged. And she said, "You know, Marita, in the South, you have a lot of black people who cared for white people for years and years like that and who did love them." She said that it was possible to have a kind of friendship that was admittedly very unequal in that, for example, Miss Daisy knows virtually nothing about the texture of her driver's life yet he knows a tremendous amount about the texture of hers. Yet, as my friend informed me, many times those white people would lend black people money. Those white people would help the black children in those black families get into schools. So the type of friendship that would result wouldn't be the ideal friendship that we see where there is total mutual openness. But it would be the kind of friendship designed to serve, I think, the survival needs of each. That is, the white family enforces its power by helping the black family out. And then by the black person knowing some things about the white person's life, that allowed the black person to serve that nurturing role. So I think a kind of friendship certainly could develop.

I have had friendships with white women. I remember when I was living in Boston and I was doing a lot of traveling. I became friends with a white woman who was the most pure Christian I have ever met. She was the purest Christian person I ever knew in my life. She was about my age, and she was just *pure;* she was good-hearted; she worked in the community. When I would travel, she would take care of my son, and I used to kid her about this. The roles were reversed: she was taking care of my son for a change. But there came a moment when I realized that as much as I respected her, as close as we were, there was a racial boundary and class thing. We were talking about the whole issue of being a single parent. She was married and had two children. She said with an innocence I hadn't expected: "I could just never imagine myself raising a child alone." Even though she had all the right politics and was a wonderful person and had been marvelously supportive of me, the ugly head of her racial, class, and cultural conditioning as a white woman became apparent. Even though she was politically liberal, even left leaning, she had still been raised as a white middle-class woman to view herself on a pedestal. We had a friendship, but there was still that line of our individual conditioning that could not be crossed, but she was a good friend as far as we could go.

**JORDAN:** Have you noticed subtle distinctions between the way black women authors portray characters and the way white women authors portray them?

**GOLDEN:** Yes. White writers—male or female—have a preoccupation with the physical beauty of female characters, and physical beauty becomes a trait in and of itself, whereas in the work of black women writers character tends to be more important. Even in a book like *Their Eyes Were Watching God* where Janie is light-skinned with long hair, that portrayal is still not as loaded with the high expectations, the mythology, all the cultural weight that a white female character who is beautiful in a novel by a white writer would be laden with. I noticed that even when I was reading a recent novel by Joyce Carol Oates that the women characters are "beautiful" in that kind of mythic way whites deal with physical beauty. I admire Oates tremendously, but even as dark as her work is with all this undercurrent of violence and even though she does a good job of shattering the American bourgeois dream, her female characters *must* be beautiful. They may not be beautiful in the classic sense, but beauty is important, and you don't find that so much in the work of black women, and that's ONE way in which black women despite our very real economic and social oppression are freer than white women. While, yes in our culture too, we are hung up about the long hair and the light skin, it still is not as deeply rooted. The whole thing that you got to be beautiful to be real is not as prevalent in our culture. In white culture, with their women, you are not real unless you are beautiful, and I don't think that's as strong a motif in our work.

It really hit me when I was reading Oates's work because I think she's a very fine writer. I noticed in Persia, the mother in that work, *Because It Is Bitter, and Because It Is My Heart,* she was just so beautiful. When the daughter grew up, she suddenly became beautiful too. Toni Morrison made a very perceptive comment that she thought one of the most damaging things about white culture was the burden of beauty that it placed on women.

I also think that sex plays a different role. You have a lot of novels in the late sixties and early seventies that came out which dealt with the sexual liberation. For the contemporary white woman, sex is a liberating act. To us sex is sex because we never had our sexuality straitjacketed. Granted, in the media we were portrayed as the whore or the asexual. Either Ethel Waters or Dorothy Dandridge. But there is a difference between what white people put on the screen and what we live in our day-to-day lives.

White men actually straitjacketed their women's sexuality. Then when these women sit down to write these books, sex becomes a very important act. You don't find that so much in black women's work.

I think the issue of sex and sexuality is still an unexplored area in the writing of black women. We've discussed its perversions—incest, rape, but there's a whole realm of sexual feelings, legacies we've yet to explore. The role between white women and their mothers is different also. There's a strain of competitiveness between white mothers and daughters. In black women's literature, even when the daughter rebels against the mother, rejects the mother's legacy, it isn't quite as brutal, and it's not as deeply lodged in sexual undertones and sexual competition. It's more about defining what *I* want to be, what *I* want to do. It's not so rooted in sexual competition over, "Oh, I'm a fading beauty; you're a young beauty."

**JORDAN:** I was just thinking of *Imitation of Life,* the novel, where there is eventually that competition between the white mother and that growing, beautiful daughter.

**GOLDEN:** And it's because the mother as she gets older is losing the primary thing that her culture says makes her valuable, her beauty. Whereas in our culture, what makes a woman valuable is her responsibility to the community and her competence. Can she take care of business? That's what makes a woman valuable to us.

JORDAN: As you were drawing the character of the white female, Carla, in particular, were there particular concerns that you had in mind about how you wanted to portray her? How was this figure born? What do you think of her?

GOLDEN: She was a character that served several purposes. When I was thinking about Neal and Crystal and some universal themes like why people marry, why they choose particular men or women, I had this character of Crystal, who was fairly integrated intellectually, emotionally pretty strong. But as we see, she had problems dealing with the choices she had made. But to Neal, she appears quite together, so then I said, "Well, why did he choose her?" In choosing a woman like Crystal, he was choosing a woman very different from his mother. His mother had been a victim, had conspired in her own victimization for a number of years, and just as he rejected his father's script—"Well, I want you to be a successful Hollywood filmmaker"—he decided he wanted a woman that he could never control; she is the opposite of his mother. It was a delicate balance to draw Carla because I didn't want her to be a complete victim so that the reader would "just write her off." It was important that she grow into some way of affirming herself. And for her the way she grew was to grow out of that marriage into a relationship with a woman. So I had the problem there of a white woman who was older and who grew into a type of sexual relationship which is not my orientation, and I think my concerns were to have a balance between the drama and the affirmation.

Throughout the book Crystal appears to have it all together. Then once she makes the choice of marrying a white man, that veneer of strength crumbles. Throughout much of the book Neal's mother appears to be totally made of clay, but once she decides to get out of that marriage, she grows into a much stronger sense of herself. So that one of the things that intrigues me when I portray women is to kind of shatter the myth that we are super strong, that we are matriarchs and do not have vulnerabilities. Crystal is very intellectual. You puncture that and there are all these demons and ghosts about this man she loves and the price she has to pay for doing that. The fact that Crystal and Carla are both artists was a deliberate choice because I think art can be a wonderful way to affirm self. Carla was a sculptress, and she has one sculpture with all these faces of different types of women—a black woman, a white woman, a Native-American woman—and often what we write, the music we write, and the pictures we paint are dialogues with our deepest consciousness. For her to be making a sculpture that included women of different cultures and different backgrounds meant that she was searching for role models, different ways to be, so the fact that they were both artists was not an accident, and for both of them the art served a self-affirming purpose.

JORDAN: In some ways then you broke some of the stereotypes about white women. Oftentimes they do not have strength in black women's novels.

GOLDEN: I like to shatter stereotypes, which is why I gave Crystal a considerable amount of vulnerability and confusion to counter her image. I get so tired of that. We're not allowed to be vulnerable, and white culture does not allow white women to be strong.

JORDAN: That's very true. Is there ever a role or function for a stereotype in fiction—perhaps to introduce the reader to a character or to expose the danger of such attitudes?

GOLDEN: Yes, but I think in the best fiction, you transcend the stereotype. I think in the sense that when you first meet a person, the person is often a stereotype.

JORDAN: Until you get to know him or her. To what extent do you use sources such as histories, biographies, or autobiographies in your work?

GOLDEN: I don't use histories or biographies so much, but I use real life. I think that my background as a journalist and my general orientation make me a writer who responds a lot to what is happening in the world. As I'm living, I will fuse reality with imagination. I find reality absolutely fascinating. Like the Marion Barry trial. You couldn't write that; and yet if I tried to write it as it was, it wouldn't work because it's too melodramatic. There's too much sex, too much drugs. It simply couldn't work in a book so then you say, "Well, how could it work in a book?" But I do use reality. For instance, Richard Wright's *Native Son* was based on a real case. The challenge is to take reality and then make it up all over again. I just did an interview last night for the new book I'm working on. One of the characters is a black actress, and I did an interview with an actress and she gave me some wonderful stuff. Now when I sit down to write I'm going to fuse the perspective that I gained from her with my imagination so it is a combination of things. In the last book there was a lot of historical material that I did use to fuel my imagination.

**JORDAN:** White women have often written novels with black female protagonists. But the reverse happens less often. Could you comment on this phenomenon? Do you think this pattern will remain the same, or will black women start portraying white female protagonists a bit more frequently?

**GOLDEN:** I think that maybe the reason white women portray black women more is because of the role we've played in their lives. Until maybe twenty years ago, it was largely the black woman who was the domestic coming into their home as nurturer and servant. While the white woman poured out all her troubles to our mothers and grandmothers, when they left those homes, that was it. We did not take those white women home with us. Yet the black woman left something behind in that house. She had left comfort; she had left nurturing; she'd left maybe a sense of emotional security. But white women were not emotionally that important or significant in our lives. I figure when you have black women portray white women in the last twenty years, it has been women who are politicized as in Alice Walker's novel *Meridian*, women who came out of the civil rights movement.

Even in *A Woman's Place* where neither Crystal nor Carla is a political activist in the traditional sense of the word, what bonds them is a search for identity through art. I think you'll find a little more of it, but I don't think you'll ever find as much of it because the roles are so skewed and also because we black women are about the business of trying to find ourselves. We don't have time to get too much into white women. They're somewhat irrelevant because there are so many untold stories about ourselves that we haven't given voice to.

**JORDAN:** What can black and white women teach each other about living and about writing?

**GOLDEN:** I don't like the word "teach," maybe gain from each other. I think white women can certainly gain an understanding of the importance of character in shaping a woman as opposed to just beauty as well as male definitions of sex. In the work of black women the female characters are often extraordinary women who go off and do extraordinary things. Very often in the work of white women the only thing they do is go off and get married. They grow up, they fool around, and they get married. One of the most important things that black women writing has done is to take women out of that strict milieu, whether it was Meridian who was a political activist, whether it was Sula who just went off and did everything, whether it was the woman in Toni Morrison's last novel who killed her children so that they wouldn't have to be slaves, or my characters. Those are astonishing things, so white women can look at the work of black women and find a whole symphony of definitions for what a woman is about. And we can look at the work of white women and see what a trap it would be if we were to begin to define ourselves their way. Suppose we said all the barriers are down. Now all we want to do is grow up and get married. I think there are warnings for us in their work, and there is advice for them in our work.

JORDAN: Your answers sounds so similar to the other black women I have interviewed. It's interesting to hear how black women respond to that question.

GOLDEN: I'm interested in what white women say.

JORDAN: Well, for one thing, white women generally answer more quickly. They do feel that there are are some things we can teach each other. But black women usually pause . . . sometimes it is a long pause as if they are trying to figure out something to say.

GOLDEN: The pregnant silence.

JORDAN: Yes. Your pause was again the signal. One black writer did mention that perhaps white women writers could teach her something about style.

GOLDEN: I don't think they are better writers. One of the problems I have with white aesthetics is that they put so much importance on style, almost to the point that it doesn't matter what the writer is saying. The author can be saying the most outrageous, abusive, offensive things, but if they said it with style, it doesn't matter, so even that I would have to take with a grain of salt. It is not that difficult to write well. What is hard is finding a subject and infusing it with perception and depth. That's hard. Too often they master the technical aspects and then completely empty the core.

But then even the way they write technically comes out of their culture, and we write in a way that comes out of our culture. That almost architectural, cold, dispassionate structuring of sentences is white. And the way we structure sentences comes out of our Africanness so I would not even say that they can teach me anything about writing.

The white writers who have inspired me have *not* inspired me by style. Tolstoy is one of my favorite writers because he is a nationalist with a profound sense of identity: *I am Russian*. He was a sloppy writer technically. *War and Peace* is one of biggest mismatches structurally and technically, but its passionate belief in family, in country, and the endurance of some things is what it is really about. These very large universal essential issues that he writes about with such passion make you forgive him. These are the novels that survive. People don't read novels one hundred years later if they are only well-written, and that's true whether the writer is black or white.

**JORDAN:** Well, you have learned something from a white male writer.

**GOLDEN:** If you ask me which white female writers I like, I'd immediately name Joyce Carol Oates and Margaret Atwood. Margaret Atwood because she gets away from all the race/gender bullshit and Oates because she skews the mythology of the American dream. But too many white women writers I find guilty of navel staring. There's not enough in their writing. Among white males, when I read Don De Lillo's work, which takes this society apart, I find his work very politically interesting. I like Doctorow for the same reason. I like Tim O'Brien. The thing that I like about Oates is she takes the typical, surburban, white milieu and shows how crazy the people are, and she does it brilliantly. Her work is profoundly political, and she is making a political statement about how people digest dreams and how those dreams just destroy them. She uses the beauty idea, but with some of the women the beauty is a curse also. For instance, this is true of Persia in *Because It Is Bitter*. I thought that scene of Persia with her black lover when they were stopped by the white policeman was fantastic. It takes a very courageous woman like a Joyce Carol Oates or Margaret Atwood to step back from the mythology that has imprisoned white women and examine it.

JORDAN: Shall we move to the women's movement? Do you envision black women becoming more integrated into the women's movement as common concerns such as child care and abortion bring women of all races closer?

GOLDEN: I think there was an American white bourgeois movement that unfortunately never really significantly reached out to women of color. Even poor white women were neglected. And if they didn't do it in the beginning, they're not going to do it now. So I don't see black and white women integrating. I see black women like Byllye Avery with her health project and other black women saying, "We have to do certain things," and as we have always done, go ahead and do it. There is this woman in Texas running for governor, Ann Richards, who straight out said she would back abortions for middle-class women; let poor women get their own. I don't see any commonality, and if it didn't happen in the sixties and seventies when the atmosphere was right, then in the treacherous nineties I doubt that it will happen because blacks and women are crabs in a barrel. These white men are fighting for their lives. That is their main agenda. Sometimes we tend to get confused and think it's really about being a woman, but it is really about their being white. They're having a little family argument right now, but when the deal comes down, they're white. They're not women. Consistently, white women vote against their own best interests.

JORDAN: Well, that smashes any optimism for our real integration, right?

GOLDEN: Integration is no longer the issue. I think a lot of people are now saying it was one thing to get rid of segregation laws. They were illegal; they were odious; they were wrong; but the mistake we made was in feeling that we had to integrate. Why couldn't we have kept our culture, because there were a lot of things that were there, and Lord we miss them now. We really do miss them now. The new term is diversity, multiculturalism, but they still say nigger.

JORDAN: When you look at young children and teenagers who often do not know their own family histories and do not have or know the words to voice their experiences, what kinds of things ought to be done to help them gain control over their own voices?

GOLDEN: I figure it all goes back to the family. Until children have families that are composed of a parent or parents who can get a job, and in the process transmit a strong sense of self to the kids, all the programs in the schools, all the mentoring programs, all the money for special projects will not make a difference. It all starts and ends in the home whether that home is a single-parent home or a two-parent home. That is where children most effectively learn who they are, what their possibilities are; so until the country addresses these profound economic and social inequalities that have been made worse in the last ten years, all these patch-up, Band-aid programs will mean very, very little. They will salvage a few kids here, a few kids there, but as long as you have so many black homes where the men cannot get jobs, the men are declared obsolete, the schools do not educate, you will not create vibrant families. It's not going to work, it's not going to mean anything. It all goes back to the family. I think we should, for example, be marching on Washington for jobs. We need to be demanding housing. That's what civilizations and cultures are based on, and the problems that we are having in our communities today are not problems of drugs. They are problems of culture because our kids don't know who they are. They pick up a gun. They pick up a needle. They put something up their nose. You can arm your kid against anything, but they have got to know who they are.

JORDAN: That does sound pessimistic. I'm thinking about the young women who are having children at such young ages before they have had time to know who they are. By the time they start to understand who they are, their own sons and daughters have begun the process of trying to come to terms with what they want to be.

GOLDEN: Then she has got to go back and have a childhood she never had. Her adulthood will be interrupted by dealing with that lost baggage. I think that we need to be knocking on people's doors, going physically into people's homes. Our culture has broken down, and I think a lot of that is because in the push to get rid of segregation, we bought into integration. What kept black people in the early 1900s from going crazy when we were segregated and we had black teachers who taught black history? They didn't use the word Afrocentricity, but they taught us history. We have lost as much maybe more than we have gained. I would never say that the civil rights movement was not necessary, that those people died in vain, because they didn't. I think one of the saddest things is that kids—black and white—do not learn how effectively, how powerfully a very small group of mostly black and some white people revolutionized this country in a period of about fifteen years. The civil rights movement is a fantastic drama, fantastic history, in which a relatively small group of people changed this country. But at the same time, there was something insidious happening in our community. We were so busy fighting out there that we were not preparing ourselves. But the economic legacy of the past decade has been disastrous for our communities too, and those forces devastated us socially in ways it will take generations to recover from.

I'm a child of the fifties. I was raised partially in segregation, and then in my late teens in integration. I had a solid grounding in the black community; there were black lawyers, black doctors, black pimps, everybody. I knew who I was, but the generation that followed me had only integration. We've got to do some deep soul-searching. We have rhetoric, but we don't have a plan.

**JORDAN:** We'll help them.

**GOLDEN:** We have to. It's going to take a massive effort of reaching back. The class issue is going to be very insidious, and the middle class must start reaching back. I think that our situation is so bad that the business of saying, "Well, I don't have a responsibility to anyone else. I got mine" is something we cannot afford to say. There aren't many of us that *are* middle class. We're all just a paycheck away from homelessness. So what do I look like saying, "I got mine?" The white man can take it away. I don't see anything wrong with saying things are pessimistic; maybe that will start people moving.

**JORDAN:** Let's turn again to another general literary question. Do you see literary critics, particularly black ones, as having a special role in shaping the ways stories of black women's lives are read, assessed, and taught?

**GOLDEN:** I think it's still white literary critics that set the agenda. I think we have had some ground-breaking work from people like Mary Helen Washington and Henry Louis Gates, Houston Baker, and others. They do have a profound impact, but in the final analysis, the white literary world determines the significance of the work vis-à-vis awards, vis-à-vis magazines like the *New York Times*.

JORDAN: Was storytelling a part of your growing-up experience? If so, how has it affected your writing?

GOLDEN: Yes. My father was a person who did not have a great deal of formal education but he had educated himself through reading, and he read everything, and he had a very profound sense of himself as an African American. He studied a lot of history, and he talked to me a lot. My bedtime stories were stories about famous people from black history so that I grew up entrenched in the oral tradition. In my work, I see myself continuing the work my father did because preserving history is very important in my work. In my last book, it was important for me to write about the migration of blacks from the South, to put a woman who married a Garveyite for Christ's sake, in a book. And in the new book I'm writing about the civil rights movement to the present.

JORDAN: Have you ever felt pressure from your publisher and/or editor or audience to portray a particular kind of character or to treat a particular set of themes, or have you remained free of such concerns?

GOLDEN: I have never gotten any pressure from my publisher or editor. My work has tended to portray black men as fairly complex. For example, my father, was a man who was very complex, who had some good things and some bad things about him. He was a pivotal figure in my life. The complexity that he possessed I try to infuse in all my male characters, so it's a natural thing for me.

JORDAN: What is the responsibility of the reader, if any, in the creative process?

GOLDEN: To learn how to read, and by read, I don't mean just read sentences. I mean to read with understanding and perception. There's too little of that. People read cursorily; they read half a book, or they don't even read at all. They read a review and become an expert on the book, so I think the responsibility of the reader is to learn how to read with precision and depth.

**JORDAN:** In writing *A Woman's Place*, race, sex, class, or age aside, was there one character that was more difficult to develop than the others?

**GOLDEN:** Probably Aisha was most difficult because her choices were so radically different from any choices that I would make. And yet I think she is probably the most fully developed character in the book. But she was the most difficult because she retreats from life. I don't. But that's why I wanted to write about her because she is so different from me.

**JORDAN:** As your writing pulls you along a particular path, and other responsibilities—teaching, parenting—are pulling you in other directions, how do you resolve the conflict?

**GOLDEN:** I send my son to Wyoming. [*Laughs*] I don't really have that tension because I've been writing long enough now that I know how to organize my life. My son has never been an interference; he has been a source of inspiration. Watching a kid grow up, if you are perceptive, is a course in psychology. I have found that being a mother has influenced positively on my work. I'm glad that I'm a mother. In terms of organizing, I always get up early in the morning. From my early twenties when I realized that writing was a serious endeavor for me, I realized that I would have to have a separate structure for writing. My life has its structure, and then there's this little structure inside of that and that deals with my writing. And I just put my writing in a structure that would accommodate the rest of my life. When people say that they don't have the time, it just means they aren't ready to claim the time.

**JORDAN:** In writing *A Woman's Place*, you moved from nonfiction to fiction. Who or what inspired you to write this novel?

**GOLDEN:** I had always wanted to write fiction. I had written a novel first—before *Migrations of the Heart*—and an agent told me that while the novel was interesting, I should really write an autobiography because I was living in Africa and that was a very dramatic, untold story, so my life simply imposed autobiography on me first.

**JORDAN:** I find your use of points of view very effective in allowing each character to speak for herself and himself. How did you decide on the alternating points of view instead of omniscient point of view?

**GOLDEN:** I had written the whole novel in the third person, and one day I realized it didn't work. The story was there but there was some interior push or pull that was absent. There was some light that was absent and then I realized that the reason it was absent was because for this particular story, those people needed to speak in the first person. So I wrote the story and then realized that these characters had to speak for themselves so I didn't plan it, but it just grew out of the story.

**JORDAN:** How would you describe uses of silence in *A Woman's Place*? I was thinking of Rashid, for instance. At times he doesn't say anything; he's keeping it all inside.

**GOLDEN:** Silence is a very effective form of communication. In the book it's meant to illustrate how people, when they think they're not dealing with something, actually are. Crystal, for instance, refuses to talk to her husband about her doubts about their marriage and instead begins to have affairs. That's a form of silence, too. When Rashid becomes ill, he goes into silence. That's typically male, but with Crystal, it's also a form of leaving the relationship, but controlling it at the same time. As long as you don't say anything about the problems and the partner is begging you to, you're in control of the relationship. Once you open up and say something, you may lose control, depending on what you say. By remaining silent, she has left the relationship but is still there. This is one of the most effective ways to deal with a person whose identity depends on your saying something.

**JORDAN:** Describe uses of memory in the book—focus on the grandmother in *Long Distance Life*, for instance.

**GOLDEN:** Memory is very important for her because she is designed to be a griot, and she is the consciousness as well as the conscience of that family. She knows her story, she knows everybody's story, so that she is the repository of the personal history of that family. By the end of the book, it's a collective memory so that the book is about remembering history and remembering who you are. But there is also an absence of memory in the grandson who doesn't feel a part of his grandmother's memories. He feels alienated from it, so that there is a failure to implant those memories in him.

**JORDAN:** I've not often seen interracial relationships explored in our fiction except maybe in the rape of the black woman in slavery—not truly a relationship. How did you come to develop the character of Crystal and her relationship with Neil?

**GOLDEN:** I thought it was a metaphor for what was happening to many post-affirmative-action women who had entered into the white world. It is inevitable. I don't think that racism is natural; it is an unnatural construct that's been enforced through economics and sociology. I think that if you put people together in a room or environment, the natural thing is for them to be drawn to one another, to be curious sexually and otherwise, so that Crystal's being involved with Neil is natural as are the possibilities, limits, dangers that come along with integration.

**JORDAN:** I wasn't surprised that Crystal's father and her brother to a lesser extent were more upset by her relationship with Neil than her mother. Do you think that the father's response remains typical?

**GOLDEN:** Yes. I have a friend who is involved with a white guy who says black guys will stare them down in public. That's the confusion for the black woman—this sense of ownership that we are the property of black men, yet the black men who are supposed to be the pinnacle of success go with white ones.

**JORDAN:** Is there one main barrier that brings out questions of Crystal's identity once she gets married to Neil?

**GOLDEN:** I think that Crystal has a concept of herself as pretty independent. Then when she goes home and is confronted with this rejection not just from her father, but also from her brother, the concept that "I'm an island" is shattered, and she realizes the older she gets, particularly at the time of crisis, if she doesn't have a family, it becomes very important. Having a family in times of crises becomes crucial. I think she had forgotten how important her family was to her, not just in nurturing and shaping her but in determining who she was. She realizes she has to break away from that family and say, "Even if you don't like what I've chosen to be, I'm going to be." That's a profound thing to do. In interracial relationships one of the biggest tensions is very often that the family will reject one of the partners. That puts a tremendous burden on that person. One of my uncles said to me once: "You've been around those white people too long." Now I wasn't married to anybody white. I was just working with them, had gone to school with them. That statement is filled with so much fear, apprehension that the rejection by a father would have to raise significant self-doubts. Family is crucial, and we want legitimacy. We want our families to respect our choices, to approve of our choices no matter how old we are.

**JORDAN:** It is interesting that Tamika gets the last word. Did you see her as the reflection of the hope and triumph and love of all three women's lives?

**GOLDEN:** Well in a sense, but I also saw her mostly as the next generation, hopefully that will inherit the legacy of all three women—the political activism, commitment to family, and personal, intellectual growth.

**JORDAN:** Friendship is powerful. Nothing seems to separate the three women—not space, not writing to each other over time. The friendship remains intact. Is the bond of friendship a major means of women's thriving and certainly their surviving?

**GOLDEN:** Yes. It's the way that black women have survived. My mother had vigorous and amazing friendships with women, and I grew up seeing that. When white women discovered that women could be friends in the seventies, I asked, "Where have they been?" Friendships have been our psychic glue.

**JORDAN:** When you look at all three women, are there parts of you that live in each character? How would you describe each character's individual strength?

**GOLDEN:** Yes, there is a little of me in each one. Serena, of course, has the questioning, adventurous nature that puts her in a realm of politics, international activism in a way that I could never be. I'm adventurous but I want to die a natural death. She will put herself on the firing line. Aisha has that wonderful quality of nurturing, which is very important. She nurtures her husband, she nurtures her kids, and she's important as a nurturer to Crystal in the years when Serena is away. And, of course, Crystal has that mind that's like a surgical tool. Each of them has something of me as a seed, and then it grew into something different.

JORDAN: Finally, without rewriting the novel, where is a woman's place—anywhere she wants to be, in her heart, in whatever space that allows her to be true to her own spirit?

GOLDEN: Yes, in the final analysis, women have to decide that and we haven't been conditioned—black or white—to unequivocally determine what our place is. We've accepted, "Well, your place is beside me." Yes in our culture, we do want you to be competent, we do want you to take care of business, but we still want you to get married. I think the challenge is that we have to determine who we are, who we're going to be, and that will be our place.

# SHIRLEY ANN GRAU

■

*Shirley Ann Grau, born in 1929, continues to live in a suburb of
her native New Orleans. She is the author of several collections of
short stories and novels. Her first novel,* The Hard Blue Sky, *was
published in 1958 by Alfred A. Knopf, as were three of her subse-
quent works:* The House on Coliseum Street *(1961),* The Keepers
of the House *(1964), and* The Condor Passes *(1971).* The Keepers of
of the House *won the Pulitzer Prize in 1965. Her last novel,* Evidence of Love, *was published by Random House in 1977. Her*

*short-story collections include* The Black Prince and Other Stories *(1955),* The Wind Shifting West *(1973), and* Nine Women *(1985), all published by Alfred A. Knopf.*

JORDAN: What specific conditions seem to be in place when black and white women become friends?

GRAU: I don't think a writer thinks that way. You don't think in terms of what conditions are conducive to the making of friendship. I think writers think of stories first.

JORDAN: Outside of literature, what makes for friendship between black and white women?

GRAU: Common interests, as would be the case for anyone. I don't think there's any difference between the formation of an interracial friendship and any other, whether it's between oriental and white or black and white or white and white. Most often a common goal brings people together. There's nothing like working together to get to a mutually agreed on point. That breeds friendship very fast, but I don't think there's anything special besides common purpose and a respect for each other. But that's the same for anyone. Color doesn't matter.

JORDAN: That response would be true of the way you would read fiction too, so that you would not see any difference in the kind of role white females play in black women's novels and the role of black characters in white women's novels?

GRAU: I've never read novels that way. I'm trying to think of the last novel I read by a black writer, and the last one I read was *The Color Purple*. There were elements of some man-hating in there that disturbed me. It's her book though. She can put anything she likes in there. But it was basically a good story and very well told. But I don't think that way in terms of character roles.

JORDAN: Let's turn to *Keepers of the House*. In some ways Margaret is such a memorable character because she has a history. She doesn't suddenly appear on the pages but she has roots. How did you go about fleshing out this character, giving her roots so to speak? How did she come to be in your imagination?

GRAU: First of all, I never go back and read my novels, so this is about a twenty-year memory gap. I really didn't think of Margaret as special in her development. She's like so many black women I knew then. They all had roots. Country families have stayed in the same place for one heck of a long time, and they have their own network of blood relationships that are just as intricate as anybody else's.

I think that perhaps what I wanted to do with Margaret is something that had always irked me in fiction. It's much less true now but *Keepers* is twenty years old. There used to be a standard for creating a black character, a standard for creating a white character as if they came from a different world, a different planet really. And I wanted to show Margaret as an ordinary, typical country woman. She was black, but she was a country woman. I think that's what you mean by she had roots. I always wanted to paint blacks and whites as people belonging to a place. I think it's commonly done now, but it was not so before.

To treat black characters as you would any other character. A fine woman is still a fine woman no matter what. So in that sense Margaret is based on any number of women, really an amalgam of all of them. I try hard not to make any special effort in treatment, but simply do them as everyday—as belonging, as living, as dying, as part of the human spirit—no more, no less.

And living invariably, I think, means an interracial picture because except for rare places in the South, it's an interracial world. Coming from Alabama, you know that it is conceivable in some counties to have a world all one color, but it's very rare. So when you talk of ordinary people's everyday life—in the South at least—it's almost certain to be black and white. It's just the way it is. If you've got this mixed-color world, you simply look at the inhabitants of this world as people. I don't think there's anything special about a black character or not special. They're there, they're interacting with others. This is the way they are. It's the point you start with, and then from there you go on with the story.

JORDAN: That's certainly how your characters come across to me, but sometimes I read fiction where the black female doesn't have the roots.

**GRAU:** I know. The wandering black, I guess, the counterpart to the wandering Jew. I think that's probably the result of wrong presupposition or observation.

**JORDAN:** Does Margaret have ambiguous feelings toward her identity as being both black and white?

**GRAU:** Yes, she must. Most people at one point in their lives have a bit of an ambiguity about themselves. It usually hits in your teens, as I remember, when you ask yourself, "Who am I? How do I fit into the whole world? What am I doing? Where am I going?" That's the identity thing. Everybody has that. Now when you have a character who is living between two worlds, she is going to have that problem, but she is also on the fringes. She's in a never-never land between two worlds. She can't join her husband's world. He can't join hers. And this dichotomy has got to make for a real ambivalence about who she is and what she is doing. Unlike most people who settle it in their teens, she is constantly reminded and confronted with it every day of her life. Her point was not to solve the ambiguity but to in effect go around it, to ignore it. There's no solution; therefore, you walk around it. I think in a sense that's what she did.

**JORDAN:** Abigail says Nina, Margaret's daughter, uses her marriage as a way to hurt her mother.

**GRAU:** Children use all kinds of weapons to beat their parents. I often thought it would be a wonderful story to go back and see how did her husband feel about it. Did he enjoy being her weapon to pounce on her mother? She simply felt some anger toward her mother. She was sent away. There really is no right or wrong way to look at it. What did you think?

**JORDAN:** On the one hand, I think the mother really did want the best for her children when she sent them North for schooling. Her way of coping with their also having to live between two worlds is to try and give them the best of the *one* world. Then they can decide what they want to do. She sent them North for schooling so that they could be prepared for what options education might offer to them. If she had kept them in the South, their professional and social choices would have been severely limited.

**GRAU:** But just because your mother does what is logical and kind and the very best for you doesn't mean you accept her reason.

**JORDAN:** I can certainly see where Nina would have been angry at her mother. But I also felt that Nina simply would need time to forgive her mother and proceed with her own life without harboring the resentment.

**GRAU:** The situation is a dead end. There is no way you can satisfy everyone. I believe one of the girls goes to France, which is one way to start over. Change your language and your location to convince yourself you're starting over completely.

**JORDAN:** One of the interesting things that struck me as I was reading the novel was how people use memory. It's interesting what people choose to remember or forget in order to protect themselves.

**GRAU:** Everyone is a conduit of memory one way or another. Everyone is a checkerboard of all sorts of things. Sometimes memory comes to the surface and sometimes it recedes. Sometimes external events will trigger it; sometimes they will not. Sometimes it will just seem to travel its own course. A person who has memories is fascinating for a writer. With a major character you have to stress memory because it gives depth to the character. The trick to writing a certain kind of fiction is to have characters who are true to life, and one way to do that is by memory. It's also a way of giving a person roots as we were describing earlier.

**JORDAN:** At times is Margaret overly concerned about using appearance—not necessarily to conform—to protect herself from what could be unnecessary frustration. When Abigail had her baby, Margaret said, "Do not let it be known that the baby was born on the floor because that wouldn't be proper for a white girl."

**GRAU:** This might also have been a situation of irony. Margaret is terribly patient, but not completely. Abigail is something of a wimp. This is just a gentle stab because she's run out of patience.

**JORDAN:** Abigail usually cannot tell when Margaret is mocking her, but in a later scene, she finally seems to understand it as such.

She says, "I never knew when she was serious and when she was mocking."

**GRAU:** Well, Abigail finally does grow up, but it does take a while. She is spoiled but it's hard not to be given her experiences.

**JORDAN:** Let's turn to at least two of your short stories. The first is "The Other Way," which looks at the black middle class.

**GRAU:** One group that has not received as much attention is the affluent black. This is an extremely conservative family. There are families like that here in New Orleans who have become integrated. They leave behind so much of themselves in order to be integrated. They've certainly left behind their identity. They could be white. And that's the thing for this group; they become so integrated that they appear white.

They are so conventional. The wedding invitation must read "Mr. and Mrs. So and So announce the wedding of their daughter . . ." But then after the wedding, they can divorce.

Actually, I based the grandmother in that story on an older white woman that I knew. If I had not added shades of color, the story would have just been about a group of white people. But you know the character that children find most intriguing is the Jamaican. They write and want to know more about him. Isn't that something? Some day I'll have to write about the lives of some of these other characters to find out what happened to them.

**JORDAN:** "Sandra Lee" is also a very insightful story and a very moving one. What led to its birth?

**GRAU:** I like to write stories in which there are no easy outs. I wrote that story because I wanted to look at the price of integration. Let her go to school and be faced with utter isolation. And these children always seem so young and they are nonthreatening because they are so young.

**JORDAN:** What impact will the mother and aunt's rigid expectations have on Sandra Lee? Why do they refuse to see what is happening to her? I suppose they might not be able to see her pain very clearly. After all, they have not been in her situation.

GRAU: They probably have had that dream for themselves, so now the child is saddled with the burden of their dreams. If the mother and the aunt have their way, then she will probably become like Barbara Eagleton, the woman in "The Other Way."

JORDAN: In some ways, Sandra Lee is forced to bear the burden of the race—not just her own. Does Sandra Lee have any alternatives?

GRAU: If we think about her beyond the story, then we can think about the kind of life she will eventually lead. Maybe she can stay there in school miserable and fail, and so, not achieve. Then she would be forced to return to her old school. But then she returns as a reject so she is still an outsider. There is simply no easy out for her. Of course, she might stay and also find her way somehow.

JORDAN: I found a very interesting passage from *Keepers* concerning the practice of detecting "Negro" blood: "It's a southern talent; and to this day I am very good at spotting signs of Negro blood and at reciting the endless lists of genealogies in the Bible." Do you think this kind of teaching was an important part of the upbringing of Southern white children at the turn of the century when segregation ruled? And do you think new kinds of teaching really have supplanted this kind as integration has become a more common phenomenon?

GRAU: Well, it still sometimes continues but only among older women who are just very curious and gossipy and nosy. They knew how to tell if So and So had Negro blood by looking at the fingers, and they are still doing this because I've recently heard of this going on. As one of my friends would say, they are a little wicked. Relatively speaking, they don't harm anyone. I can remember a time when if someone cooked something a bit different, it would become the topic of conversation for a week. I remember when someone cooked a leg of lamb and that set the telephones ringing for a week. And they were very good at discerning ahead of time when a ten-pound baby would be delivered supposedly at seven months. And all these things were discussed on the same level because they were simply curious and gossipy. That's the scary part—it was all discussed on the same level.

JORDAN: When I asked that question, I had not anticipated that the practice was still going on.

**GRAU:** Oh yes, it still goes on, but only in that circle of gossipy, nosy older women.

**JORDAN:** There is an incident in which Abby asks Abigail the name of the boy to whom she had been talking, but Abigail doesn't know his name. The narrator then says: "I had done what most white people around here did—never got curious about who he was . . . as if Negroes didn't need identities." Why is it that some whites might behave as if Negroes do not need identities? Do you think the reverse is also true that some blacks behave as if whites do not have identities?

**GRAU:** I'm sure if it's true of whites then it's true of blacks. Think how many people you meet in a year that never come to have identities other than casual surface ones. They're nonhuman. I just finished the business of taxes. I have an accountant, and he did not have an identity to me. He was just this figure who sat and punched numbers all day. Then he said that his son was graduating from high school. I was amazed that he was a parent because I had not thought of him beyond being my accountant. That was his only identity until he mentioned his son. So people often remain non-human to us in that respect.

**JORDAN:** Was storytelling a part of your growing-up experience, and if so, how has it affected your writing?

**GRAU:** Yes, very much so. My grandmother, father, and to some extent, my mother told her own stories. I get many of my ideas for stories from newspapers. I read four or five newspapers a day—not the front page. If you look at the front page of most papers, they all look the same. But I like to read the other sections. I read the obituaries because here you have in a few lines or small space a representation of a man's life. Sometimes you can place them side to side in a story. It's a filing system of sorts, and the stories are there when I need them.

**JORDAN:** As your writing pulls you along and other commitments emerge to make demands of you, how do you resolve the conflict?

**GRAU:** Writing is a lifelong exploration of things, and I find that people are endlessly interesting. They are such a mixture of angel and bastard. I am never bored. Never bored. Sometimes I am appalled, but never bored. And some things are intellectually appealing, and you must follow them. So if an idea is intellectually attractive, I explore it. You have to, but writing is a tenuous process at best. Sometimes you choose the writing over the personal and sometimes the reverse. You have to prioritize. I'm sure I could have written more if I didn't have children. I corrected galleys in the doctor's office. One isn't a writing machine. Living from day to day makes the writing subordinate to that. But some times are dry for the writer, and during those times I do other things to amuse myself.

JORDAN: Have you ever felt pressure from your publisher and/ or audience to portray a particular kind of character or a specific set of themes, or have you remained free of such concerns?

GRAU: Someone might say, "I've got a wonderful idea," which means "Here is something I want you to write." I hear them but I do what I please. They may try to get me to do it their way, but I say in a polite way, "It's my name that's on it. If someone else's name is on it, then . . ." You set your own standards and hold to them.

# JOSEPHINE HUMPHREYS

■

*Born February 2, 1945, in Charleston, South Carolina, Josephine Humphreys studied creative writing as an undergraduate with Reynolds Price at Duke University where she graduated in 1967. Almost twenty years later, Humphreys, with Price's encouragement, submitted her first novel,* Dreams of Sleep, *for publication. The novel received outstanding critical reviews and was awarded the*

*Ernest Hemingway Prize from P.E.N. Center for the best first novel*
*in 1985. Since that time Humphreys has published two other nov-*
*els,* Rich in Love *(1987) and* The Fireman's Fair *(1991), both of*
*which have been well received.*

*Formerly an assistant professor of English at Baptist College at*
*Charleston, Humphreys is now a full-time writer, noting that "I*
*waited until writing was the only thing in the world that I wanted*
*to do. Nothing else tempts me." For her outstanding work, Hum-*
*phreys has received a Guggenheim Fellowship in 1985 and a Lynd-*
*hurst Fellowship for 1986–88.*

*The mother of two sons, Humphreys lives with her husband in*
*her beloved Charleston.*

**JORDAN:** What specific conditions seem to be in place when
black and white women become friends?

**HUMPHREYS:** I can only tell you my own experience. I have to
start way back in history, 1945, when I was born in the same place
where I live now. My whole forty-five-year life has been in Charleston, South Carolina. And I did not know a single black person as a
friend until I went to college.

**JORDAN:** To Duke?

**HUMPHREYS:** Yes. My class at Duke was the first integrated
undergraduate class. In the freshman class of, I think, three hundred women there were five black women. Our graduation ceremony was interrupted by a bomb threat, supposedly made by
the Klan. But let me back up to my childhood, and that bizarre
growing-up of whites and blacks separately. I never thought of my
family as racist, and in fact I have often said it was not; I think I
called it "conservative" instead. Yet this is not honest. Of course it
was racist; with rare and heroic exceptions, every white family in
the South was. We thought of black people as different from us.
But in my own family the difference was expressed as a difference
in color alone. That may be the most pernicious form of racism,
but it is strong enough so that when I went off to college, knowing
my class would be integrated, I was nervous. Afraid, really. I didn't
know what it would be like.

All the black women I have been friends with came after that first year of college. It has always been through school and through teaching, and now through writing, that I've met and become friends with black people. My students, my co-teachers, other writers, people I've met through writing, those have been my black friends. But the first, the woman I met freshman year at Duke, I have not seen since then. I haven't seen her since college.

So the conditions you asked about—which make these friendships possible—have for me been school and work. The setup is already there, yes. But I have to add that I don't have many friends, white or black. That has come about mainly because of my writing. I narrowed down my life to writing and raising children, and for a long time that has been all I've done. I have letter-writing friends and telephone friends, but as far as friends in person, whom I see regularly in my own town, there are only two—both white, one of whom I have not now seen in at least a year. Of course I regret this solitude, and I know it may be almost as bizarre as my childhood was. I am not exactly a recluse, but I am separated from a good bit of "normal life." And sometimes it is very difficult. I manage well for long periods of time, but now and then I have a crisis and realize how alone I am, and it becomes clear to me what a solitary, and perhaps perverted, life this is.

JORDAN: Is your family still in Charleston too?

HUMPHREYS: Yes. My two parents and one sister, and I have another sister who lives in Cincinnati.

JORDAN: Well, family can be friends too.

HUMPHREYS: Yes, mine are. My best friends are my husband and sons, my parents, and my sisters. Fortunately, my children have had black friends, growing up here, even though I did not, because the place has changed, and that rigid separation no longer exists.

JORDAN: It sounds like there has to be the right set of social situations in which the women can come together in the first place.

HUMPHREYS: For me, that's how it's been. All my friends have tended to be people I was working with or other writers with whom I share the same craziness and can call them up or write to them and they understand—because there are a lot of writer neuroses that people share.

**JORDAN:** Let's go back for a moment to your first year at Duke with the first integrated class. Even though you had not grown up interacting with blacks, you were still able to develop friendships once the situation presented itself. I'm sure some of your peers who grew up in the same situation would not have been open to such friendships. What makes you different?

**HUMPHREYS:** [*Pauses*] Let me see. I don't really know. I don't think I was all that different. As I said, I came to Duke with no previous contact with blacks. I honestly did not know what it would be like. My town had seemed strange to me, in that the races were separated . . . and yet I had never been taught to hate or fear. So there seemed to be no reason for the separation. I grew up in this old Southern way, but my parents didn't teach me the old reasons behind segregation. It just existed. The problem, as it was discussed in my family, was that Yankees were forcing integration upon the South. There was far more animosity expressed against Yankees than against black people, and a resistance to forced change. I think now that the cry of "states' rights" was a false argument altogether, an argument that sidestepped the issues. Yet that was how I heard it, then, as the main issue. I was never taught to hate black people.

**JORDAN:** Now I'm thinking to myself that perhaps some blacks hold misconceptions about what whites teach their children.

**HUMPHREYS:** Yes, and why not? That was the evil of segregation, I think. We didn't know each other. Of course we had misconceptions, blacks of whites and whites of blacks. And I was able to accept "states' rights" as the only rights in question, because I didn't know the people whose civil rights were the real issue.

**JORDAN:** I think that some blacks would assume, given the racism they experience, that white families must be teaching their children in very overt, direct ways to dislike them, and we extend that picture to all whites.

**HUMPHREYS:** Here is the single example I can remember of having been overtly taught anything concerning the nature of black people. There were black women selling flowers in front of the post office, and I called them "the flower ladies." My grandmother corrected me, and said they were not ladies, and could never be ladies, because they were black. I adored my grandmother, but I could not understand why she insisted so strongly on making this point. It outraged me, because it seemed so deep, that a racial difference should extend to language. I've heard other white Southerners recall similar stories about words and terms. We were not allowed to use the word "nigger," but we were told that "nigra" was acceptable.

But all of this, while not overt teaching, was subtle teaching. It represented fear, I think, racial fear. I think hatred is not the right word; I really think it was fear. Even without overt teaching, the fact of segregation alone was proof of the fear. And Charleston is still a very segregated city, as are all American cities, especially in residential and urban areas. What kind of fear can it have been? Fear of what? There is always a general fear of the unknown. But since I was afraid, myself, of black people, until I was eighteen years old, I think I know a more specific reasoning behind the fear. My fear was that black people would some day want and seek revenge for what we had done to them. Once when I was very small, seven or so, I was trapped in a bus when the door closed before I could get out at my stop. I was so little that the driver could not see me waiting to get off, and he just shut those big rubber doors. I was panicked—you remember how important it was to get off at the right stop; I had visions of riding the bus off to no-man's-land. But a black woman sitting on the bus called out to the driver to open the doors, and miraculously I escaped. I remember very clearly wondering why in the world she would have wanted to help me, a white person. And thinking that if I had been the black woman and she the white child, I would not have saved her. But she saved me.

JORDAN: When you were drawing the pictures of the black females in both novels, were there particular concerns you had about the portrait you wanted to produce? In other words, how were these figures born? What do you think of them?

HUMPHREYS: Well, Iris is white, and Queen is black. I think my idea for that friendship actually did come from my childhood experience of walking to an all-white school through an all-black neighborhood. The strangeness of it struck me. I walked through the public housing project. Where the characters came from is hard to say, although I know where Iris came from; she was based on one of my students at the Baptist College. She happened to live in the same housing project I had passed through on my way to school. And so, even though they are separated by twenty-five years, time doesn't matter much in the imagination, and I put those two things, the memory and the person, together. But most of the time—almost all the time—my fictional characters are not based on real people. Iris is the only one that I can say for sure is really based on someone I knew, but it was someone whom I did not really know well, but whom I liked very much. And Queen—it's funny to remember this only now—I also had an older black woman in that same class whose first name was Queen Elizabeth. She was a terrific person I think I combined with yet another student to make Queen; both of these were older students, around forty, which is probably Queen's age.

The second student was probably the best I've ever had. What impressed me and what I wanted to make part of the fictional Queen was this woman's incredible dedication under nearly hopeless conditions. She had five or six children. She lived way out on John's Island; it's probably about forty miles from the college. She would get up every morning and get her children off to school and drive to school for a full load of courses, and she'd be through by twelve. Then she would go to an eight-hour shift as an LPN at the hospital. Do that. Get home. Feed her children. Do her homework and go to bed—it couldn't have been before 2:00 A.M. and then get up at five or six and do the whole thing all over again. It was her courage and strength that I liked and used even though I didn't include any of the details of her real private life. There are often two or three characters behind the fictional one, and they're all invisible. They are there lurking in the background.

JORDAN: You like Queen?

HUMPHREYS: Oh yes, yes. Love her.

JORDAN: Do you ever use sources such as histories, biographies, or autobiographies when you are developing characters?

HUMPHREYS: I actually do, but I don't search historical sources with any kind of discipline. As a matter of fact little tidbits of history fascinate me. When I was writing about Queen, I happened to go one afternoon to the Charleston Museum where they had on exhibit the most beautiful pottery. I think I remember reading that they were among the biggest hand-thrown pots ever made in America, made in 1820 by a potter named Dave the Slave, and they were signed. Some had Dave's own poems written into the clay; it was a beautiful collection, an inspiring thing to see. And so he is also in the book, not as a potter but as the man who made Queen's bed—Dave-Nero. That was the result of one afternoon at the museum. If I run across something historical that does seem to fit my story, I have used it. But I didn't look it up.

**JORDAN:** What can black and white women teach each other about living and about writing?

**HUMPHREYS:** Well, there again I can only say personally. I don't know that many writers, and the only black writer I know really well is Gloria Naylor. I can say that I've really learned a lot from her, both about writing and about teaching. She's just incredible. She's a wonderful person. It would be hard to say, as it's hard to say about anybody, what specifically we learn from one person. The best thing we can learn from anyone is courage and bravery—that's always something we need to learn over and over again. And still I don't think that has to do with black and white. It just happened to be something I learned from growing. Women can always learn from each other about shared troubles, and that's what I mean by bravery. I use that word a lot, but what I really mean is strength.

**JORDAN:** When you said, "learning courage over and over again," that struck me as curious because I don't know if I thought you could learn courage over and over again. I thought that somehow there's this one experience that forces you to be courageous or whatever and then you are.

**HUMPHREYS:** I don't think it works that way.

**JORDAN:** When you started to talk about strength, I started to think about some things my sister is going through right now, and I'm sure she's had to learn that same lesson once before, twice before, three times before, but the situation seems so new that it seems like a whole new test altogether.

**HUMPHREYS:** In a way it is. There's always a new test. A new one coming.

**JORDAN:** Have you ever been actively part of the women's movement in terms of a formal organization?

**HUMPHREYS:** Not really that I can think of. If I were to be rigorously examined, I don't know whether all my ideas would qualify me as feminist or not, but I tend to think of myself as one. I'm not up with things; I don't read the current literature and I don't know whether I would qualify for membership, but I've lived thinking I would.

**JORDAN:** Were you very much an activist during the sixties?

**HUMPHREYS:** No, not till I was in graduate school. I was in graduate school at Yale and at the University of Texas and became much more involved in things there. But I was even then fairly withdrawn, shy, an observer more than participant in anything. And I suppose that's why I became a writer because I watch more than I play in any game. And there are advantages to that too. I spend a lot of time watching. I didn't start writing until I was thirty-three, and I only did it then because I was driven to it. It was what I'd always wanted to do, but I had not found the courage, the bravery to do it. If you deny that kind of dream—which is what it was—it can really hurt you. It did hurt me. Luckily, it hurt me enough that I finally had to quit teaching, quit doing everything extraneous, and just sit down and write. It was scary but worth it. I'm very lucky that that happened to me.

**JORDAN:** Maybe this kind of writing commitment means putting yourself on the line.

**HUMPHREYS:** It does mean putting yourself on the line. But what I found is you have very little to lose! I finally realized one day that I really had nothing to lose by trying for what I'd always wanted. What had held me back was the fear that I would fail. That I couldn't do it. I had always thought of myself as a writer, but I hadn't written anything besides student stories and poems so there was no proof. All I had was the longing to do it, and some indication that I had some talent; but I was afraid that if I undertook it and failed, then I wouldn't even have the dream left. I wouldn't be able to say to myself, "I'm really a writer but just never got around to doing it." I would have to say to myself, "I never was one. I didn't have what it took. I never was a writer." That kind of hedging is not worth protecting—especially in that curious, almost suicidal way—I mean, protecting your dream by killing it doesn't make any sense at all. I was actually getting physically sick from not having sought what I wanted, so I just started. I made a deal with myself. I said, "Well, I'll try it for a year and if I fail then I'll have to go back to teaching." After that year, I looked at my work and found that it really was awful. Terrible. I didn't want to give it up yet so I thought, "I'm going to give myself one more year; but I'm going to try something different. I'm going to try a novel instead of short stories." I knew immediately that this was the thing that I ought to do. I couldn't write short stories, but I felt much more comfortable with the longer form and the vaguer purpose. In a short story, I think, a writer really has to know what she's doing, at every instant. Novel writing is a more mysterious kind of thing to me. Anyway, I was able to work at it without consciously knowing what my purpose was, without spelling it out to myself; and that way I think your purpose flows almost subconsciously into the novel. I could see it building up, so by the time I got to two or three hundred pages, I could read the thing and see that it had a purpose. I could know then what I was going to do, even if I hadn't known at the beginning. And now after twelve years of doing that, I think I can see what my real and secret goals are in fiction writing. They have to do with the human soul. I want to find it in every character I can find it in. If there's a way to discover the goodness of people—even of characters that seem bad at first glance—I want to make that discovery.

**JORDAN:** When you're writing and then something else in another part of your life demands your attention too, what do you do?

**HUMPHREYS:** I have already narrowed myself down so that those other pulls would be minimal; there are only two of them. And those are so important that when they pull, I quit the writing. So it's not too complicated, and I know what the priorities are. My family is my first interest. When I finished my second book, I told my oldest son, "I finished this morning," and he said, "Great. Could you take me to get some new shoes?" and he held his shoe up: there was no sole. This shoe was just worn through completely.

So a lot of things have to wait but if it's important, I stop writing. Now my sons are fifteen and sixteen, but when they were younger, I was the kind of mother who wanted to go everywhere with them. And I did. I did all kinds of things with them and with other kids too. I love children. But at this age, they don't really want me hanging around, and I know I'm not going to be able to do that much longer. This trip (to visit colleges before my son graduates from high school next year) is in many ways very sad because it's like the last big trip together for us; but it's not that sad to me because I'm eager to do more work. As there's less pull from children, there's more pull to write fiction.

**JORDAN:** My first question about *Dreams of Sleep* is where did you get the title?

**HUMPHREYS:** It's a very interesting thing. The phrase sort of came to me one day after I had written maybe three-fourths of the novel and was trying to think of a title. I had been trying to think of a title all through the novel. The phrase popped into my head, and I recognized its relevance, especially to Alice, who dreams and longs for rest. That restfulness is both a good thing and a bad thing. In Alice's case, her desire for rest is excessive. She could almost go to bed and stay there for life. I also liked the title because it's a rather tangled notion to dream about sleeping. And when I showed the book to my former teacher, Reynolds Price, one of the first things he said to me was, "Where does this title come from?" I said I had thought it up, but he said, "No, I've heard it before. Maybe in Shakespeare." I insisted it was my own original. Reynolds Price had been my teacher when I was a freshman at Duke. I got back in touch with him when I finished my book fifteen years later, so it was a most wonderful renewal of the friendship; and I've stayed in touch with him since then. Well, for several years we argued about that title, until last summer, when my son was reading a book on his summer reading list, Robert Penn Warren's *All the King's Men*. Allen looked up and said, "Did you read this book?" I said, "Yes, I read it when I was a freshman in college. And he said, "Did you like it?" I said, "I loved it." He said, "What do you remember of it?" I said, "I don't remember anything about it, except the main character's name and oh yes a wonderful section about sleep as an escape from worrying and hiding." He showed me the page he was reading, which included the part I recalled, and there it was—dreams of sleep. I had read *All the King's Men* in Reynolds

Price's English class. He and I had actually read it together! In 1963. So twenty years later one little phrase came back, pretending to be my own. At least Reynolds knew it had come from a book. He just didn't remember which book. The power of memory is remarkable. That I can remember something and not know that I remember it, can even believe wholeheartedly that I made it up, is very strange.

**JORDAN:** I just thought the title was so different.

**HUMPHREYS:** I meant it to suggest not only Alice's longing for escape and oblivion—but also the more general longing for peace and harmony.

**JORDAN:** Why is Queen so protective of Iris, or why is Iris willing to accept Queen's guidance? Why does she allow Queen's input in her life even though she's clearly going to do what she's going to do? She at least seems open to listening to Queen.

**HUMPHREYS:** In Iris's world, Queen is the only person who deserves both love and respect. Iris loves her mother, and in a way she loves her father, but she doesn't respect either of them. Others she respects but doesn't love. With Queen, it's both. Queen also feels the same kind of love for Iris. There are sometimes people who encounter each other, and each will know right away that the other is worth listening to. Both of them know. Even though these two are so different both in age and race, there are still things that hook them together. And Emory, of course, is one of them. He makes a link between them.

**JORDAN:** What is it about Queen's home that puts Iris at ease with herself? The love and respect?

**HUMPHREYS:** Yes. Also there is the attraction of history in the bed: Queen's furniture has a past, a significance. Iris doesn't have that sense of history in her own home. It's almost like an anchor to her, and a real sort of fascination.

**JORDAN:** She admires Dave-Nero and she's fascinated with him in a way and perhaps very much wants to emulate his independent spirit or she sees herself as having the same kind of spirit.

**HUMPHREYS:** Yes. Yes.

**JORDAN:** My question then is don't you think this is unusual though for a white teenager to see this older black male figure as one that is worthy of emulating even though he's dead and long gone?

**HUMPHREYS:** I don't know if it's unusual. It's hard to know what is usual and what's not. I'm sometimes surprised by what people find likely and unlikely. It often reflects more about what they think personally, individually, than about what's usual. For example, there's the friendship between Lucille and Rhody in *Rich in Love*. Someone said to me that it wasn't likely in Charleston that these two people would be friends. I said, "Oh. Maybe not." The person who made the comment was an older white woman. But a black girl said to me, "You know, one thing I don't understand is why you said that Lucille's sister, Rae, was brave to sing with a black band. This is a college girl," she said. "That happens all the time." So I don't know: Would Iris be unlikely to admire a black man? It doesn't seem unlikely to me. Iris is a very unusual girl—not just personally, but her whole upbringing and position in the world is strange. Aberrant, so maybe if something is unlikely for most people, it is likely for her.

I think I learned a lot about unlikely things from teaching at the Baptist College. Some of my students were white and some were black; their lives had often been quite unusual, so that you couldn't predict what was likely for them. You couldn't say what their racial attitudes were or their politics or anything because they just didn't fit the mold. Some came from deprived backgrounds or fanatic religious backgrounds or abusive backgrounds. Very few were average middle-class Americans, and that's what I loved about them. They were unpredictable, and they were very open to new ideas. They were eager to change their lives.

**JORDAN:** Did you like Faye?

**HUMPHREYS:** Yes, I liked Faye. I like almost all my characters. What I liked about her was her unfailing devotion to this guy who didn't deserve it. Didn't deserve any of it. But as a matter of fact, I liked Owen too. That's what I mean when I say I look for whatever spark of goodness there is in a character, whatever seems to me to be redeemable.

**JORDAN:** That redeeming quality is also true of Randall, who is maybe not a "good guy" but we hope for the best for him anyway.

**HUMPHREYS:** Yes. He was eager to go with his father because he loved his father; he had no motive—certainly he had no evil motive, even selfish motive. But Randall doesn't even say much in the book. He's a minor minor character.

**JORDAN:** Clearly Faye has problems with Iris being a friend of Emory, and Faye also seems to have problems with having to live close to blacks. What is it then about Iris that allows her to be friends with Queen and Emory even though her mother holds such prejudiced views about blacks? I suppose even lower-class persons, not just blacks.

**HUMPHREYS:** That's a good question. Iris has been raised there. That is her world, whereas Faye has presumably lived some other history. Iris at one point says to Alice, "If you live in it, you're not afraid of it." She's talking about the neighborhood, but it could be taken in a more general sense. She knows the people. Faye doesn't; she stays inside and doesn't let anybody in. And then, of course, Iris, like any child, can see her mother's failures. She sees that Faye is not the most reliable source of information and wisdom, so she has reason to doubt Faye's worldview. And I think that Iris is certainly an adult child. I think that children are the greatest source of wisdom and understanding. The more childlike the characters are, the more they are to be trusted, I think.

**JORDAN:** As you were speaking of trusting the wisdom of a character, I was thinking of Evelyn and Lucille.

**HUMPHREYS:** Evelyn is a character who's only about two paragraphs long. That's what's sad about writing novels: there are characters you are drawn to and fascinated by, and then they disappear. I have a sort of collection of them now. I want to go back to them. Reincarnate them with other names. Actually, Lucille was a continuation of Iris, because I didn't feel quite finished with Iris.

**JORDAN:** Once you're done with a novel, is there a sense of completion or does the work seem to somehow never come to an end?

**HUMPHREYS:** It doesn't seem to come to an end for me. Luckily, the publishing business brings it to an end. I have never felt finished and I actually keep rewriting right up to the last possible minute. I've finished the new book and sold it, but I'm still working on it. It makes the editor really nervous. She says, "Oh, don't change anything." But I have plans for big changes. [*Laughs*]

**JORDAN:** For the most part, have you had to deal with a lot of pressure from publishers to create a certain kind of work or have you remained free from such concerns?

**HUMPHREYS:** None at all. Completely free. The pressure anyway is not overt, and does not come from my publisher. But any writer, I think, understands some pressure. I think it's pretty clear that the book-buying public prefers a certain kind of book. And some writers, I guess, could figure out what that is and write it. I think that truthfully if I were writing without any thought of ever publishing, my books would have very sad endings. But in the act of publishing, you're presenting a vision of the world to other people. I think I could stick with a sad ending, but in revealing it and sort of sending it on to other people, I suspect I pressure myself to alter the vision. I don't believe that existence has a sad ending. I believe that in the long run most human stories turn out well, and that there's wisdom to be gained from that redemptive process. And yet I can read in all three of my books this kind of building up of sadness that would have just as easily ended sadly. It's odd. I think I do shape the story with some thought of the reading public, but it's not because I want to sell books. It's because I think of it almost in the same terms as teaching. I have a highly developed sense of the tragic and of despair in life, but I don't tell my children that. I would rather have them believe in the other thing, hope—which I also believe in; but there's more to it than that; there's that possibility of good. So that kind of pressure doesn't come from my editor or publisher or even from the thought of sales. It comes from me. But it is a pressure in the sense that it's a force. Again it's like being a teacher: you have a responsibility to give the truest lesson you can but also the best lesson you can.

**JORDAN:** As I am reading the novels, I do have a sense that everything is going to somehow be all right, but I don't know how. Emory and Iris love each other as mutual friends—a platonic love—at least on Iris's part. Emory, however, seemingly wants more. What is it that keeps them apart? Is it that their future paths diverge too widely? They seem to be going in such different directions.

**HUMPHREYS:** I really don't think that's it, for if the story went on they would be together. At the end, Iris is heading to Atlanta to see Emory. What keeps them apart in the book is not their divergent ways but the incredible, horrible pressure in their own separate lives. They can't really get together—Iris especially. She's not ready to deal with a romantic life. And I also think they're too young. They are children, in spite of their forced adulthood.

**JORDAN:** When Iris goes to Queen about getting the job, Queen says, "Tending a white girl's babies is not a job for you," to which she replies, "Why not? I'd be good at it. I hate waitressing. The cook is white trash." Does Queen really believe that housework is a hundred times better than watching babies?

**HUMPHREYS:** In that scene I meant for each of them to make racial remarks while actually forgetting the race of the other one. Queen says, "Tending a white girl's babies is not the job for you," but Iris is a white girl. It is a remark that Queen might make to another black woman. And Iris says, "The cook is white trash." Iris is white trash. Iris and Queen are not perfect; they think in categories, but they do not put each other into those categories. Queen is a little embittered by her long experience with domestic work. She really is different from Iris in that she wouldn't love the Reese children. She doesn't love Will who presumably was the child she helped raise; she feels nothing toward him, none of that maternal love that Iris feels, and really very little affection for the white woman she works for.

**JORDAN:** When she tells Iris this, they almost sound like mother and daughter.

**HUMPHREYS:** Yes, and each of them probably needs the other. One needs a daughter and one needs a mother.

**JORDAN:** Which brings us to *Rich in Love.* Personally, Helen troubles me a great deal, but at the same time she's absolutely fascinating. I don't know if she's ever really been a conformist. She'd been a hippie during the sixties and there is some carryover from those days. I was wondering if the mother's influence on the daughters encourages them to be independent.

HUMPHREYS: Yes, I think so. Helen's method of raising children was almost a game, especially with Rae, but it worked. And it obviously did shape Rae, and while it was not as rigorously pursued with Lucille, I think it did also make her independent.

JORDAN: I guess whenever mothers leave, we are inclined to say, "What a bad thing," and I think that's what bothers me.

HUMPHREYS: It's something that obviously fascinates me since in every book I've written, a mother leaves. It is a horrible thing. It's what mothers are not supposed to do, but to me it is also fascinating. There are some personal reasons for my interest in that. I grew up in a family where my grandfather had left my grandmother suddenly and horribly. And though I wasn't even born when it happened—which is probably good—it became more like a legend in my family rather than an event that I had seen actually happen. A legend is a kind of powerful thing—more powerful, perhaps, than a real event. I knew this story, and I was always fascinated by it—a man who had seemed to be a perfect father had just suddenly gone. And it happened so quickly that it was devastating. I think that's where part of my fascination comes from. It's a way to let her leave him, which she should have done.

But also personally as a mother, I find the duty of motherhood absolutely compelling. It's something that I have discovered almost by accident. I had never touched a baby before I had my own little baby. It was like a ton of bricks. It completely changed my life. I hadn't thought about it before. Then all of a sudden I felt the major force of it; it was biological and wonderful and mysterious and delightful and also just incredibly different. But it was the force of it that also made me think, what would happen if you just quit? Maybe it is horrible to think about leaving your children, but I have the kind of mind that can't help considering opposites and alternatives and possibilities, at least. I'm always thinking, "What if?"

But another thing I'm really sure of is that mothers are in a difficult situation. They have this duty, and it's not simply a duty, it's a passion, to which they dedicate themselves. But then if they do too good a job of it, they can harm their children. You must be the greatest mother in the world, but you must also, simultaneously, withdraw from your children's lives. You don't want to be the major force in their whole lives. You need to do the job adequately and as best you can, and then provide them with independence from you. You have to give them enough so that they won't need you anymore. So I've always thought, "What a strange job. If you do it correctly, you must eliminate the job." It struck me as being real and sad that I had to do that. But if you realize it from the beginning then it's okay. I'll be able to do it. I hope, of course, that they will also like me well enough to invite me over for dinner sometimes when I'm old. Motherhood is something that I think about a whole lot, in all its aspects. And if you think about it enough, you're bound to run across the idea of the runaway mother. Actually, the worst episode of it in these books is when Faye leaves her two children alone. A friend of mine once told me this story of how her mother left her and her brother alone in a motel room for three days when she was ten and her brother was six. No food, no money. Just alone in a motel room. It was a nightmare. I realized that there was only one thing that would make a mother do that, and that's a man. So that was the kernel of my story about Faye. When Alice leaves, she actually leaves with her children, so that's not exactly a mother leaving. And Helen does it in a way that's not completely irresponsible—not as irresponsible as it looks. She just makes a mistake in thinking that her children are old enough for her to leave. She turns out to be wrong. Lucille is not old enough. Helen still doesn't understand how much Lucille still needs her.

**JORDAN:** My last question concerns the speech of the characters, which seems so real; the dialogue for each one. I'm thinking about some of the minor characters in particular. There's a brief scene, for instance, where Rhody recounts something that her mother had said to her. The mother's voice is so compellingly real.

**HUMPHREYS:** Most of it I made up but I'm always listening for what people say. There is one conversation between Rhody and her mother that I did hear somebody say. It happened one time when Gloria Naylor was visiting me, doing some research for *Mama Day*, her third novel. She came down and stayed with us and asked me to put her in touch with someone who could tell her about root doctors. Well, I didn't know more than fifteen people anyway and none of them were root doctors. But I didn't tell Gloria that. I remembered that one of my students had written a wonderful paper about her grandmother, who had been a midwife on the island and had delivered babies. Alfreda had learned from her grandmother a lot of information about herbal remedies, and while that was not root medicine exactly, I said to Gloria, "Yeah, I know someone." Gloria and I went to talk with Alfreda about herbal medicine. I just sort of sat there and listened. Gloria asked what she knew, but Alfreda wasn't giving out any information. After they had talked for about an hour, Gloria sneezed. Alfreda went to a locked cupboard and took out some herbs. Gloria's eyes lit up. She knew that she had gotten a source. After a while, she was getting lots of stories that Alfreda hadn't wanted to tell right away. But the specific remark that I lifted from that conversation was Alfreda talking about her children, one of whom was working as a maid in a resort. She had told her mother that she was depressed, and Alfreda said, "In my day, black women didn't have time to get depressed." And I filed that away because I thought it was so true, such a sharp insight into her own life and her daughter's and the times. Everything sort of came together in one sentence. But I'm always eavesdropping. I listen to conversations in restaurants. I don't always know that I'm going to get a scene right or a conversation right, and I know that I've gotten some wrong and I know I'll get some wrong in the future. It's always hard to know if I've not only got the black characters right but the men characters right or the teenage characters right. It's just something you can't be sure of. And in my new book, the main character is a man, a white man whose best friend is a black man. I have no idea whether it's accurate or not. I won't know. I can only imagine. That's what writers are meant to do. To imagine any character who is not you takes some kind of guessing and risking too. You can't be sure that it's going to seem real to readers either. You only hope.

# JILL McCORKLE

■

PHOTO BY BERNARD THOMAS

Jill McCorkle is a native of Lumberton, North Carolina. She graduated from the University of North Carolina at Chapel Hill in 1980 and from the Hollins College Master's Program in Writing in 1981. She has written four novels—The Cheer Leader *(1984)*, July 7th *(1984)*, Tending to Virginia *(1987)*, and Ferris Beach *(1990)—and* Crash Diet, *a collection of short stories.*

*After receiving her MFA from Hollins, she taught writing at Duke University, Tufts University, and the University of North Carolina.*

*In the fall of 1992, she became a Briggs-Copeland Lecturer at Harvard University.*

*She is a frequent reviewer for the* New York Times Book Review *and has also reviewed for the* Washington Post, *the* Atlanta Journal/Constitution, New York Woman, *and many North Carolina newspapers. Her short stories have been widely published in literary journals, commercial magazines, and anthologies. Her novels have had wide international distribution, foreign rights having been sold in Britain, Sweden, France, and Japan.*

*Jill McCorkle is married and the mother of two children and lives near Chapel Hill, North Carolina.*

**JORDAN:** Quite a few of my questions focus on Fanny, the black maid in *July 7th,* so we will begin there and return to the more general questions. Where did the idea for Fanny originate?

**MCCORKLE:** I had the idea for Fanny and was timid because I felt that somehow as a white person I didn't have the right to try and portray her. And I was so afraid because I felt when a black portrays a black person or a Jew portrays a Jew or any group portrays one of his own and crosses that line into stereotype, nothing would ever be said. But when an outsider does, then there's always that chance that you can be perceived as minimalizing this person when that wasn't the intention at all. I had a real struggle because what it comes down to is language. There's a fine line between accurate language and that "sho' nuff" stereotype.

I feel that Alice Walker can write dialect and that's all right, but for me to attempt dialect was a little scary. What it comes down to is if your heart is in the right place, then it's going to work out. When I finished the novel, what I realized was that Fanny was not a believable character because she was an absolute saint; the way I went back and flawed her was with her attitude toward Thomas and her inability to fully see where he was coming from. I felt that that flawed Fanny just enough to make her human but not so much that it pulled her down because I very much wanted her to rise above, and I was pleased with the ultimate portrait.

**JORDAN:** Yes. Why is Thomas so angry toward Fanny? Is it that she really has been negligent in encouraging him in pursuit of his dreams or has she not shown him the same kind of affection she showers on M.L. whom she clearly sees as her future?

**MCCORKLE:** I felt that a lot of that anger is that Thomas is at a point in his life where he is not able to see the shaded areas; and for him Fanny represents the old ways and the old roles. He doesn't understand that by her wits and by her smarts she has always felt that she was in control, and it didn't matter whether these white people she worked for perceived her that way or not. She was getting what she needed to get her own way. But Thomas sees her as representative of what he does not want and so he is angry at her. The social point I so much wanted to make with Fanny is that to fall into that Aunt Jemima stereotype means that you're robbing a whole generation of black women of a lot because there's this whole generation who have made their livelihood that way [as maids]. And they have supported their families and sent their children to school by cleaning and doing domestic work. It was a stepping-stone generation to the changes that started happening, so I don't think you can say or pretend that that never existed because that's to completely wipe those people out of the picture, which is unfair. That's where I saw Fanny, someone who has always been self-sufficient and done what she had to do for her own survival and yet kept all her standards intact. But I always felt her choice would be to do what she had to do to protect M.L. I saw her as a protector of the future, and she has in her mind that he is going to be the bridge between her generation and Thomas's generation, that he will take the anger and the passive existence and somehow put them together. That's what I had in mind.

But there's always that fear that you use the word, "nigger," and someone could flip open the book and see "nigger" and say, "I don't want anything to do with this" and to me that is an invocation. If I have a character use that word, that should reveal a lot to you about that character in a hurry. Then I thought but even though the stupid redneck people—here I am stereotyping—even though there are people who are that way, again I didn't want Bob Bobbin to be a stereotype, which is why I went back and added the thing about the black man he had encountered showing how he had been persecuted. I tried very hard in *July 7th* not to condemn any one person, and it was hard, but the one man I had no sympathy for is Mr. Foster. I felt that with his life, I could find nothing redeemable. Billy is sad. Billy is begging for something, and the fact that his dad is once again going to pay for everything and get him off is the worst that could happen.

**JORDAN:** And even Billy does not realize that.

**MCCORKLE:** No, he doesn't. But Thomas was in a lot of ways in the same position as Sam Swett—this young guy who is sort of floundering and thinking about all these big things and trying. And yes, Thomas has got a white girlfriend but what a dip she is and it's the same thing. This whole business about just because she's white . . . what does that mean. Nothing. Absolutely nothing.

**JORDAN:** That was one of my questions. I'm not sure of the impetus behind Thomas's relationship to his white girlfriend, Janie. Is it love? Her salary? Her support? Or does he need to find someone different from his mother? He seems to see the relationship in part as one in defiance of her.

**MCCORKLE:** Fanny does not like her.

**JORDAN:** Well, Fanny says, "He knows I would not like this." And when Fanny meets Janie at the jail to see about his case, he already thinks that the relationship is one more thing she can throw up in his face. When he introduces Janie, he says, "That's my woman" and stares his mother down. "Her name's Janie." Given the tone of his voice here in particular, I wonder if Thomas's relationship with Janie does not derive in part from this love/hate relationship with his mother?

**MCCORKLE:** Yes. The way I felt is that Janie probably felt that the relationship meant a lot more than Thomas did. He's using her. He's just kind of exploring all the boundaries that have been placed on him as a black man. That's what I thought. It's like he's having to fight his way out of something. And he is jealous of M.L., and he's hurt by that.

**JORDAN:** That brings me to two other questions about Thomas. There are so many contradictions in Thomas's actions. He blames the whites for placing him in jail but he is also willing to have his mother beg her "white folks" to arrange a lawyer or recommend one who can clear him. And his mother clearly sees this request is one of asking her to sell out. In the jail scene, is Thomas merely asking for this favor because he's desperate, or does he really not see he's asking his mother to give up her own sense of integrity?

MCCORKLE: He's desperate and he's scared, and the whole purpose of that scene is he's asking her to do what he's always accused her of doing. Thomas is much more bark than bite—sort of like Sam Swett again in a lot of ways. It's one thing to sit in your armchair in your mobile home or wherever and philosophize but when you're confronted with a real situation, which Fanny has almost always confronted . . . And he has never seen her going out there struggling every day and having to work very hard. He sees her as being a wimpy namby-pamby, this dishrag. But you don't live all those years as she has and so the whole way through *July 7th*, I felt I was playing flip of the coin. If I presented this angle, then I immediately turned it over and viewed it from the other side. Which is the way life is. And I think our problem results when people don't look from the other way. When people become set in one angle and see it that one way and nothing else. I think that's what prejudice is all about.

JORDAN: On the night that Thomas is released from jail, why does he go to his mother's house?

MCCORKLE: He wants his mother's sympathy, I think. He wants Fanny to say, "Come here, little Baby," the way she does to M.L. But she's sort of beyond that. Her backbone is stiff to that at this point. They've butted heads so many times, and I think now she even sees him as a threat to M.L. It's like everything has become a threat to M.L.

JORDAN: When I first saw Corky with M.L. who later tells Fanny that Thomas came and took him, so he's all right, I was thinking that that was good. Maybe Thomas is going to become a kind of role model for M. L. But then I always look for happy endings. I was really surprised; I thought, "Aren't they just going to embrace because here's a situation where he could have been put in jail for a long, long time, and it's turned out all right, and his mother did show up." But they don't come together. Fanny is more vocal than I had seen her. Thomas goes away, and Fanny cuddles M.L. That's the end of that? Will Thomas be all right? Is this one of those things where it's just a matter of time working them out?

**MCCORKLE:** Yes, I think so. It's a matter of time for Thomas and Fanny. I think that what she really felt is that because of her working hard, even though Thomas had accused her, she had protected him from a lot of hardship, and the fact that he doesn't give her any credit, that she sees this night in jail has shown him a side that he's needed to see. But she still cares a lot. With Thomas's father, there's a lot that's unspoken and I really hated to perpetuate that black male myth and yet I know so many women where it is true. I grew up with all these young girls who were being raised by their grandmothers and then it always skipped a generation. And the mother would be in Washington and Detroit trying to make a new start and then later she would send for the children and then ultimately she might keep their children while they went out. I knew so many young women where this was the pattern and so again I was nervous about what is this stereotype, what is this myth. It evolved from somewhere, but you can't rely on it. It can't be all true, and yet I have witnessed examples of it, so I was trying to write something believable and yet not something condemning of the whole, and it's a fine line there.

**JORDAN:** I think you're careful to balance each side if you can balance a side. There are so many ironies and contradictions that run throughout the novel. I liked the way you were able to go inside Fanny's head. You really seemed to understand where her burdens were coming from and where her son was coming from too.

**MCCORKLE:** But there are just times when people can't say everything and that's okay too. I could have taken either of their sides and argued it well. And that's what made it work because for everything he said, she had something to say that made just as much sense. They'd hit a dead end, which is why I feel that they are slowly going to come around. But she wants his respect and she does not have it. I was not a parent at the time that I wrote it, and I don't think you have to be a parent to know it. I think being a teacher is just as good an example. To know that this person you tried to give so much to has no respect for you. To imagine being in that position where you have loved and cared for someone and paid a whole lot of attention and then to realize, "no respect," I can't think of too many things that hurt more.

**JORDAN:** Do you think that Fanny has talked to Thomas all along and that lack of communication is part of the problem? When we see her in the car with Mr. Foster and M.L., she talks to M.L. and they so freely communicate.

**MCCORKLE:** I think the key there is what I say when Fanny is first introduced about how she named her son Thomas because there was all this doubt and resentment. I think that without meaning to she has fixed so much resentment toward Jake [her husband] that Thomas represents Jake in her eyes. Back to this myth. You can't help but wonder if when the man runs off and I'm not just saying in black homes, white homes too. When the man has left, then what is that little boy left with with no daddy? And if negative things are said about men, what effect does that have because he is hopelessly a man and he knows he is going to grow up and be a man? Does he perpetuate it because he's heard that's what a man is supposed to be? Does he feel bad without hope? I don't know. There are situations in lots of broken homes where I always cringe when I hear a parent talking about the other parent in front of the child. I am very fortunate, meaning that I have both parents intact, but now I see in my classroom that it's a rare thing to have a student who is from a home that's not broken. So all these kids from divorced homes, if they've ever been confronted with one parent talking about another in a negative way—and I would say with human nature, it's pretty damn hard for that not to happen at some time or another—that's got to hurt especially if you're of the sex of that parent. And I think Thomas without even knowing it is having to carry the weight of that.

**JORDAN:** Elizabeth, Thomas's sister, isn't central to the story. Although I get the sense that Fanny is very disappointed in her, she doesn't have to assess her in the same way that she does Thomas. Fanny doesn't believe that Thomas killed the man. She says he's not that kind of person. She sees his potential and all of that, but she seems so saddened that he hadn't done what she thought he should have done with it. It just seems that she placed more of the weight of her expectations on Thomas than Elizabeth.

**MCCORKLE:** But it also makes her mad that Thomas wants everything the white world has at any expense and I think Fanny feels like, "No, what you need to do is want everything you can get and still be very proud of your history and your heritage," and she more or less says, "I'm that, I'm your history so don't turn away from me."

I was in sixth grade when we integrated, and I have memories of stories being perpetuated about what we should be scared of and watch out for. There was this fear among adults to be expectant of something, and somewhere along the line someone figured out that the way we should handle it is go in and pretend we didn't notice. Which was very stupid. And black kids were coming in the same way. And that was impossible. It was impossible. They were just as afraid as we were. And all of this anger was coming out of fear of being rejected. And once everybody got over that and started asking questions like "Why do white girls shave their legs?" and "Does it hurt to pick your hair?"—once people started asking these cultural questions and understanding one another, then the fears were gone. And I was always proud because I had a high-school class that was so close, and our reunion was absolutely wonderful. I always maintain that maybe one reason our class was so successful is because maybe around sixth grade or younger is the right age. You're not quite old enough to have let anything eat into your head and you're still young enough to accept and come around.

JORDAN: Is Sam's kind of naïveté also part of what sometimes keeps the races apart, that kind of thinking that recognizes commonalities but does not appreciate differences or sees acknowledging differences as in some way prejudicing himself against the other and therefore does not acknowledge any? In some ways, can't that kind of thinking be dangerous too?

MCCORKLE: Yes, this is something that I had said in that *Southern Review* interview because I made some comment like "by acting like you don't know or recognize . . ." is a form of prejudice and what I mean by that is you're robbing that person of his/her individuality and history. Again I don't think it's fair just to look at a person and assume that that person fell from the sky! The ideal is that there is no prejudice. We seem to be going toward that yet you wouldn't want to give up a heritage and that's the other option. If you become like everyone else, you say, "I'm going to sacrifice my Southern roots and I'll never make reference to being a Southerner." That would be impossible for me because I think of myself as a Southerner. When I have to come up with the adjectives to identify myself, I think a lot of times we choose that adjective that is most likely to be a target by someone from the outside. When I was living in Boston, I know if ever I saw something going on bad in the news, especially something racial, I would say, "Please don't let it have happened in the South." I feel very protective of the South, and that's why I get so angry when I see any of this "Klan did this" because I think we've come so far and yet that's what gets the national attention. And yet when I was living in Boston, I've never seen a place more segregated. And I made that comment. In the South, when you go to the store and to the movies and to school, you're out there with black people. In Boston it's very segregated and yet when I was growing up feeling so guilty and thinking, "Oh well, there're the Kennedys working for civil rights in this very area." Maybe I have an ideal that can never be reached: everyone together on the same level and still able to have an individual past and history that can't be robbed. I don't think we could have any ambition if we didn't feel that we were different and have something different to say. It's hard for me to verbalize what I'm thinking, so bear with me.

JORDAN: I think that's what makes your portrayal of Thomas, Fanny, all of your characters so special. Fanny has an individual past and so does Thomas. He has a personal past, and he has a larger cultural past and heritage, and it's woven into your portrayal of their lives. I think that's why Fanny works; she moves beyond a stereotype. As I started to do research for my book of criticism, one of the things I started to notice was that a lot of times regardless of whether the writer is black or white in the earlier novels, if the writer is portraying a black woman, that woman does not often have an individual past. She doesn't even have a Jake, and if she did, you don't really know much about how he affected where she is in the present. She just sort of comes. There she is. But how did she get here? That's part of why I think characters remain flat and more stereotype.

MCCORKLE: I just thought of something that might make this idea a little clearer. As long as we are proud of our differences, then it's going to keep it balanced. If I say I'm proud to be something . . . I always get these "Southern woman" questions and there are the black Southern woman questions and the white Southern woman questions. As long as people don't take that to mean that I would only be of interest to other Southern women, I'm not offended because obviously I'm inescapably both adjectives. I am a woman and I am Southern, but this does not mean that this man in Milwaukee would not find something of value in my book.

JORDAN: I hope you are not tired of Fanny.

MCCORKLE: Oh no. Fanny and Juanita are the two that I miss the most out of that book once it was finished.

JORDAN: I like Juanita too.

MCCORKLE: I almost wished Juanita lived near me. I wished she'd drop in.

JORDAN: For some reason, she reminded me of Cindy. You somehow know if you were friends with these women, you'd be much bolder.

MCCORKLE: I think that's why I always have a character like that. I always call them my alter-ego characters because I don't have that. If someone asks, "Do you like this dress?" I say, "I think you could find something that would suit you a little better" rather than "What is going on in your brain! God no! You look horrible. I wouldn't wear that to a dog fight." You never say what you think at the time, or I don't. There's a part of me that really admires these women. Now if I did it, people would say, "What has happened to you? You've gone crazy." And yet you know these people who without any problem can just fly off and say anything and people just say, "Oh that's just her. That's just Cindy." I envy her.

JORDAN: Corky and Fanny are like family—Corky in fact in some ways is more of a family to Fanny than her own children, Elizabeth and Thomas. And despite their significant age differences, they are also friends. They share a closeness, an honesty that some of the other women who are blood relatives and are much closer in age do not share. What accounts for this intimate, surrogate grandmother/mother—granddaughter/daughter relationship?

MCCORKLE: I don't know how much Fanny has revealed to Corky about her own life, but I know Corky has told Fanny everything. I would tend to think that Fanny has never dumped a lot on Corky and that she probably has served as the comforter. Here you have two people who feel they are on their own, surviving. And yet it's more than that. They have a lot of things that can potentially make them happy. I think that Fanny has M.L., but I think what Fanny sees in Corky is that pre-hope. Corky is very much searching for something, and what I liked most about Corky is that she was so hopeful. Both are realistic though. Sam, on the other hand, is hopeless and has no sense of reality. Everything has to be the ideal for him. He's thinking of the best way, whereas Corky sees everything in black/white harsh reality. And yet she has hope. Somehow out of this reality, she's the one with genuine hope such that she has what's real—he doesn't—of the imagination. She has every reason to be negative on life, whereas he really has none. I'm always taken with that notion: something terrible happens in a person's life, and either he turns to his faith, or suddenly finds a faith, or he turns away. There's no in-between and I see Corky as someone who is turned fully toward this faith and hope in life. Sam is someone who has temporarily turned entirely away. To look at them, you would say he has no reason and she has every reason, but it doesn't work that way.

**JORDAN:** One other question about Fanny. Do you ever wonder if she is going to return to the Foster household after that night or is this just one more of those things that you live through and then you go on to the next day?

**MCCORKLE:** I wasn't sure. When I finished writing the book, I felt she would eventually go back. That she would feel threatened if she didn't go back. All I could think about when I was writing it was feeling a sense of urgency for her: "Oh just let me get home. Just let me get home." And that's really what I was feeling as I was writing about Fanny.

**JORDAN:** I like happy endings, but *July 7th* was not a book given to that.

**MCCORKLE:** You know a lot of people just read *July 7th* as this rollicking comedy. I felt for the social impact to fully be there, for the social issues that I felt I had introduced, to tie everything up too neatly with the bright red bow would defeat the purpose and in a way would make light of what I thought were very serious situations. So I did sort of leave Fanny hanging there because I think she has sort of been hanging like that her whole life and has taken life one day at a time.

**JORDAN:** Now to Fanny and Mrs. Foster. Fanny clearly has some respect for Mrs. Foster, and she rather likes her as a person, and to some degree that respect and like are reciprocated. Is it simply class and/or the employer/employee relationship that keeps Fanny and Mrs. Foster from becoming "intimate" friends or bosom buddies?

MCCORKLE: Yes, I think there is genuine affection there on the part of both, and I just think that Mrs. Foster is from a time and now a social class that wouldn't allow it. I didn't fully explore it, but I think Mr. Foster is imposing in every way, and I feel that these social boundaries would be what would prevent Mrs. Foster from indulging more of herself when talking to Fanny. I think there's a wall there that she does not cross and it's social, but I did not see her as a negative character. Really, I felt sorry for Mrs. Foster at the end because I think she wants to do things differently and handle things differently, and I think the thought of Fanny not coming back just really throws her because I think there's a dependency there that she's never fully acknowledged. And I don't just mean keeping the potpourri in the bowls. Fanny is a strong force for Corky and sort of everywhere she goes. I just saw her as representative of stability and strength.

JORDAN: I don't know if Thomas was really being flippant or not, but he tells Fanny, "Your white people could help because didn't they say one time you were part of the family." And Fanny replies, "They say that to people. They don't really necessarily mean that." I get the sense that Fanny understands her relationship to them.

MCCORKLE: You know that's something that people oftentimes will say or you hear it often, "Well, she's part of the family." And there have been times when I've seen cases where I thought, "yeah" and other times when I didn't believe it. You know what I'm saying? and I said, "Well, if she's part of the family, why isn't she sitting down at the table eating with you? And why is she calling you Mrs. So and So?" You know there are lots of those family members. So I use that phrase as tongue in cheek from my own because it's something you do hear often to the point that if I ever said it, I'd make damn sure I found a new way to say it. That phrase has lost a whole lot of weight because it's been misused too many times.

JORDAN: Maybe because of the boundaries that keep them apart, Mrs. Foster clearly doesn't know Fanny in the same way that Fanny has gotten to know her.

**MCCORKLE:** Well, it's also like I told you. You look under somebody's bed and in their closets and you know them. Walk in their bathroom early one morning before they've had time to clean it up, and you get to know that person. That's why marriage is such an eye-opener. There is no way you can be in such an intimate situation and not know everything. Mrs. Foster has only been to Fanny's once because Mr. Foster always goes. There's one time she went and she was so taken with the quilts, and it's almost as if she's surprised that she felt so good in Fanny's home. She hasn't seen Fanny's world, and I think that's where a lot of that difference comes. Fanny says herself she has been allowed to be a fly on the wall—to stand there and listen. She's just considered a part of the atmosphere. But they've never seen her in her natural habitat. That's where you get to know people.

**JORDAN:** I thought it was very funny when Fanny mentions the swamps or river behind the house, and Mrs. Foster says, "I didn't know it was back there."

**MCCORKLE:** And just leaves them hanging about the bodies in . . . but there too she was sort of playing that role—sort of telling this old black magic story to spook them. I laughed so. I feel like Fanny is playing with them there. She's giving them what they expect from her on the one hand.

**JORDAN:** And having fun with them.

**MCCORKLE:** And I think that is what I wanted to show that she has always done. Thomas doesn't see that she pulls her own strings and has her own way of maintaining respect while in this lesser position. But she does. Her self-respect is fully intact.

**JORDAN:** Still, Fanny is more of a human being to Mrs. Foster than she is to Mr. Foster. To him she is almost a nonentity.

**MCCORKLE:** She is to him until she becomes a witness.

**JORDAN:** When he tries to bribe and blackmail her, he reminds her that she has to take care of "what's his name" and Fanny remembers that, "Now he's been driving us all this time, and he doesn't even know this child's name." It's like they're just figures; they appear and then they go away and that's it.

MCCORKLE: Unfortunately, there are so many people like that. I know from my stint as a secretary, you're invisible in a lot of situations to a lot of people. And I think we've all experienced this at one time or another where this hand reaches out and hands you something, and no one even looks you in the eye. And it's a feeling you never fully get over. And I guess I used that sensation and multiplied by a thousand when I started working on Fanny.

JORDAN: There were times when I felt Fanny could have been the Invisible Woman; she was just there. Do you think women such as Fanny, who are poor, destitute, marginal to society, have alternatives for living out their lives except through the hope they place in what their children might become?

MCCORKLE: That's a tough question. I know she has all of her hope in M.L. She is the kind of person who if she didn't have M.L. she would find something else. It would be Corky or something else. She is a caretaker, a nurturer, so she would find something. That's a tricky question. I think she's satisfied. I think that's why she is so threatened by Thomas's inability to understand her because she's very proud of herself and in certain ways she's very satisfied. So the fact that he questions who she is and where she is is a big threat.

JORDAN: Let's move to some broader questions. You seem comfortable portraying all of the women of *July 7th*. Was one more difficult than another to develop?

MCCORKLE: I think the hardest for me was Kate, because there was always that impulse to carry it a step too far. She was so close to the caricature that it was real easy to get heavy-handed, and I would have to step back and try to tone it down. Throughout the first draft, I felt that Kate more than anyone else was like a real stereotype of the new-money social climber and so I went back and added that one little bit where the other women are like, "Oh God, here she comes." Any time I see someone trying so so hard, too hard, your first reaction is one of disgust, but it quickly turns to something else. It's painful to watch, and the whole time I was writing about Kate, I would feel myself cringing, just making the hair on my neck stand up, because I thought this is just so embarrassing. But that was what was so much fun about *July 7th*. I really felt like it was role playing and that I was putting on all these different hats.

**JORDAN:** I was pleased, however, that for once Kate recognized the other women were talking about her and she knows that members of her family talk about her but they don't really count.

**MCCORKLE:** Since she looks down on them.

**JORDAN:** Right. She's not going to change, but at least she knows how they feel about her.

**MCCORKLE:** But there, too, I think with Kate and with Ernie also, it is a parallel to what's going on with Thomas—someone who really wants to deny an entire past and all the people who have fed into it.

**JORDAN:** Do people ever take people like Kate seriously? Because that's what she craves, that someone will take her seriously in the way that she wants to be perceived.

**MCCORKLE:** I think only people who are below her on that same ladder. There is always someone looking up from the rung below. I mean I realized when I finished that I was venting some feelings toward this kind of social climber, which is why I did go back and try to soften her a little bit.

**JORDAN:** What specific conditions seem to be in place when black and white women become friends?

**MCCORKLE:** I think it's a matter of honesty and carrying on a conversation as people without thinking, "Isn't this something? You're black and I'm white and we're sitting here talking." To be able to talk about things that are personal and are real in your life as an individual. Again it comes back to what we said earlier; it's the individual existence that I think allows everything else to grow out of it. I think friendship as much as anything in terms of the conditions is people coming together without feeling like they're so far removed. That's a hard question.

**JORDAN:** Do you think it is easier for women of the same class to get together?

**MCCORKLE:** I think class is probably the bigger issue for us. I was on a panel not long ago, and this guy stood up and asked a question; he could not identify with any of the Southern fiction. The only Southern writer he could identify with was Peter Taylor. He didn't understand where all these Southern writers were coming from, and I paused to answer the question: "I think we're talking about a difference in class rather than geography." I think more people are willing to admit there are far more walls and gaps between classes than race. Do you think so?

**JORDAN:** I think so. I think that you're more likely to be in more of the same situations that would automatically bring you together in a way that if you're in different classes you wouldn't even get to know each other in the first place.

**MCCORKLE:** But then there are other common variables like being in school together.

**JORDAN:** That's what I'm finding in works by authors of children's books and young adult fiction. Some of the most compelling friendships between black and white females occur between schoolgirls who are pretty much on the same footing regardless of what happens at home. You can sort of put differences aside at school. But in looking at adult novels once again, what kind of role does the black female play in white women's novels? What kind of role does the white female play in black women's novels?

**MCCORKLE:** I think I voiced that earlier in terms of for the sake of reality in creating my own picture I always feel a need to have a black character. As a writer starting out, I was a little intimidated about how to go about it, but I felt like, "God if you avoid or skirt issues that you really feel close to, that's a dishonesty and once it starts it's never going to end." And as I said earlier, I just had to approach it in my own way with the knowledge that I was being as realistic as possible. I have to make sure you have a copy of the galleys of my new novel because it is told from a first-person point of view of a young girl from ages twelve to fifteen and even though the backdrop is the time of integration and the shake-up of the sixties, I touched on some of the issues I have before but on a younger scale because I do have a scene where the older ladies quiz the younger girls: "What's it like in junior high? I hear they use horrible language. I hear this and this." Just ridiculous things that you're asked. That's in the new novel.

**JORDAN:** To what extent do you use sources, such as histories, biographies, or autobiographies, when you are developing a black female character?

**MCCORKLE:** I never have. Just imagination.

**JORDAN:** White women have often written novels with black female protagonists. But the reverse happens much less often. Could you comment on this phenomenon? Do you think this pattern will remain the same, or will black women start portraying white female protagonists a bit more frequently?

**MCCORKLE:** I'm not sure except maybe. . . . Certainly if I were a black woman writer, I would feel that I had enough to explore on my own turf before I ventured out. In the same way that I feel that I as Southerner have to explore on my Southern turf without venturing out. It's what you know. The issues are out there and big and we've witnessed it. The white woman has witnessed what has gone on in the black community. And maybe sometimes—well for a lot of people quite often—there's the need to step into those shoes and see and try to understand. I don't think that the black woman has had time to run out of patience such that she has needed to step out and look elsewhere. I think there's plenty to explore. That's an off the top of my head theory. . . . A lot of women never have male characters either and a lot of males never have women characters. They don't feel the need to step out. I like to every now and then try to step out just to sort of test the range. But I don't know.

**JORDAN:** What can black and white women teach each other about writing and about living?

**MCCORKLE:** That's another hard one. I think the same thing. I think the most important thing is discovering how very much there is in common just by way of being human. I don't know. I think all writers and all people stand to learn a lot from each other because again it's like I tell my students: there are only so many plots and whenever you summarize your plot, everyone yawns because they've heard it a million times before. But what allows people to keep on writing and will forever is the individual soul behind it. It's your style and it's the way you see it and it's all the little bits of you, the individual nature of different people that allows it to become something different, and so I think we can just learn from each other period that that is one of the cases—that maybe it is regardless to race or sex.

**JORDAN:** Do you envision black women becoming more integrated into the women's movement as common concerns such as child care and abortion bring women of all races closer?

**MCCORKLE:** Yes, I do. I think that's already happening very much among women. I think that these are the things that form friendships—variables that have no need to differentiate.

**JORDAN:** When you look at young children and teenagers who often do not know their own family histories and do not have or know the words to tell their experiences or what they see, what kinds of things do you think ought to be done to help them gain control over their own voices?

**MCCORKLE:** Certainly, if they don't know their own history and they have access to people who do, they need to ask. Even if it's in the roughest form, to get it down. I'm a big believer in preserving the good and the bad, which is what *Tending to Virginia* is about. So often we're just given these good wonderful stories, and then it's a big shock when you realize that there was always the flip side, and I'm very much into that flip side. Show it both ways and somewhere in between you have what really happened. I think to ask questions and pursue the history and then I think finding the voice is a matter of experimentation. In teaching writing, I see students trying to step out of themselves way over here and be someone totally different, and oftentimes they come into a writing class thinking that's what it's all about—writing something that's different from who you are, and I think that first you have to learn about writing about who you are before you can learn to take your emotions and transpose them. To take this sense of loss you know in this situation and then to magnify it and compound it and give it to this character who is able to experience something far greater than you have experienced and yet the emotion is there and it's accurate. So I'm always telling my students you have scenarios going on in your head all day long. It's a form of experience. It's never happened but your imagination is a part of your experience and a lot of people when they tell stories about their lives, they want to hide the ugly part and camouflage the flaws, whereas oftentimes that's what makes it real. That's what makes it work—all these little idiosyncratic details that we have. I had a professor one time say to me, "Most of us spend our time trying to forget adolescence and you have spent so much time trying to remember all the sordid details." To me it's a very important time, and we all have our pet topics, and I'm very drawn to adolescence. I feel like it's a kind of ball of the most wonderful of things and the most terrible of things all in one, and I don't think it changes so much as we learn to control it. A lot of time with that control you lose a little of the fire. I think people have to ask about their history. I was so disturbed recently because for years I had heard this story about one of my mother's relatives who walked home from the Civil War, and his house was still standing. And the last time I went home, we went to find it and within the last year the house had been torn down. There were my great-grandparents' graves. There was something just real humbling to go and see. It makes you feel real small at the same time so much a part of this big cycle, which I think ties in with all that we've been talking about all morning. About everything being different but the same to quote you. We all share common experience in that we do have histories. It's the individual fact of our histories that make us different, and I think it's important to hold on to those.

**JORDAN:** Do you see literary critics, particularly black ones, having a special role in shaping how stories of black women's lives are read, assessed, and taught?

**MCCORKLE:** Yes, I think so. But I'm speaking from a very limited experience. I'm speaking specifically of Thadious Davis's class because I have seen it in a very positive light, a class that is a healthy mix of black and white women doing what we have been talking about: finding all these common variables in their lives because they're reading this fiction that pulls them together in a common experience. I think it would depend on how the fiction is portrayed. There's always the fear that like with being a Southern woman writer, being a Southern black woman writer, I would think there would be that fear people would make it sound like "Why another Southern black woman would want to read what you have to say," which certainly Toni Morrison and Alice Walker have proven is not the case. But I would think there would be that fear, and certainly how a critic chose to handle the work could affect that. But I always hate to see a book pegged or placed on a certain shelf without first being offered a certain universal appeal.

**JORDAN:** When there is conflict between your writing and demands outside of writing, how do you resolve the tension?

**MCCORKLE:** I thought you were going to ask me when the story starts pulling this way and you've got it all structured to go that way, I say throw in the towel and go where it leads you though it takes you two hundred pages out of your way. The adventure is worth it. But to the question you're asking: The demands are there, but I'm a firm believer in the adage if there's a will, there's a way. I think if it's important enough to you to write, then you will certainly get it done. But I don't believe in sacrificing your personal life and your personal happiness for it. Although I grew up hearing all the stories about the tortured starving writer, I knew that I did not want to be one and that I had to see to it that I had the kind of life I wanted. I also feel if I allowed my writing to become a burden and to become a demand that maybe it wouldn't bring me the same pleasure that it does. I treat it as a reward and when I really feel that impulse to write, it is the golden carrot dangling out there and that's what makes me get that kitchen floor mopped and get Claudia bathed and off to bed and get everything taken care of. Then writing is a luxury. It's a prize rather than the other way. It would be harder to mop the floor after or wash the dishes or go to the grocery store or do any of the other things that you have to do. At this point I see writing as much a part of my life as breathing and making the bed and part of what allows me to do that is both. There are days though where it's really magical and it really carries me off. There are other days when it's just sort of a physical act where I know I have to sit down and write this chapter today even though if it's not the way I want it, I have to physically get it on the paper. So it's not always magical but it's something that I do the same way I would do anything else I had to do. If the car has a flat, you change it. If you need to write this thing, you write it. When I started thinking about it that way, then I had no excuse not to do it. But I do enjoy my work, and I think that's why. As a matter of fact when I started getting paid for doing it, at first I felt guilty. Something's wrong. This is like getting paid to take a nap.

**JORDAN:** Does your teaching feed into your writing? Do you think it strengthens it, gives you more ideas?

MCCORKLE: I think so. I think if I taught three classes, I'd have a hard time juggling. I teach two classes, and I'm still able to write. You know sometimes it cuts into other things, but I think you have to make your priorities, and I think that's what it's all about: organizing those priorities.

# JOYCE CAROL OATES

■

*Joyce Carol Oates is the author of twenty novels and many volumes of short stories, poems, essays, and plays. She has received awards from the Guggenheim Foundation, the National Institute of Arts and Letters, and the Lotus Club, and she received a National Book Award in 1970 for her novel* them. *Her most recent novel,* Because It Is Bitter, and Because It Is My Heart, *was nominated for the 1990 National Book Award.*

*For many years her short stories have been included in the annual* Best American Short Stories *and the O. Henry Prize story collec-*

*tions, and she has received the O. Henry Special Award for Continu-*
*ing Achievement twice.* Heat: And Other Stories, *her most recent*
*collection, was published in 1991 to critical acclaim. She is a mem-*
*ber of the American Academy and Institute of Arts and Letters.*

*Most recently, in 1990, she was awarded the Rea Award for the*
*Short Story, given to honor a living American writer who has made*
*a significant contribution to the short story as an art form. In nam-*
*ing Joyce Carol Oates the 1990 winner, the jury for the Rea Award*
*stated: "One of the magical things about Joyce Carol Oates is her*
*ability to constantly reinvent not only the psychological space she*
*inhabits, but herself as well, as part of her fiction."*

*Joyce Carol Oates is married and lives in Princeton, New Jersey,*
*where she is the Roger S. Berlind Distinguished Professor in Hu-*
*manities at Princeton University.*

**JORDAN:** What specific conditions seem to be in place when black and white women become friends?

**OATES:** No doubt, intellectual and professional equality, proximity.

**JORDAN:** What kind of role does the black female play in white women's novels? What kind of role does the white female play in the black woman's novel? What strategies do the authors use to develop the character's voice to make her "real"?

**OATES:** This is simply too broad a question. I would guess, how-ever, that very few white women have written intimately about black women, and vice versa. I tried in *Because . . .* to present a wide spectrum of black and white characters, mirroring the com-plexity of life.

**JORDAN:** To what extent do you use sources, such as histories, biographies, or autobiographies, when you are developing a black female character?

**OATES:** I've sometimes, though not often, done research for fic-tional characters, but without regard for race.

JORDAN: White women have often written novels with black female protagonists. But the reverse happens less often. Would you comment on this phenomenon? Do you think this pattern will remain the same or will black women start portraying white female protagonists a bit more frequently?

OATES: I'm afraid I am not aware of white women's novels with black protagonists. Of course, there are black characters, but are they protagonists? I wonder which titles you are thinking of. Perhaps Jean Rhys's *Wide Sargasso Sea* would qualify?

JORDAN: What can black and white women writers teach each other about writing and living?

OATES: Sympathy—sympathy—sympathy!

JORDAN: Do you envision black women becoming more integrated into the women's movement as common concerns such as child care and abortion bring women of all races closer?

OATES: Perhaps. But economic factors are likely to undermine the women's movement overall.

JORDAN: Do you see literary critics, particularly black ones, having a special role in shaping how stories of black women's lives are read, assessed, and taught?

OATES: Black literary critics are extremely important, and they should write helpfully about black writers, not attack them as has sometimes happened, perversely—black male antagonism toward black female literary success, for instance; or, in any case, not attack them out of self-serving motives. The black scholar-historian Henry Gates, Jr., recently decided to write about white writers occasionally, in white publications, and this may prove exciting, and controversial. I am one of the first of his subjects, and consider that his assessment of *Because It Is Bitter* . . . is probably the most intelligent the novel has received.

JORDAN: You relate at least two incidents in which a black female is wrongfully accused of cheating but does little to defend herself. The first occurs when Mrs. Rudiger accuses Lucille Weaver of having stolen the correct response to an arithmetic quiz from

Iris. For a time, the girl is mute and then suddenly cries. The second incident occurs later when a hotel guest accuses Minnie of having taken a piece of jewelry. Fortunately, the woman finds it in her suitcase and apologizes. Still, Minnie is aware that had the jewelry not been found she would have lost her job. Why are these females so effectively silenced in these situations? Clearly, they are extremely assertive, even aggressive, at other times.

**OATES:** There is no evidence that Minnie Fairchild did not deny the theft—certainly she did, and must have. Generally, however, anyone so employed or in such a position of relative powerlessness, whether black or white, male or female, will be "silenced" by the very fact of this powerlessness.

**JORDAN:** Later a fight occurs between Lucille and Iris in which Iris's nose bleeds, "but she sees that the black girl's nose too is rimmed in blood." She also notices that Lucille's blood is red just like her own. Do you think that such experiences in which blacks and whites interact naturally as part of their growing up experiences—negative on the one hand—nevertheless can have positive outcomes in terms of shaping flexible attitudes and broadening outlooks on life?

**OATES:** Yes, certainly.

**JORDAN:** And how do you think these early interactions with blacks contribute to Iris's later attitudes toward them?

**OATES:** Iris admires Lucille, who is one of the very few people, black or white, who will "touch" Iris, in her entire life.

**JORDAN:** The black boys' assault on Iris on November 23 had to be traumatic, but she is seemingly able to put the incident to the back of her mind. "A lifetime of flinching at black skin and yes, it's true, to a degree it's true, though when she smiles, . . . you'd never know."

Iris is clearly more than an overcomer. But how is she able to forgive these boys and move on with her life—apparently without benefit of counseling or even much discussion from her newfound friend and mother-in-law?

**OATES:** It may be that Iris feels she deserved this assault: as she has ruined Jinx Fairchild's life, so her life might be ruined, or at least sullied. It may be, too, that inviting such a defilement of her body is Iris's unarticulated hope of finally exorcizing her romantic attachment to Jinx, whom she can never have.

**JORDAN:** It seems as if Iris responds to the assault by adding one more big secret to the ones she has already buried. And yet I do not doubt that Iris will hold herself together despite the major secrets she will carry forever in her mind and heart. When you look at Iris, what do you admire most about her? Are you ever a bit afraid for her sanity? her health?

**OATES:** Iris Courtney, like my characters generally, and my major characters in particular, should inhabit a dimension beyond my attitudes toward or opinions of them. I believe that it is the writer's task to create character as fully and honestly and with as much attention to psychological subtlety as possible, and, from that point onward, it is up to others to consider them; even, at times, to misunderstand them, as in real life.

**JORDAN:** Do you think that silence is sometimes our only alternative for keeping ourselves together?

**OATES:** "A thing once said can never be unsaid, only denied."

**JORDAN:** And are there times when as long as we know the truth and admit it to ourselves, keeping up pretenses, appearances, or simply not telling the "whole truth" is a healthy alternative for protecting ourselves and for keeping intact our life-styles?

**OATES:** Yes.

**JORDAN:** Jinx and Iris have strong feelings for each other. Maybe they love each other. They seem to understand each other in ways that their spouses probably never will. And yet these two people do not have a place in Hammond, New York, either as a couple or as individuals. Is race the only thing that keeps them apart?

**OATES:** A complex of factors, surely . . . but race is definitely at the core.

**JORDAN:** Sometimes when I've read novels in which the white employer/black servant relationship is explored, it is not very clear what the black person gets from the relationship besides a paycheck. This is not true of Minnie and the doctor. Could you comment on the significance of the doctor to Minnie's world and the benefits she receives from her working relationship with him?

**OATES:** Minnie genuinely likes her white employer, and he genuinely likes her. They are both good people. Yet Minnie is living in a fool's world, like so many women, both black and white, who are wholly dependent upon a "good" person's kindness. So long as Minnie works for the white doctor, without adequate insurance and medical coverage, and without belonging to a union, she will be unprotected as soon as the terms of her employment change. When the doctor leaves his practice, Minnie is unprovided for; she realizes, as we realize, that, all along, she was exploited. She was exploited by her white employer's very "goodness."

I want to emphasize that the trap Minnie falls into unknowingly is not limited to black women and/or black men. It is a common predicament among employees of any race.

**JORDAN:** Does her perception of the relationship in any way hinder her dealing with the reality of her life on her street?

**OATES:** Minnie is of the older generation than Jinx, who believes that Martin Luther King's nonviolent activism may hold the key to the future. Because Minnie fears change, even change that might better her economic position, she would side with critics of King; yes, her perception of her relationship with the white doctor has hindered her grasp of her real situation.

**JORDAN:** Your ear for black speech is soooo sharp. As I was reading, I could hear other black women speak some of the same phrases as Minnie and I remember some of the expressions Verlyn used as being true to life. You really seemed to be inside of Verlyn's head, and this speech reflects this very much so. How were you able to train your ear to hear the black speech patterns so clearly or was capturing the speech pretty much an unconscious act of composing?

**OATES:** Black English is very beautiful, very musical, very poetic, canny, sharp, startling in its metaphors and images . . . just plain more interesting than so-called White English. I have heard it all my life, but, apart from a play [*Miracle Play*, in *Three Plays*] I wrote some years ago, I've never actually employed it in my writing. As, for years, I'd been very interested in boxing, but only wrote about it a few years ago.

**JORDAN:** I found Mrs. Savage to be absolutely intriguing in part because I still had so many questions about her and in part because I was not quite sure I could trust what I did see of her. At times she seemed too good to be true. And yet I was glad of that perception for Iris's sake. Iris was overdue for someone who might appear good and true and wonderful. Although there are a number of instances in which I feel this tension between the real Mrs. Savage and the surface Mrs. Savage, I am really struck by Mrs. Savage's response to blacks. On the one hand, as Iris notes, "Mrs. Savage introduces her [Mercedes] to the company as Mercedes: 'Mercedes' and no last name." And later at dinner "her melodic voice rings out, . . . on the edge of sharpness, 'Those bottles Mercedes.'"

Even though Mrs. Savage admits that she doesn't know what she would do without Mercedes, she clearly sees the maid as no more than a tool, a presence that gets paid for services rendered. I understand this treatment as typical behavior for a white woman of her maid. But later after the assault on Iris, Mrs. Savage is able to say "You must pray for them, dear. You mustn't harbor bitterness. . . . It's the only way. The Christian way. The way of health and forgiveness." Now I'm a bit thrown. Iris and the entire Savage family have been almost nonhuman in responding to this entire incident. Leaving the race of the assaulters aside, they nevertheless are the most understanding group of people I've ever seen. What do they do with their anger that understandably is probably as much a part of their response as this forgiving spirit?

And how is it that Mrs. Savage who dismisses Mercedes—a woman who cooks, cleans for her—as if she were not a living, human presence so able to suggest forgiveness to Iris who has been so viciously attacked by unknown, strange black boys? It occurs to me that, of course, Mrs. Savage might have made the suggestion out of love for Iris and not out of any genuine forgiveness for the boys. Still, I'm struck by the kind of subtle contradictions that seem to be at work in this woman's behavior and attitudes without her seeming to be aware of them.

**OATES:** Mrs. Savage is a very fine, gracious woman—yet she is a white woman of her time, place, and class; thus exhibits, without the slightest awareness, racial prejudice of an absolutely self-evident kind. We are accustomed to harshly drawn caricatures of prejudice, but these may be, in fact, relatively rare. We are surrounded by people like Mrs. Savage, a truly good woman, whose prejudices we tend to overlook. As Minnie, in her justified affection for her doctor employer, chose not to see that, in a few years, she would be cast out on the job market, with no security. As to her forgiveness—such women are frequently self-abnegating, even, in a way masochistic—though "masochistic" is a word I deplore, for its pop-psychology reductiveness of extremely complex factors of sociological/political/historical significance that go far beyond simple Freudian-labeled sexuality. The heart of Christianity is such "forgiveness" of enemies. Though in fact, as we are all well aware, it is rarely demonstrated by Christians.

**JORDAN:** Was storytelling a part of your growing-up experience? If so, how has it affected your writing?

**OATES:** Yes, though in less expansive and communal ways than one might meet within, for instance, the South, or among really large families. Our extended family was large but not really large.

**JORDAN:** Have you ever felt pressure from your publisher and/or editor or audience to portray a particular kind of character or to treat a particular set of themes?

**OATES:** No, never.

**JORDAN:** What is the responsibility of the reader, if any, in the creative process?

**OATES:** This is an interesting theoretical question, but, for the most part, I doubt that any writer considers it. My focus is upon the "integrity of the work"—my hope of realizing certain material, and by way of this material certain characters and visions, as fully as possible. This draws my attention, and is often exhausting. To think of the reader and his/her responsibility would be unprofitably distracting.

**JORDAN:** In writing this work, was one character more difficult to develop than another regardless of race, class, sex, or age? If so, which character(s) and why?

OATES: No.

JORDAN: Particularly in novels—but not necessarily limited to these situations—in which white female employers are portrayed with their black maids, do you think that ambiguity is a major device, among others, that black women use in relating to white women? And why?

OATES: Very likely all employees use ambiguity of a kind (some of it surely unconscious) vis-à-vis their employers. The problem may in fact be less "racial" than merely "class"—the consequence of what is called a free-market economy in which one must sell oneself.

JORDAN: When your writing pulls you along a particular path and other responsibilities—teaching, children, speaking engagements—are pulling you in other directions, how do you resolve the conflict?

OATES: I don't experience any conflict between inner and outer worlds, at least not any significant enough to discuss.

JORDAN: Finally, who or what inspired you to write this novel?

OATES: Several memories converging: One of an extremely charismatic black boy whom I knew in junior high school. I went to a "mixed" school in Lockport, New York. Another of having been followed, at dusk, in an area of warehouses, by an unseen tormentor (like Little Red Garlock), also in Lockport, in fact as I'd been making my way—an extremely complicated way—to catch a bus home, after school; another of the painful, nightmare experience of witnessing, even at a distance, the alcoholic death of an older woman of my acquaintance—not my mother, as some people have believed!; another of recalling the vivid hallucinatory hours following the news of Kennedy's assassination. Another factor is my contemplation of Princeton, New Jersey, where I now live, in relationship to the world of my childhood and young girlhood.

# GRACE PALEY

■

*Grace Paley was born December 11, 1922, in New York. Though she began writing poetry at the age of five, Paley has distinguished herself as a major short-story writer.* The Little Disturbances of Man: Stories of Women and Men at Love *(1959) and* Enormous Changes at the Last Minute *(1974) are both currently in print. Paley's stories have also been published in periodicals such as* Esquire, Atlantic, The New Yorker, Genesis West, *and* Ikon, *among others.*

*Paley has taught creative writing at Columbia University and at*

*Syracuse University and later became a member of the literature faculty of Sarah Lawrence. She has received several awards, including a Guggenheim fellowship, a National Council on the Arts grant, and a National Institute of the Arts and Letters Award for short-story writing.*

*The daughter of Russian Jewish immigrants, Paley grew up keenly aware of political causes and how they affect people's lives. She has worked on numerous projects to rectify social ills. Still much in demand on the lecture circuit, Paley lives with her husband in Vermont and New York.*

**JORDAN:** What specific conditions seem to be in place when black and white women become friends?

**PALEY:** That's very hard. . . . Well, there has to be an awful lot of trust. It has to be able to go two ways. But I think mostly the black woman has to be able to trust the white woman. By that I mean that the white woman has to be trustworthy. I could probably think of a better answer but that's a beginning. A matter of trust that can happen with work when people trust each other—or have a common experience such as children, age. . . . And it's also a class thing too, economic class.

**JORDAN:** I was just going to ask you if the issue of class also plays a part in the forming of these friendships. If the women do not meet in situations in which they are on the same footing socially, it's hard.

**PALEY:** Yes. But that would be true of white women too. It would be more difficult for a black and a white woman. But two white women could have a lot of misunderstanding or different interests too.

**JORDAN:** That's also true. Have you noticed distinctions between how black women authors portray characters and how white women portray them?

**PALEY:** I'm trying to think of authors. I think the last book I read was by Ellen Douglas who is a Southern white woman author writing about friendships between black and white women. You'll have to refresh my memory. Her novel is unusual and truthful. In it, the black woman who works as a maid is really portrayed with a lot more feeling than the white woman. The white woman is a decent sort of woman but there is no real understanding. I just met the author, Ellen Douglas, so I paid particular attention.

**JORDAN:** As you were drawing the character of the black female in "Long Distance Runner" [in *Enormous Changes at the Last Minute*], what particular concerns did you have about her portrayal? How was this figure born and what do you think of her now that she is actually here?

**PALEY:** First of all I come from the Bronx, and so I will give you an example from my background to show how I started her. I have been going back there every year to visit my father and mother's house. The neighborhood has changed since then. Now there are about four houses left on the block. My father was the neighborhood doctor. Just a couple of years ago I returned. I see this little black girl sitting on my stoop and . . . well I'm overcome with happiness. She's sitting there and a woman is looking out the window—the mother I thought (this happened after I wrote the story). I was elated, I almost ran into the house like the woman in the story yelling "Mama! Mama! Let me in!" Anyway I had been going earlier—often—and I had looked at the neighborhood and had seen what was happening—it's hard to talk about a story that pretty much said what I felt. What I tried to see and maybe know is another life. Not terribly unlike my own, which was full of mommies and daddies and so forth, but still to see another life in the same place. Place being a very important thing. The same place.

I remember what the neighborhood was like. The people who lived on my block then, now have some kind of idealized view of what our street was like. It was really not a rich people's street. It was a poor people's street—at least during the ten years of the Depression—most of my childhood and adolescence. Maybe it started out and planned and wanted to be more middle class, but in those days, my days, the street itself was often lined with evictions—people thrown out of their homes for nonpayment of rent. Those were hard times for my neighbors so that it wasn't hard for me to move into the world of the story, which ends with the narrator asking "What in the world is coming next?" I wanted to show that in a loving way—loving and truthful, not bullshit.

And I wanted to break certain stereotypes that the narrator has—for instance, when she says she's going to teach the kid to read, it turns out he's a great reader. You want to break this thing without a hammer but crack it anyway. That was intentional. But I also wanted to show the truth of that. I don't know if it's that story—it is—but there is one house left on this street. Nothing there but rubble and dirt and so forth. There's a big sheet hanging out the window and it says, "People still live in this God-forsaken neighborhood." That was just one house. Nothing around it but rubble and dirt and junk.

**JORDAN:** Do you think others go back too?

**PALEY:** Well, I think people do want to go and look at where they grew up—at least if they can. I lived there my whole life until I got married, so I lived there for nineteen years. I was on the streets a lot. Kids used to play in the streets all the time so I had a kind of identity with that kid on my old stoop. I see very little street life in the white neighborhoods in Manhattan. None practically. I mean, it's really pathetic for children. I had such a nice, rich street life. So the streets themselves are interesting and exciting to me.

Now I live downtown. I've lived for years in and around the Village. It's a very strong neighborhood, and Chelsea is a neighborhood much like it. There are some city areas that aren't neighborhoods; new people are moving in and new houses are built. A community takes time anywhere. You don't have a community the minute you move in.

**JORDAN:** To what extent do you use historical sources when you are developing a character like Ludie or Cynthia?

**PALEY:** I just write from my knowledge. Tough little girls and stuff like that—they are all going to have some of the same characteristics, right? "She's gonna not let the boys push her around and she's gonna . . ." I mean you go to school with these kids too. I did. My children did.

**JORDAN:** What can black and white women teach each other about writing and about living?

**PALEY:** Another complicated question. I know this sounds silly to say this but in general white people have a lot to learn about what it means to live in this country. . . . I'm Jewish and I've been in situations—for instance, I lived in a small town in Illinois when I was about twenty or twenty-one, when I first left home. The anti-Semitism was acute and painful to me and surprising since I had lived a ghetto life. I lived in a Jewish ghetto, and there's nothing more protected than a ghetto. And in its own way, there is probably nothing more protective for little black kids too. It's kind of nice to be in a kind of cocoon for a while, protected until you get your muscle together. But then we do have to go into the world; we must go into the world. You have got to have your strength to go into the world, and you get some of it from the people you've been living your childhood among.

I have a very brutal story in that book [*Enormous Changes at the Last Minute*] about a killing. You may have read it. This story comes from a guy who was a friend of mine. I met him just after World War II. Late forties. I worked at that time for the Southern Conference for Human Welfare in New York; it was basically just a fund-raiser for the South. There were a lot of black people around even though the group was run by these very idealistic white people who were going in and out of jail. Joe Louis was the chairman, and he would come around sometimes.

But I made friends with this guy, Bill, who was working there; he was from Eclectic, Alabama. I can't believe these names. We became very close friends. We were friends until he died a couple of years ago. He told me that story, and he didn't tell it to me once. He told it to me so many times that it was as though I knew it by heart.

A writer in general has to be a person who pays attention. I would say if you're not the kid sitting under the table who listened to grownups, you're not going to be a writer black or white. I think it's that listening. . . . For white Americans, of any kind, to listen is to begin to understand the country. To listen to blacks particularly is to understand the whole country historically. Slavery was a great curse the United States greedily, foolishly accepted.

**JORDAN:** One thing I have noticed as I've been reading novels in which black and white women appear is that we see fewer novels written by black women that have a central white female figure. Do you think this pattern will remain the same, or do you see black women starting to tell stories through the white female voice?

**PALEY:** Well—first of all—people tell their own stories, their unknown stories, and certainly black women's stories haven't been properly told by white men or women or black men so they have had a big job on their hands. In general, I think people go through this business of writing about their own people. I mean you had this whole big wave of Jewish literature and what it was, of course, was the first time they could write about their own Jewish experiences and be generally read. I'm just going to make one Jewish comparison here. When I wrote my first stories, they were really explicitly about my own neighborhood life, which I was just trying to understand and then there were a couple of other stories. And then I didn't need to explore that life so much.

When I wrote my first stories, I was afraid I'd stop writing because I have a lazy nature. I went to the New School for Social Research thinking maybe a class would keep me writing. And I had a teacher who kept saying to me "You've got to get off this Jewish dime." So I asked, "How can I write about a middle America?" What I didn't have the brains to say then was "I'm not even interested in it yet." Black women are important and interesting to black women writers. And to be able to write truthfully from where you are toward what you don't know about yourself, toward what you're trying to find out, toward your own mysteries and be read, which is possible at this time, is a very great thing. There's no reason yet for them to write with a central white character unless they were very specifically trying to understand what that person was in relation to blacks. Otherwise, they'd be writing a kind of middle America voice, the sort you hear on the radio or used to. So unless they were after something specific. . . . But it seems like there is so much yet to tell that hasn't been told and the new ways of telling are exciting.

So many women are writing now, women of all colors. It's a wonderful time. Before this, they didn't know that they could write about themselves. I remember when I wrote my first story—about a woman's life—I thought, "Gee, this must be boring. This is so boring to everybody. But I don't care. I can't help it. I have to write it." So I think that experience of suddenly being able to talk about ourselves—not just black women, I'm talking about myself and all women—is exciting and curious. And to be read by strangers as well as friends is a great thing.

**JORDAN:** That leads me to my next question. How do you maintain your own voice or manage to remain true to the voices of the characters without succumbing to pressures from publishers or readers to write either what they want to hear or what they consider proper to write? Has this been an issue at all?

PALEY: Well as far as the pressures from readers and publishers go, the only time I responded to a publisher was when I was told to write a novel. I had written my first book of stories. And I tried to write a novel and I failed. I mean I really gave it a shot. I did two years of writing a novel. And it was no good. Since then I just do what I want to do. I don't feel that pressure at all because I don't think in terms of a career or something like that. I don't think that way, and I never expected to make a lot of money writing so I teach like all writers do. [*Laughs*]

JORDAN: Did you grow up aspiring to write?

PALEY: I grew up aspiring, knowing that I was going to write my whole life because there was all this childhood encouragement. Every time you wrote a sentence, somebody said, "That is very good," so then you wrote two sentences. But people should not worry about this kind of pressure, not if they really want to write. I mean if their reason to write is to speak truthfully, writers must give their characters a full life and a truthful life—that's the only job a writer has.

JORDAN: Suppose you're writing something so radical that you think you can't find a publisher for it, then you still don't consider the publisher but pursuing the truthfulness of the story?

PALEY: See, when I wrote my first book, I got every story back again and again and again. Every single one. I mean until suddenly the University of Illinois printed two stories and that was it for the whole book. None of the others were accepted. I could have been very discouraged, and I mean I could have succumbed if I hadn't by luck gotten a publisher. I wouldn't have stopped writing though. But you really have to stick by your vision because life isn't so long really. It's always something. It's just as hard to fit somebody's—a publisher's—idea of what writing is as it is to write your own way. They're equally hard. So you might as well be hung for who you are. [*Laughs*] 'Cause they'll get you. They get you anyway . . . so . . . I mean look at publishing today. It's in such a weird shape anyway that you have to go to small presses if you're starting out.

JORDAN: As you are writing, are you ever conscious of race or ethnicity in a very overt way as you allow characters to come to life, or is it the story that is more important? Therefore, you're concentrating on the story and not so much on "This is the Jewish person who has to speak" and "This is a black person who has to speak."

PALEY: No. No. Well . . . I'm thinking of what I'm writing, and I'm letting the characters work their way through to the story. When I wrote "Long Distance Runner," I just began with the narrator running. I really had no plan. I did not know where I was going and when I got to the street, I didn't know I was going upstairs. And so you just sort of open yourself up to it, and by not knowing you have more tension somehow. There is some kind of great pull like a great stretch. And you stretch toward something that you don't understand totally and that then pulls you along somehow. The stretch and the tension in it I think is the way it works. So when I get the people I have to figure out how they evolve and sometimes I do the best I can. And what I also do is I read it aloud to myself. I read it aloud so that I try to get it right. Sometimes I show it to other people. It's funny when I wrote this story with a lot of black speech. I didn't feel so comfortable about it at all, and I wouldn't have for some reason. I didn't know if I could do it.

JORDAN: As the story is pulling you along, what do you do when other things also demand some of your time like picking up the kids or whatever?

PALEY: Oh, you mean my life? Ah, it's very hard. Some people are very organized. I talked to Mary Gordon. She puts aside the time. She has two kids, adores them, gives them a lot. But she organizes her time well, and she gets a novel out every couple of years. She is young and in another time than I am. She is the age of my children. But as for me it was always push and pull and pull and push. And then I had two children, and then I also had jobs, and I did a lot of politics too. I mean I just did it. It was a very rich period; I don't feel bad about any of it. And I would sit and talk with my children, take them to the park; they would give me a lot. In fact, they sometimes became my subject matter. So I can't really say I shouldn't have done that because that's what was interesting to me then.

But I was lucky enough to have child care. Everybody—not just writers, to hell with writers—but all women do have to have decent child care. And I don't think I could have accomplished all that I did without having a certain amount of child care. Basically, it was a settlement house in the neighborhood, which was cheap—what I could afford which wasn't much. It's hard but you gotta stick with it. [*Pauses*] Just think of a woman who really has some rotten job who is running back and forth with the kids. I'm particularly lucky to have some wonderful thing I want to do.

JORDAN: Back to the protagonist of "Long Distance Runner." She seems so much at home in the community even near the beginning when she first gets into the neighborhood and there are all these people around her. She seems alert and on guard but she never seems to me afraid for her life—at least most of the time she isn't. . . .

PALEY: Yeah, when she runs up there and the kid starts yelling at her.

JORDAN: I thought that that scene really moves far beyond the stereotype.

PALEY: It's a little surrealistic.

JORDAN: That's it! She couldn't be that naïve, and I didn't think she could be that open-minded but I suppose she could have felt at home. After all, if she has returned home, she wouldn't be as afraid anyway.

PALEY: I think it's a couple of things. It was quite surrealistic. No one would stand there and say . . . On the other hand, there is a certain naïveté. Even her deciding to give the little boy a reading lesson—I mean there was a kind of good-hearted naïveté about her in a sense. But it also had a surrealistic quality. . . . I mean the whole thing is invented. It's not very likely she would say those things. None of that is likely but all of it is in the realm of the barely possible. She might have gone up there in her shorts . . .

JORDAN: And maybe it's the naïveté that allows her to get even that far. If she were truly just sitting around reasoning out everything, she probably wouldn't have run that far off course.

PALEY: Yes. Yes. I'm nearly seventy. I come from a less fearful time. I used to have to pick up the collection boxes for the Southern Conference about forty-five years ago. I walked up and down apartment houses in Harlem, jangling shopping bags full. I never thought about it. I was afraid of the Irish neighborhoods though when I was a kid—because of Father Coughlin.

JORDAN: I'm sure you have heard the following said of your work before, but I will add my compliment as well. You capture the speech of the characters so brilliantly that the words seem naturally to flow from the characters' mouths. How did you develop your ear to capture Black English on the page without it sounding like "and now here is a black person speaking" versus "here is a person speaking in his or her own way who happens to be black?"

PALEY: I don't know. It goes back to listening. I think a lot of people could do better than they do. I say the dialogue aloud to myself. I can't tell you how many times I change the words. The smallest sentence I change many times. I mean any ten-word sentence I must have changed ten times. I rarely got it right. That's the main thing. I rarely got it right the first time, and I rarely got it right the third time. But it's this business of saying things aloud again and again. You know poets read aloud, right? And fiction writers don't do that so much in working. But just to say it again and again. You will get it. You may not get it perfect but you'll get it a lot better than—say—if you write it once and you say, "Oh I can't write dialogue." If you haven't been listening to people, you'll never get any kind of sound, but if you have been listening, then I think you can get it. But as I said I really have more self-consciousness right now.

JORDAN: It didn't seem self-conscious in the story at all.

PALEY: But that was because I rewrote it after it was in my head a long time. I wrote it, and then I made certain changes. I got it right, I think. It didn't begin with me being self-conscious. I began with the idea that I could do it, and then I only had to make the effort to and do it. I don't remember where, but I feel like I went off someplace. But that story, "Lavinia," was very much like my grandmother's story, and I wanted, in my mind, to bring people closer together. I wanted to show the same kind of story really in one case in the older immigrant woman and in this case, the working black woman. Married, didn't want children, wanted to make something of herself and had children. And then wanted her daughter to make something of herself. And it's not that the daughter went bad. I don't want her to become the bad person. What she did was live with a guy, just begin to have a lot of children. It didn't seem like she was going to do something with herself—from the old woman's view.

JORDAN: When we look at the protagonist leaving the neighborhood, Ludie tells her that it's time for her to go suggesting that she understands the protagonist perhaps in ways that she does not know she really understands. How does Ludie intuitively seem to know when it is time to leave? She's accepted this stranger into her home as if that were the natural thing to do, and then she seems to know exactly when she ought to leave. Is that just her instincts at work?

PALEY: I think also it's the surrealistic part of it. I wanted her to leave. [*Laughs*] She'd been a guest an awful long time, and nothing is more annoying than people telling people how to raise their children. Like telling them to go downstairs. Tell them to do this; they need more air. They would get really pissed at that.

JORDAN: The protagonist is renewed by her journey back. At the end of the story, we see her at home. In particular, what has she learned from her journey back to the neighborhood—to her roots?

PALEY: Well, she says that at the end, she's learned "what in the world is coming next."

JORDAN: Do you think our stereotypes of interracial relationships and of sexuality keep us apart as women rather than becoming closer?

PALEY: Yes.

JORDAN: From the perspective of both races?

PALEY: Yes, but I really think from the point of view of black women. . . . First as real people and as valuable people I can see their suspicion is historically so reasonable, but on the other hand, what it means is that white people, white women who are really interested have to prove themselves, and when people start to prove themselves, they become somewhat false. I mean not a bad false. I don't mean anything like untrue or anything like that. I mean they become unnatural and then a certain falsity sets into the relationship. And that has to happen, and that happens a lot. I think it can't help but happen. It's not anyone's fault. Our terrible history—oppression and hatred.

**JORDAN:** It's probably one of the hardest hurdles to cross in learning to trust.

**PALEY:** Yeah. It's a hard thing for people to act naturally together.

**JORDAN:** Once you start to make the effort to do so then that's when the falsity sets in.

**PALEY:** Yes, so people have to sort of recognize that falsity not as an evil thing sometimes but as an unnatural effort. Not meaning ill. And that goes both ways too. Listen, this business of suspicion between people who have hurt each other in one way or another. . . . What bothers me about say my own family or a lot of Jewish people I know who are really open-minded. . . . People think that the persecution of Jewish people started with the Holocaust. The Holocaust is *the* moment like the bringing over of slaves in our recent history. If Jews just thought about the way they've been treated in a daily way not just forty years ago but about a thousand years ago, they could identify better. Put away the most recent experience and think of what their ordinary life—just their daily life was like—not just the genocidal moment, but everything, then they would really understand better the daily life others live. And that's one of the things they don't do. So one of the arguments I have, like the idea that their neighborhoods were so great, is that they were just like any good people. I remember my mother going to Orchard Beach and saying, "Look what a mess! Our people were here." But when I tell that to my sister, she says, "No. No. We were never like that. We were never like that." [*Laughs*] Mama said that. She said that: "Our people were here. It's dirty. Let's go to another beach." [*Laughs again*]

**JORDAN:** That makes me think about blacks and how we remember slavery. I think sometimes people my age and older become frustrated with black teenagers who—not that they don't want to remember slavery—don't make it the pinnacle of all black experience. We think that they don't fully understand and that often frustrates us.

PALEY: Well, I think a lot of the kids think things are bad enough. "What are you going back there for? Why do you keep talking about that when here I am on this block, you know?" So going back has many possibilities.

JORDAN: What are some of the uses of memory or history you see at work in your fiction?

PALEY: Well for me, I like to go back into my parents' life, and I have a number of stories like that—stories from my father and history. There's a story called "A Conversation with Father," which to me is historical. It is seen by a lot of people as a psychological father/daughter thing, but to me it is clearly a historical statement. More than that the father comes from a place where change is not possible. That's one thing. He has that rigidity and also he comes from a world where he says she'll never change, it's like that. It's more historical than psychological, and I'm more interested in the historical than I am in the psychological.

JORDAN: When you look at young children and teenagers who do not know their own family histories and do not have or know the words to recount their experiences or what they see, what kinds of things do you think ought to be done to help them gain control over their own voices?

PALEY: Well, I just think, first of all, we tell them stories from history, not just the stories that happen to Grandma and Grandpa, but also tales of the past. From my own experience, I am not religious at all but I really enjoyed stories from the Bible when I was a kid. I felt related to them, so I told my children these stories. My son has told my granddaughter too, though he has no religious feeling. It's the way that our own old stories connect us to our past, and the stories of other people connect us to their past, so that we read not just our own stories but the stories of other people to know history, to make connections. And I really think that's very useful to children to ground them and to place them among the generations. I want to tell you a good assignment that I did with kids. Exactly related to this. I didn't know it was going to work out so well. Just before Thanksgiving I said when you get home ask the oldest person there to tell you a story he or she remembers by the oldest person he or she knew. One of the women went back through great-great grandparents to slavery. In fact that's one of the stories in "Long Distance Runner." When the little kid says, "I remember that story, 'Freedom Now,'" that's the one that student had told me. She's the one who told me that story. Her grandfather told her what his grandmother had told him. This is the story of how they ran from cabin to cabin. So you can go way way back. That was one of the best. I've done the assignment again, and you go pretty far back.

**JORDAN:** Did you want to make any comments about "Lavinia" at all?

**PALEY:** The story came from that common experience that seems to me to be a class experience, a common women's experience. Someone said to me, "Well, why didn't you just tell your grandmother's story instead of doing this?" And I guess I was just extremely interested, and it would have been boring to do it in my grandmother's voice at that particular time because what I was after was trying to understand what it would have been like for someone else. And I had been talking to this old black woman, Mrs. Pinchner, who had told me the same story anyway—exactly the same story. And it just seemed that I wanted to tell her story. In that whole period of my life I felt as a white woman that I wanted to understand more and also try to make some kind of contribution in a sense. Somehow I should understand and help other people to understand to see certain commonalities. And also the whole female subject, the whole business of these two women saying, "We wanted to be teachers. We didn't want to have all those children," interested me.

**JORDAN:** In growing up in the Bronx, what made you open to wanting to understand all cultures?

**PALEY:** Well, first of all, my parents were socialists who came from Russia. They'd been in prison in Russia when they were eighteen, nineteen years old so they were very young when they emigrated. And when they came here they didn't do a lot of politics. They had to work too hard. All my aunts worked in the garment district to make my father a doctor. They were all about twenty years old. Think of all these young people coming over, and they worked very hard so he could become a doctor, and he became one. He was always a neighborhood doctor. And the office was in the house so there were always people coming and going. And there was always sickness, and there was always a lot of feeling for other people's suffering. My father, unlike some doctors, had a lot of feeling, identification with pain. In fact, so much so that by the time he was sixty he just had to stop. He couldn't handle it anymore.

So I think it began with that, and then we read the papers at breakfast and all these things were happening in America. People were being actually lynched. And the Armenians got into my head too. All those worries—the pogroms my parents went through— uncles killed or deported from this country in the repressions that followed the First World War and the Russian Revolution.

And then I had a very small but strong experience. Children in the street used to play among many other games—

eenie meenie minie mo
catch a nigger by the toe . . .

My sister gave me such a crack across the face. When I remind her of this now, she asks wondering, proudly I think, "Where did I get such an idea?" She said to me that day, "Never let me hear you talk like that ever again." I mean that was a traumatic smack. So that's an early remembered corroboration from the family. As you go on, you realize that you've said a bad thing, which will mean a sad painful thing to someone else and that leads to other ways of thinking. It moves from person to the community to the world. It's not so good if it stays in the area of personal kindness—in fact it could be dangerous if there's no wider political understanding. Anyway—with experience of other people's suffering, my sister's smack remained a lasting education. And we did have black women and occasionally men working in the household and office a lot of the time, and they totally engaged me as often happens. But because of my family's old politics, they had gotten a lot less radical actually, these conversations were socializing and useful— and also established remembrances of personal love.

# ELAINE PERRY

■

*Elaine Perry graduated in 1981 from Oberlin College, where she studied with such writers as Stuart Friebert, Michael S. Harper, and Margaret Randall. From 1982 to 1984, she attended Columbia University as part of the Literature/Writing Program in the School of General Studies. She received the Claire Woolrich Scholarship in Writing while at Columbia and attended workshops with Colette Inez, Gary Glover, Andrew Harris, and Michael Stephens.*

*In addition to fiction, Elaine Perry writes poetry and plays. Her work has appeared in numerous academic and literary journals since 1983. She is also a visual artist and photographer and has pursued advanced studies in computer graphics and broadcast art as well as fine arts.*

*Originally from Lima, Ohio, Elaine Perry has lived in New York City since 1981. While writing, she has worked in publishing, holding both editorial and production positions, and as a computer graphics instructor, graphic artist, and camera operator.*

*Farrar, Straus and Giroux published Perry's first novel—Another Present Era—in 1990.*

**JORDAN:** What are the kinds of conditions that generally make for friendship between black and white women?

**PERRY:** Speaking from my own experience, the white women friends that I've had are the ones that I've had very strong common interests with and also some sense of connection. Most of my friends are fellow writers, artists, and musicians. For me, the important thing is shared interests and experiences that cross so-called racial boundaries.

**JORDAN:** Can white employers and black employees be friends?

**PERRY:** It's hard to say in general if employers and employees could befriend each other. It would really depend on the individuals. I think it depends on how flexible people are. If they insist on stratifying the relationship, that can create problems. Of course, that can happen between people within the same race too. I think it really comes down to a matter of personality and what each person would want out of that relationship. But friendship would be more difficult if one or both people are overly concerned with or insistent upon an unequal power differential.

**JORDAN:** But the two people can move beyond the racial differences if it feels comfortable for both of them. Some people criticize *Driving Miss Daisy* for depicting a situation that could not happen. But it could if people are even mildly open.

**PERRY:** It does happen, though I had an experience in which it didn't happen. In the summer before my senior year in college, I worked as a maid to an elderly woman in Greenwich, Connecticut. It was quite something to see that side of life—old money, upper class. This woman did have some set ideas of servants and what was expected of them and that did create some conflicts. But on the other hand, she did genuinely like me as a person and she was impressed that I was a writer and also a pianist and a singer. On some levels we did get along. There were things we could talk about. But there was that rigidity that came from her class background, and she was predisposed to see servants, particularly black servants, as being a certain way. The relationship was interesting because it would shift. One day she would be talking to me about how she felt the distribution of wealth was unfair. Sometimes I felt "Well maybe she really does mean that. She seems sincere." Then at other times she would fall back into that old pattern with "the servant should know her place." It was hard to keep up with her.

**JORDAN:** That was an interesting experience.

**PERRY:** Oh it was. Eventually I got fired because of all the conflicts. The latter part of the summer I was up in Seal Harbor, Maine, which is a very exclusive area, as exclusive as Martha's Vineyard. I was not allowed at the yacht club, not because of race, but because I was a servant. Had I been in Seal Harbor as a friend of the family, for instance, I would have been able to go. Even my employer believed this was snobbish and unfair. I got along well with her children, who were in their forties, and her grandchildren because they were a little more contemporary in their attitudes. I was on a first-name basis with them, for example. They even took me with them on a boating trip, and just generally treated me as an equal. Eventually my employer resented all of this so much that she fired me. It was something. We had a lot of loud arguments, and she would say, "Oh I never liked your cooking anyway. You never did this. You never did that." She was just pulling stuff out of thin air because I was a good maid. I was a good cook. I did the job. Even her children and grandchildren took my side and tried to get her to change her mind. I just think she was very resentful that I wasn't fulfilling expectations she had.

**JORDAN:** I think a lot of times it is the expectations that keep us apart, regardless of race or class.

**PERRY:** Yes, it is very hard for people to see beyond what they think a person is supposed to be because they're a particular race, or age, or gender.

**JORDAN:** White women have often written novels with black female protagonists, but the reverse happens less often. Could you comment on this phenomenon? Do you think this pattern will remain the same, or will black women start portraying white female protagonists a bit more frequently?

**PERRY:** Well, I can only speak for myself. I've never really thought about them in those terms. I think I'm more interested in how black women survive and even flourish in a world when there is so much against them. When I do write about white characters, generally it is primarily through the experience of the black woman. I am interested in cultural and racial clashes among people of differing backgrounds, differing ideas, and worldviews. People of disparate backgrounds trying to connect in spite of the problems and conflicts that occur is a central theme in my work.

**JORDAN:** I know that the urge to create comes from some impulse that we can't always actually define and that most writers trust that impulse. I spoke to some black writers who said, "I'm not interested in writing about white females and probably wouldn't." Is it that you find black female characters interesting at this point, but if the impulse to portray females from other cultures was there, you would pursue it?

**PERRY:** I don't necessarily set out to say I'm going to write about black characters in a novel. It doesn't happen that way. People are who they are. Characters tell me what they are or what they're going to do. In that sense, I don't put constraints on myself or on them.

**JORDAN:** Do you envision black women becoming more integrated into the women's movement as common concerns such as child care and abortion bring women of all races closer?

**PERRY:** I'm very concerned that nowadays the feminist movement seems to be running aground. All this talk of postfeminism I find really disturbing because I don't believe we've come close to achieving our goals. The attitudes, the misogyny, of this culture are so deep-rooted in the same ways that racism is. That is something that concerns me greatly. Women walk down the street getting harassed or not getting a job or getting fired from a job or not getting a promotion, knowing why but not being able to prove it. I think it would be good if we found that common ground because it is very important, especially on such economic issues as unequal pay or inadequate family leave time. What's been called the "feminization of poverty" greatly affects or potentially can affect many of us.

**JORDAN:** You're optimistic then about our coming together?

**PERRY:** I would say so. I tend to be optimistic in general about life's circumstances, and I also think a coming together is possible.

**JORDAN:** When you look at young children and teenagers who do not know their own family histories and do not have or know the words to recount their experiences or what they see, what kinds of things ought to be done to help them gain control over their own voices?

**PERRY:** I think that people really need to know their history. I think that we as African Americans just don't know our history. We may know some of the high points—the life and accomplishments of George Washington Carver or Frederick Douglass—but we don't know enough of our history. It disturbs me that our history is being rewritten and/or being suppressed. For me growing up in the seventies with the black power movement and black studies, I found it to be such a revelation to discover that, "Yes, we have been making contributions in history." I also think this current trend in scholarship in establishing that ancient Egypt was primarily a black culture is very important because we have really been even more unaware of the achievements of the distant past than the achievements in recent times. I feel that is vital, and it does come down to a matter of building self-esteem by knowing our ancestors and knowing where they've been and how far they've come. I think it's important for us to know that we have achieved something in this world.

**JORDAN:** Parents of teenagers right now would have been teenagers in the sixties and seventies who, I would think, would have been culturally aware of the achievements of our ancestors and our struggles. What has happened? This should be a group of parents who are very much in touch with not only the past but who have a sense of what the sixties meant. What has happened in the carryover?

**PERRY:** I see a resurgence of it nowadays in the scholarship I mentioned and in people wearing the African emblems and clothing. In a way, we are going back to the attitudes and trends of the sixties. But this time it seems more substantial and not so much like a fad as before. This cultural awareness also seems more integrated into people's lives. They're not just going into an African phase where they change their names and wear the African clothes and hairstyles and throw out all their Western values. Somehow you have to integrate it into your whole life. You have to accept that you were raised in Western culture. Maybe it wasn't your choice, but you do have a certain worldview based on what you've seen and heard and done all your life. I don't think African heritage should be used as an excuse for unacceptable behavior either. I knew a woman whose husband justified the infidelities that broke up their marriage by saying that monogamy was a Western thing, that it wasn't African. Also, I have heard people condemn gays and lesbians by saying that homosexuality is also a Western phenomenon. You have to integrate that African heritage in a meaningful way. Otherwise it becomes very superficial and self-serving, or it becomes very rigid and self-limiting.

Then, of course, so much depends on how interested people are in history. I'm especially interested in twentieth-century history, as you can tell from my first novel. My second novel is set in the early sixties, and it deals—at least peripherally—with the civil rights struggle. But maybe the average person—whoever that is—may not be interested in history as I am. But I see changes. I see a lot of interest in Malcolm X and his philosophy, for instance.

**JORDAN:** You also mentioned that you read a lot. We came from a time when children did read more.

**PERRY:** My parents encouraged me a lot. They're both academics, and they're responsible for me learning so much about black history at an early age. My father had a lot of books on these subjects, and I read them and I would talk to him about his own personal history, his being involved in the NAACP right through the heyday of the civil rights era. One of my earliest memories is a civil rights march in Lima, Ohio. I remember people assembling in the church basement and the big signs they were carrying. This was sometime in the mid-sixties. History has always been a part of my life with my parents being involved in civil rights and encouraging me to read and to know more about my culture. But that's not necessarily everyone's experience.

But I think it is probably part of the answer for everybody. Imparting personal history is something every parent can do. Maybe you can't go all the way back in knowing your family's history, but you can go as far back as you can. I think if more parents did this more, children would feel more in touch with something larger than just the individual and the day-to-day struggles. It would also help them to combat all those negative images of ourselves in the media and everywhere and to not lose touch with the knowledge that they are part of a heritage and an ancestry they can be proud of.

**JORDAN:** I was talking to a children's book author who said, "But when children encounter negative images of themselves in the classroom and people call them names, isn't there someone at home to negate those images, someone who tells them, 'What they say about you is a lie'?" I think very often no one tells them, "They're telling you a lie." Therefore, the child has only that negative picture. Let's move to the critics. Do you see literary critics, particularly black ones, as having a special role in shaping how stories of black women's lives are read, assessed, and taught?

**PERRY:** I would say that that's very important. I think that their perspective would be shaped by their own background and they might have a deeper sense of what we're trying to say. I don't think that just because they're all of the same culture that they're going to be interested in taking on that role. You can't assume that.

**JORDAN:** But one would hope that a critic of the same heritage might have insights into the culture that an outsider might not and could, therefore, use that knowledge in very useful ways to open the world of the text to readers.

**PERRY:** Well, I think of the few certain white persons who asked me quite bluntly, "Well, why didn't you write strictly about the black experience? Why is this character a German American? Why is this woman an Anglo-American scientist? Why are you not writing specifically about the black culture?" It's as if they have to put me in a category. Because I'm not fitting into this category, they've got to ask me why. Justify yourself. Why did you do that? Well, I don't like putting limitations on myself. No one else should. It's really quite an insensitivity, at best. Certainly, it is condescending. These same people would never tell a man not to write about women and vice versa. "You're a man. How could you understand a woman?" Unfortunately, some men don't understand women or vice versa. And men aren't held to task for that. I can think of several novels published recently in which the women characters are appalling stereotypes, and the points of view are clearly misogynistic. These novels are still critically acclaimed. The point is we do have imagination and we have the capacity to write from a perspective and an experience that isn't our own. Black, white, male, female, we all have the capacity.

**JORDAN:** That's the kind of question that I would hope that even if a black critic didn't like what you had written would be understanding enough not to ask. But I also recognize that any critic who is open to seeing writers grow and experiment with form and ideas should not ask that question either.

**PERRY:** Well, as far as I know, I don't know of any [African-American critics] who have. It seems to be the whites who are concerned about what I am writing.

**JORDAN:** To what extent do you use sources, such as histories, biographies, or autobiographies, when you are developing your characters?

**PERRY:** I use a lot of those sources particularly when I am writing about Paris in the thirties and in the forties during the German occupation. I'm very interested in the culture and time period. I immersed myself in the culture by watching films of the era, looking at photographs, and going to art exhibits of the period. It just happened that during the time that I was writing the novel there were quite a number of exhibits here in New York of artists and designers of that era. I also learned a lot about architecture so I read both general and technical books on architecture. I drafted all of the buildings and interiors I described in the novel. I think I work the same way as a Method actor. I immerse myself in the lives, thoughts, emotions, and worldviews of those characters.

**JORDAN:** As you were drawing the characters of the white females—Lenore and Kelly—were there particular concerns you had about the portrait you wanted to produce?

**PERRY:** I approached them just as I would any other character. Ultimately, I had to be true to them. And I'm one of those writers who pays close attention to what characters themselves are telling me. Lenore is a very strong, very determined woman, who went against the normal expectations of someone from her upper-class background. She is someone who really, really wanted to serve humanity, and ultimately she did. That's how she lived, and that's how she died. She was able to transcend what would have been a limiting view of the world and ultimately a limited, though privileged life. But she did just what she wanted with her life, and I always admired people like that. That's how I try to live. That's the way I do live.

**JORDAN:** My sister is a microbiologist, and I could hear echoes of her voice in Lenore's. Even though this is 1991, some of the problems women scientists face are the same as they were fifty years ago. Certain barriers remain.

**PERRY:** Yes. Lenore really wanted to be a physicist, but she wasn't allowed to, so she became a microbiologist. Traditionally, that's the scientific field women have been allowed to enter. Men must have thought, "We don't want them theorizing about the nature of the universe. That's our domain. Let them be in the laboratory with these microscopic substances. They won't get into too much trouble. We don't want them dealing with abstract thought." That's really the thinking behind that.

**JORDAN:** Let's talk a bit more specifically about the novel by starting with how you came to write the title and to create the "alternate realities" we see in *Another Present Era*.

**PERRY:** Are you familiar with the group Oregon, an instrumental group? They did a fusion of jazz and folk music and traditions from around the world. I saw them in concert at Oberlin. They had an album called *Music from Another Present Era*. I was visiting my folks in Ohio and went to a record shop. I was looking through a bin of records and tapes, and there was that album. Not only did I get a great tape, but I got a title for my novel. I thought "This sums up my novel." I had been desperately looking for a title.

**JORDAN:** Who or what inspired you to write *Another Present Era*?

**PERRY:** This novel started out when I was writing a series of short stories. I was working at an ad agency as a secretary for eight people; all but one of them were stereotypical yuppies. I had been writing poetry on the job when I could, but I found with phones ringing it was difficult. So I started writing prose instead, which seemed to work better for me than poetry, and I wrote a series of short stories mostly on company time. There was one particular story I was writing that I realized after a week or two that it was not a short story but a novel. It started out with two characters, Wanda Dubois and Sterling Cronheim. Originally, the story was a meditation on time travel—not going in a time machine and setting the dial, but more a philosophical treatment of time. Everything that ever happened or ever will happen happens now in the present; there is no past or future. Just like New York and San Francisco exist simultaneously, but we can't be in both places, time and space kind of work the same way. I found it really interesting because I had done a lot of reading on quantum physics and how Western science is confirming what Eastern philosophy has said for millennia. I was dealing with some of those issues in this short story.

As I started to realize it was a novel, it went through a major evolution. It's hard to say how I came to the alternate reality. I didn't sit down and diagram what the world would be like, but I had an impression or an intuitive understanding of what it was like. It's like in films like *Blade Runner* or *Brazil* or *Batman* where the filmmakers create worlds that are not ours, but have recognizable elements. As an artist and designer I was certainly interested in the design aspects of such a world. I was also interested in the subtle cultural differences between the alternate reality of *Another Present Era* and our world. That world is a synthesis of many different elements of the past, the future, and the present as well.

For me, another character in the novel is the city of New York, which is an amalgam of past, present, and future. The trolley lines, the elevated trains in Manhattan, the live radio broadcasts clearly are of another time. The environmental problems, especially the constant coastal flooding, are accelerations of present-day problems. What we have to look forward to if we don't start making aggressive changes quickly. The decay, the ecological disaster. That is part of this character and the character's impact on the rest of the novel's characters. That's something very central to my work. In the second novel that also plays a part. The beginning of it is set in Mississippi. I'm really going to do Mississippi as a character as well as a place and as a culture in a particular time in history. I'm very interested in how people are influenced by their literal physical environment and how they've learned to cope with it. The environment, particularly in *Another Present Era*, is not hospitable, and it affects people on some deeper levels that they're not necessarily conscious of.

**JORDAN:** In spite of the amazing technological advances we see in the world of the novel and often the harmful side effects that come with them, the people themselves don't necessarily seem to have advanced. Do we remain the same, that is, does human nature remain recognizable, regardless of progress in science and other disciplines?

**PERRY:** One of the problems is that the evolution of our science and technology is way ahead of our social evolution. Power and domination become easier to actualize. Look at the Gulf War right now. I find the Nintendo-like bombing footage they've been showing to be appalling. It's a trivialization of mass destruction. All this new high-tech weaponry that the military is so thrilled about. Beyond this war, I also think that we're setting a bad precedent. This thinking of "Oh, we'll go and bomb the country" doesn't solve anything. There's always going to be another Saddam Hussein. It's all about power and domination and controlling world resources. Unfortunately, in this world, as in *Another Present Era*, there are those who are very shortsighted, and they're obsessed with controlling huge percentages of the population of the world, and they're not really seeing the deeper aspects of life. Ultimately, we're not here to make a lot of money or to dominate a lot of people or be famous. I just feel that the emotional, spiritual, and philosophical development of humanity is lagging behind the technological advancement. The fact that we do now have the capacity to annihilate the world, considering our development on other levels, is very frightening. It's also very frightening what we're doing to the environment. If we wreck this planet, there's not another one we're going to be able to go to. We've got to start solving these problems and not on a short-term basis. There are elements of change—the Berlin Wall coming down, for instance, and the move toward democracy in Eastern Europe—but there is also the repressive element—the Gulf War is a prime example. This talk about a "New World Order." It's a chilling phrase, and I have read that this same phrase is found in Nazi ideology. I see the nineties as being very turbulent. They're certainly starting out that way. A lot of good and a lot of bad.

**JORDAN:** Can't the technological advances and the spiritual advances of humanity come together to work at the same time?

**PERRY:** I hope that happens at some point. I certainly think that we have the capacity to save ourselves. I'm not a doomsayer who says, "This is Armageddon. Let's throw in the towel." But it's going to take work. It's going to take work to deal with the environmental problems and all the political problems of the world. The problems of the Middle East are not going to be solved in this war. Those problems have been there for centuries. This war is only going to complicate it and perpetuate it. It is not a matter of getting Hussein out of Kuwait. It's just a far, far more complex issue than that, and the war is not going to help. I would have thought that after Korea and Vietnam we would have learned that being a global police force causes more problems than it solves. It certainly has led to massive death and suffering and no political advances.

**JORDAN:** That the landscape is a character in the novel is almost immediately apparent, and I'd like to talk with you further about how that character influences my understanding of the human characters in the work. I do see parallels between the lives of the characters and the stark, desolate landscape in which they operate. In looking at Wanda, the main character, I think I was divorced from her in the same way that I could separate myself from the environment. There were times when they made me so uncomfortable that I found myself ignoring rather blatant aspects of their personalities. For instance, I did not concentrate on Wanda's drinking problem. For some reason her problems did not seem overwhelming even though I knew that she was drinking too much because the other characters mentioned it too many times.

**PERRY:** She wasn't a falling-down drunk, and she wasn't incapacitated. She was sustaining her life by working long hours and pouring her energy into architecture, pursuing both her firm's work and her own rather innovative ideas. I understand that certain writers of the twentieth century would get up in the morning, write a few hours, and then drink for the rest of the day. Some people can do that. They sober up enough to do their work, and then they get drunk. They can't deal with their life, they can't deal with their internal conflicts, so they are quieting the parts of themselves that they don't want to face. Some use drugs in that same way. After all, there are twelve-step programs for any addiction you can imagine.

**JORDAN:** Maybe it was the quieting effect that made me feel confident that she would take care of herself eventually.

**PERRY:** Well, she certainly had a lot of inner strength—maybe even more than she realized. But in the short term she wasn't dealing with her problems; she was just ignoring them. She was drinking because she didn't want to think about them, just as she threw herself into her work. Yes, she is doing great architecture but she is denying herself a deeper enjoyment and satisfaction out of life. Happiness even. I think that may be true of some creative people. They function well in their art, but the rest of their life is tumultuous.

**JORDAN:** Somehow I trusted that Wanda was going to resolve life's bigger problems and that she was going to be a whole person. Is Sterling then just another way for her to ignore her problem? Is she using him in a way?

**PERRY:** I don't think so. I think that she does genuinely feel a connection to him and in some ways he does help her out. He sees that she is on a self-destructive path. I don't want to get into Freudian father symbolism, but in fact, she had been estranged from her own father for so long and here was someone who was willing to say, "You really should try to deal with your problems." I think he had a calming presence in her life. At the same time, I think that she wanted to help him too because she could see that he was so withdrawn from the world and she wanted to bring him out. Sometimes it is easier to help other people with their problems than to deal with your own. It's easier to see other people's problems and to feel you must help them. It's a great way to keep from dealing with your own problems because you say, "Well, I'm busy helping this other person."

JORDAN: It did strike me that Wanda is isolated from female friends—from friends generally except for the strong women in her family who are very supportive of her. But, of course, they're considerably older—not that one must have friends her own age. Do you think that this lack of interaction with female friends her own age, regardless of color, might have heightened some of her sense of isolation?

PERRY: Yes. She certainly needed friends, and I would agree with that. But early on in the novel, it's clear how disillusioned she has become in trying to maintain friendships. It has become easier for her to simply devote more energies to her work.

JORDAN: She works in a man's world, and it's not always supportive of her.

PERRY: Yes. She has learned a certain toughness just to deal in a male-dominated profession. That is one side of her. She has this very, very strong aspect but at the same time, she has not acknowledged her needs and her vulnerabilities.

JORDAN: But doesn't her mother do that too?

PERRY: Yes, her mother, Francine, kind of does the same thing. She is a psychiatrist, totally devoted to her work as director of a psychiatric facility in the South Bronx. She is dedicated to serving that community, but neglects herself and her own needs.

JORDAN: For a while I didn't recognize her mother as having any weaknesses either. I just decided that they were all strong women who went out and did what they had to do. They had problems but they still managed to operate.

PERRY: I think Reggie, Francine's sister, is probably the strongest of the three. She seems to have the more integrated life; a successful career as a free-lance graphic designer, a commitment to social and political issues, and a stable, loving relationship with another woman, a dancer. I think Francine kind of defies the stereotype of the strong black woman, the strong matriach, certainly deviating from that norm in a number of ways, having been married to a white man, for instance. She had her vulnerabilities but yet professionally has quite a bit of strength.

**JORDAN:** I found it absolutely fascinating and wonderful to see black women who moved comfortably in the mainstream even though they had all clearly experienced some discrimination that curtailed advancement. Still, they were comfortable with success and it seemed to be a part of their family tradition to be high achievers. Wanda continues in those same footsteps. They also seem to accept themselves and the realities of life around them. Then I thought of Francine and realized I can't say that about her because there had been some problems with her ignoring possible abuse going on with Wanda. She is a psychiatrist, after all, and yet this abuse is occurring in her own home. This left me wondering if this image of the strong black woman as always strong is a myth.

**PERRY:** I think it is a kind of simplification, a kind of archetype. People have their complexities. Even if you are a strong person, you still have vulnerabilities to some degree. How you deal with them is another issue. Someone who is completely strong may have impoverished herself by ignoring aspects of herself such as the need for intimacy, or companionship. To be strong doesn't mean being strong twenty-four hours a day. Or I should say, exhibiting behavior that we define as strong. Something can happen to her that can shake her confidence and cause her to regroup and reevaluate who she is or what she is doing. If she is only strong or acting strong, that implies a kind of static existence. She is not changing and growing. After all, growth and change can involve a lot of trauma. The strong person has the courage to do that, to not always be satisfied with what is comfortable. The strength comes from making the effort to change, even though she may be scared out of her mind. She still does it. To me, that's what strength is all about.

**JORDAN:** Speaking of changing or not changing, how does Sterling manage to live as long as he does and still remain alone without linkages except to memories? I understand that he has aged so, of course, a lot of the people he would have known have died. Still, he grows old detached. His memories are as real as Wanda is alive. By the end of the novel, can we talk about Sterling as having grown spiritually?

PERRY: I think so. I think that by the time he dies he's starting to come to grips with the demons. There is this perpetual guilt on his part because he really thinks that he could have saved Lenore. I think finally he realizes that he couldn't have. She did what she wanted to do and what she had to do and what she thought was important to do, and he had to accept that. He also had guilt because during the years that she was alive he wasn't the husband that he had wanted to be and wasn't and couldn't be. When she died, he was left with these regrets. He hadn't resolved the conflicts with her. Even though she was dead, the relationship was ongoing. I think that was part of the problem. There was so much unsaid and undone and he couldn't go back and fix things. It's a hard thing to deal with for anybody.

JORDAN: Now Bradley. [*Pauses*] I won't dwell on him.

PERRY: Poor Bradley.

JORDAN: Yes, poor Bradley. In examining Bradley's background, we come to see how he became the man that he is in the opening chapter of the novel. What can anybody do for "a Bradley" except leave him alone? That's pessimistic, I know, but what else can one do?

PERRY: Changing his life is up to him, but he does not deal with his problems. He's also greatly conflicted. On the one hand, he can't give up the white male privilege but, on the other hand, he is aware of his African culture, and he does want to embrace it. But he believes he can't do both, so he tortures himself.

Of course his parents set up the whole thing from day one. He was raised to think that he was a white man and as an adolescent he finds out the truth about his heritage. It was a cruel and self-serving deception on their part so throughout his adult life he feels that his life and the self that he presents to the world is fraudulent, and he hates himself because of his lack of courage to live a more authentic life. He sees Wanda completely embracing her heritage, and he is so drawn to her because he believes she can help him do the same.

JORDAN: I always like to think something could have been done to change a person or situation, but in this instance I can't help but think Bradley is the kind of person that as soon as you meet and detect problems, you should run from him.

**PERRY:** You can try to help, but you have to realize that you probably won't succeed. The person may eventually turn against you. They will resent you for telling them things about themselves they don't want to know and don't want to deal with.

**JORDAN:** Yes, in situations like the one Bradley finds himself in, your mere presence brings to the surface things that he really doesn't want to deal with anyway.

**PERRY:** Yes. Wanda, in embracing her African-American identity, is a lot further along than he is. Of course, like you said, he admired her so much and felt that she could help him but the help has to come from within.

**JORDAN:** It seems that Wanda accepts the blood of her mother and her father in terms of shaping an identity of herself. She's fairly comfortable, and she doesn't deny one part of her heritage for the other. Do you think that her father's insistence on her "lying" about her being white somehow contributes to her complete acceptance of both parts of her heritage once she is an adult? It's almost like a slap in his face to then own up to who she is as an adult just because she can now do it without fear of punishment. That's a good way to get back at her father without doing too much damage to herself.

**PERRY:** Yes, it is true that that's a way to rebel. The truth is left unclear about her early memories of having to pretend that she is white because then her father denies that any of it has happened. It isn't resolved. I know for myself sometimes I'll tell my parents, "Well, you did this and this," and they will either have forgotten or have a totally different perception of it. Let's face it, memory is a very creative construction of the past. I would say that the truth is somewhere in the middle in this case. But obviously something must have happened to her. In some way her father has done something.

**JORDAN:** And, of course, Francine doesn't help us to resolve anything because she ignores things. But do you think that Wanda does have rather intense issues to deal with in relation to color even though she is much further along than Bradley?

**PERRY:** I think for her as long as she is alone and isolated she is able to manage some kind of equilibrium. But when she goes out and interacts with people and they say things that are insensitive brings up all these memories, this is what she faces. That developer who treats her as a curiosity is demeaning her. He's not dealing with her as a whole person. That kind of experience is still painful to her. Therefore, she chooses to become isolated and stay away from possible conflicts or ill treatment.

**JORDAN:** That makes a lot of sense because she is really on an island where she has created her own space, which works for her. I also want to move to a question from the chapter on the wrong men. What draws women to the wrong men?

**PERRY:** I think it is our background, how we are raised to defer to authority, usually male authority; to not stand up for ourselves, to blame ourselves, in an effort to avoid confrontation. Such a high percentage of women are the victims of sexual abuse—from sexual harassment to rape. It is so common. We see ourselves disrespected so often it has to have a profound effect on self-worth, it does. And I think that we are also brainwashed to think we are supposed to look up to men and we are supposed to find our identity in men. You may become a feminist and be able to critique those values, but then because you have acquired them at such an early time in your life, they are very deeply ingrained. It is something you have to guard against.

**JORDAN:** I want to ask one question about Charles. I think I've seen him before, outside of literature. I'm not sure if courage is the right word, but something actually gives him the courage to marry Francine. But then he appeared to have been uncomfortable with publicly acknowledging her. Of course, I could be misreading how comfortable he felt with her. If I look at him through Wanda's eyes, it might be unfair to say that he denied Francine publicly and wasn't very comfortable with having a black wife.

**PERRY:** I think he wasn't aware of what the ramifications of marrying a black woman were. He was in love and overwhelmed with those feelings but he also wanted to do something very principled, to marry Francine in spite of the difficulty it would bring him. But yet when it came to the reality of having to deal with family and friends and the people on the Air Force base, he had underestimated the difficulties he would have. So I think there is some truth in what Wanda says about his being ambivalent about the situation.

**JORDAN:** Had Francine denied really seeing that picture of her marriage? In other words, did she just ignore the fact that he seemed uncomfortable in certain situations? Was she too so in love with him that that's all that mattered?

**PERRY:** I think maybe she too underestimated the ambivalence that he felt, because to her face he probably tried to reassure her that everything was okay. No doubt he believed he was telling her the truth. That was part of his denial process really.

**JORDAN:** There's a lot of denying going on in this novel. [*Laughs*] That's probably also part of what draws women to the wrong men. How would you define the characters' uses of memory in this novel?

**PERRY:** I would say that in one way or another all these characters are dealing with uncomfortable memories of the past. For some, the memories are more haunting and more devastating than for others. Cronheim is the salient example of that because he's still trying to resolve both guilt and grief over Lenore, and the memory of her is very clear to him. He is also an older person for whom memories are very clear.

**JORDAN:** Is there ever a role or function for a stereotype in fiction? Perhaps to introduce the reader to a character or to expose the danger of such attitudes?

**PERRY:** I think if you deconstruct it or use it ironically . . . Actually, in my second novel there is a character who seems to be a stereotype at first, but then you start to realize the complexities of this person that make him what he is. He himself is scornful of the stereotype that superficially he represents. It is important to look at what's behind the façade or to allow the façade to be instructive.

**JORDAN:** What is the responsibility of the reader, if any, in the creative process?

**PERRY:** I think that the reader should be open to the experience and allow him- or herself to be challenged. The reader should be accepting of the characters and situations and be willing to look at life in a different way. Characters may be facing situations that may not be familiar to the reader.

**JORDAN:** In looking at the alternate realities in the world of the novel, do you still believe that it is a world that offers optimism and, if so, how would you define it?

**PERRY:** It's a matter of people doing something about it. We have to recognize that to make a momentous change is going to take a lot of effort, a lot of sacrifice, a lot of vision. But it can be done. I'm not a fatalist. There is always the possibility, but whether people acknowledge it or do anything is another story.

**JORDAN:** Do you think that Wanda having received recognition for her work will now concentrate on other aspects of her life? She has received an award that signifies the kind of achievement she has worked so hard to attain. She is also starting to deal with some of her personal problems. With her now being able to take a break perhaps, do you think that will free her to deal with some of her personal concerns?

**PERRY:** I think seeing that she can achieve something in one area will give her confidence to tackle other areas. I think that's how it works. It's not that getting the award is the be-all and end-all, but she sees, "I worked hard. I achieved this. I have the capacity to make these other changes in my life if I would like to do that."

**JORDAN:** In writing the novel, was one character harder to portray than another? Is it a matter of letting the character come out of whatever creative impulse is there?

**PERRY:** The latter is true, but some of the characters are a bit more accessible than others. Bradley was a problem. Trying to understand him and his torments was tough.

**JORDAN:** When your writing pulls you along a particular path and other responsibilities pull you in other directions, how do you resolve the conflict?

**PERRY:** I have always resolved it in favor of the writing—sometimes at financial peril. For instance, I took the entire summer of

1990 off. I did a little free-lancing but mostly I worked on the first draft of my second novel. Basically, I finished the draft from beginning to end. I was on a roll, a creative spurt so I felt if I had to work, it would just interrupt this flow. So I tend to do that; I take risks.

We have to be true to ourselves in all ways and not fall into this tyranny of so-called political correctness. I'm only going to write about this kind of character because I'm this kind of person and I'm from this kind of background. You have to accept where your imagination will go. That's how I try to live. As writers, if we do otherwise, we censor ourselves. It's bad enough that there's censorship in the world, but to start censoring ourselves and limiting our imagination is far worse.

# BELVA PLAIN

■

*Belva Plain was born in 1919 in New York. She began writing when she was very young and has had stories published in such magazines as* Cosmopolitan, McCall's, Good Housekeeping, *and* Redbook. *She did not try her hand at a novel until she was in her late fifties. Her first,* Evergreen *(1979), remained on the* New York Times *best-seller list for forty-one weeks and was adapted for television.*

Evergreen *was only the first in a succession of extremely successful novels.* The Golden Cup *(1986),* Tapestry *(1988), and* Harvest

*(1990) continue the Werner family saga begun in* Evergreen. *Her other novels are* Crescent City *(1984),* Eden Burning *(1982),* Random Winds *(1980), and* Blessings *(1989). With the publication of her latest,* Treasures, *in 1992, there are currently sixteen million copies of her books in print in eleven languages. This list by no means exhausts her "savings bank" of ideas that have yet to be developed into novels. She says, "There's something in every newspaper. As a matter of fact, there is something to be heard every time you so much as take a bus."*

*A Barnard College graduate in history, Belva Plain, who was recently widowed after a marriage of more than forty years, lives alone in New Jersey and writes full-time.*

**JORDAN:** What specific conditions seem to be in place when black and white women become friends, regardless of whether we're talking about fiction or real life?

**PLAIN:** Friends: Can you say someone who is an employer? Yes, you can be a friend. That's very true, but it won't be friends, I think, in the sense that you meant, that is socially. You meant that you can party together. That I have never experienced, and I think most black and white women have not. Perhaps those in academia or people who work together in an office have. But if you are at home as I am, working, it just doesn't happen.

**JORDAN:** So you have to have something like a common bond or some kind of situation that brings you together in order to be true friends.

**PLAIN:** That's it. That's why I say academia or if you worked in an office. But other than that . . . no. We don't go to the same churches. We don't belong to the same clubs. It doesn't happen. As I told you, I was going to answer candidly because that's what you want. If you talk about friendship in the larger sense, I have had black friends. . . . When I was a child, my parents hired European immigrants who came to the United States out of economic necessity—Irish, Germans—to work in our home. Then after I married, I had black people come to my home, and I would say we did become friends. What they thought I don't know, but they couldn't have disliked me too much because one of them stayed for twenty-three years and the present one is now in the eleventh, so we must have a good relationship. I can tell you how I feel. I cannot say how they felt. I know they certainly were fairly content because they remained, and I know they would come and tell me their problems—family problems and their troubles. They confided in me because, as they said, they didn't want to confide in somebody at their church for fear of gossip. And it also worked the other way because I would tell them, and I do now tell them some things that I won't tell my friends—about a family quarrel, for instance, because I don't want my friends to know. Each of us knows that the other doesn't have an opportunity to go talking. It's a funny thing, isn't it? It is a peculiar experience, in that an outer separation creates a greater intimacy.

**JORDAN:** It is. First of all, you have the trust between each other. But also because you're in such different worlds, those worlds will not likely come together so you trust more fully in some kind of funny way.

**PLAIN:** You really can. Once a secret is out, ordinarily it spreads. A particular friend of mine will say to me, "Well, I'm not supposed to tell you but I trust you. You know So and So is leaving her husband." There you are.

**JORDAN:** That's very true. In looking at novels in particular, what kind of role does the black female tend to play in white women's novels and what kind of role does the white female tend to play in black women's novels?

**PLAIN:** Well, I'm afraid to say. I have to say that it reflects the known role throughout American history—that of employer and employee—as far as I can see. Now I think it's too soon to judge further. Maybe if I were a professor . . . You're a teacher in a college, so you would have other relationships and could be able to write about that. But I haven't read anything like that. Have you?

**JORDAN:** Not often. There's one Gail Godwin novel, *A Mother and Two Daughters,* that has a black woman professor and a white woman returning student, and they become friends.

**PLAIN:** I haven't read that.

**JORDAN:** There is now a whole lot of adult fiction where the employer/employee relationship doesn't exist. Along the same lines, have you noticed subtle distinctions between how black and white women see each other in fiction?

**PLAIN:** Well, we get back to that same relationship of employer/employee. A white woman who is an employee in another white woman's house also sees things differently because the perspective is different. Yet the woman who is working in the house—whether she is black or white, maybe more so if she's black because she comes from even greater poverty than many of the Europeans—would look upon the employer even though she might like her personally with a certain faint contempt. She would probably be thinking, "You really don't know that much about life. You've been wrapped in cotton wool." And that is probably true. So that is not really a racial difference but an economic difference. A woman whose husband has abandoned her and a couple of children and who has to go out and clean other women's houses before going home to take care of her children will look with a kind of jaundiced eye upon this lady who doesn't clean her own house.

**JORDAN:** Do you think that the employer in those kinds of situations ever really ponders what that employee may be concerned with, or does she tend to look upon the employee as someone who provides services and not think about this person as having needs and basic kinds of problems perhaps because she herself doesn't have to worry about money?

**PLAIN:** I think that certainly depends on the individual. I've seen and heard people among my friends who have been totally insensitive, who just look upon an employee as someone who comes to work for so many hours for so many dollars and that's it. But, on the other hand, I know a great many people who are quite, quite the opposite. It may sound arrogant, but I know I am. Some people show great concern, help them out by lending them money, give them clothes for their children, do all kinds of good things, and are very compassionate. It is totally an individual thing. I haven't counted what the proportions are [of those who are insensitive to those who are not]; I don't know. I don't think there's any fast rule; it simply depends on who the employer is.

JORDAN: As you were drawing the character of Fanny in *Crescent City*, were there any concerns about the portrait you wanted to produce, and what do you think of her?

PLAIN: I will tell you how she was born. Obviously I wasn't alive then, so I don't really know what the relationship was in a slave society, but I think it couldn't have been very different from what we were just discussing in your last question. It depended on the "owner." Some people were abysmally cruel and unfeeling, and a great many of them were very, very decent people working in that particular society—accepting the society. Yet they could be very compassionate people. I have read a good many contemporary accounts. There's a remarkable book, a journal kept by a rich white woman during the Civil War. In it she has certain accounts of her relationship with slaves; I was very impressed by the book. It was extremely well done psychologically. I think that's where my idea for my character was born. The title is *Mary Chestnut's Civil War*. She was a fascinating lady. She was a Southern lady; in her heart she was an abolitionist although she could not admit it in that society. She acted upon the impulses of a person who abhorred the system, but she had to live within the system. I have read other diaries; another is *A Year on a Georgia Plantation*. There too I found the emotions that made me understand the character of Fanny.

JORDAN: White women have often written novels that portray black female protagonists or main characters but the reverse happens less often. Could you comment on this phenomenon? Do you think this pattern will remain the same, or will black women start to portray white women characters a bit more frequently?

PLAIN: I think they will. There are now more relationships in the marketplace, so to speak. I know I go into the department stores here and am reminded that years ago, one never saw black women working in sales. Now blacks and whites work together, lunch together, and possibly they meet after work. I wouldn't be able to know that, but I think if any of them should become writers—I mean, writers don't grow on trees whether they're black or white, but if any of them should, then it would be logical that they would write about these relationships. There just aren't that many yet.

JORDAN: That's what I tell my students. With their having gone to integrated schools—this is especially true for English majors who aspire to be writers or who are writers—their growing-up experiences will have been so different that probably black and white relationships will just naturally enter their work just because they were a natural part of their background.

**PLAIN:** I think so.

**JORDAN:** What can black and white women teach each other about writing and about living?

**PLAIN:** That's a very big question. I think that's an unanswerable question.

**JORDAN:** Does it help if I say learn from each other, or is it still an unanswerable question?

**PLAIN:** I think you learn as you live together. I don't think you can do this artificially. You just said before that if you go to school with people and work with them, and if you happen to be a writer, you have a subject. But otherwise I don't think it's anything you can teach.

**JORDAN:** Do you envision black women becoming more integrated into the women's movement as common concerns such as abortion and child care bring women of all races closer?

**PLAIN:** Oh yes, I certainly think so. The abortion issue especially has little to do with color. It has to do with a woman's body. Interestingly enough, and this again has nothing to do with color, Republican Senator Simpson of Wyoming made a statement the other day in the Senate that I think was long overdue: "As a man I feel I have no right, nor does any man have a right, to tell a woman what to do with her own body. Therefore, I am in favor of keeping this Roe vs. Wade law." Abortion has nothing to do with color. Black or white, a woman has a right to choose when she wants to have a baby. That's just my opinion. I don't know how you feel about it.

**JORDAN:** I strongly agree that a woman has a right to choose.

**PLAIN:** I know that some people, out of a tremendous religious conviction, disagree. I have respect for them. But still if you have that conviction, I say, "That's fine for you, but don't tell me what to do." I don't think that has anything to do with color. And I absolutely think black women will be a part of the women's movement.

**JORDAN:** When you look at children who do not know their own family histories and cannot tell their own stories, what kinds of things ought to be done so they come to know their own history and gain control over their own voices?

**PLAIN:** Well, I have to ponder that. It's a family thing. That's purely individual. Now, of course, it's a hard subject today with so many shattered and scattered families. I don't know whether there is much of an answer. Again this has nothing to do with color; I see plenty of shattered families among whites, although not in my generation because we stuck things out. But today the younger ones marry bringing along her children from her former marriage and sometimes his children too; then they bring theirs into the world. I don't know how you can know who you are with things so jumbled! And frankly I think that people must just stop all these casual divorces. If you don't have solid families, you can have no cohesion in society. You must keep families together, and then the children will know what their history is and who they are. That's my feeling. Of course, I guess I'm old-fashioned. I'm not young anymore. I was married for forty-two years until my husband died, and God knows we had lots of problems. We went through the Depression and war. We quarreled at times too, but we cared about each other, and it never dawned on us that we would separate. Never. Well, you didn't in those days. You didn't. You stayed and you worked it out somehow. If you weren't happy every day, you said to yourself, "Whoever said I was entitled to be happy every day?" That's the truth. And I talk to women, middle-aged women—I know I'm digressing here—who were dissatisfied in marriage and were divorced. Then they went out into the world and, finding it not so easy, they say now, "You know, when I look back on it, I know I could have worked it out; the problem would have passed. It was better than what I have now." That's not always true, but I think it is frequently true.

**JORDAN:** Speaking of marriage, let's turn to the novel. Miriam gets married at sixteen knowing that she doesn't love her husband. Then maybe two or three years into the marriage, she finds out about her husband's affair. She knows that the older married women knew that this kind of thing went on all the time and that they probably could have told her something to prepare her a little better for marriage. She thinks about talking to someone, but she really doesn't want to talk to her stepmother, Emma, because she feels she would probably say stay with him, that's just the way life is. Why didn't the mother prepare the daughter for the harsher reality of marriage?

PLAIN: Oh, I can answer that. It was the times, that's all. I can tell by your voice, you're pretty young. Even in my time, mothers didn't talk to their daughters. If I asked my mother something about sex, she'd say to me, "We don't discuss that. When you're married, your husband will explain to you." There was an absolute hush about everything. Girls weren't told *anything*, anything at all until the night they got married. Then they found out, and sometimes it wasn't so nice. It depended on the man. At least it was so in white society. Now, I don't know what it was like in black society. I think probably it was different. Now my friend, and I do say friend, she works in my house—will often say when I tell her something, "Blacks don't do it that way." So maybe it's different. I know that the family in this book would *never* have told her such a thing. It would have been humiliating. They didn't even tell girls about menstruation. They told them nothing. I remember when I first started, I was thirteen, and my mother told me how to take care of myself, and she said, "You mustn't get your feet wet, because you'll catch cold when you're menstruating." Now, how do you like that? Never told me that it meant you could get pregnant. That never dawned on her. That was the way things were.

JORDAN: Well, sometimes this is what girls are still told or led to believe something so similar or they are told so little that they do not quite get accurate information. You would think that mothers tell their daughters everything in this day and age.

PLAIN: They do now. At least they do around here. Mothers have to because everything is on television. Too much! It's disgraceful.

JORDAN: Was storytelling a part of your growing up and, if so, how has it influenced your writing?

PLAIN: First of all, I came from a reading family. My mother read, read, read all the time. All my presents were always books: birthdays, Christmas, etc., so I learned to read and loved it and I wrote little stories when I was in school. They were published in the school magazine—that kind of thing.

JORDAN: Have you ever felt pressure from your publisher and/ or editor or audience to portray a particular kind of character or to treat a particular set of themes, or have you remained free of such concerns?

PLAIN: No one has ever told me anything. I've been quite independent. In fact when I am ready for a new book, they just ask, "When is it going to be done?"

JORDAN: What is the responsibility of the reader, if any, in the creative process?

PLAIN: None. If while you write you're thinking: "Who is going to like this?", if that's your aim—that's pulp, that's trash. You must write honestly what you think and feel.

JORDAN: Is there ever a role for a stereotype in fiction—perhaps to introduce a character to the reader or to point out the danger of such attitudes?

PLAIN: No. Stereotypes are not real, and the thing that makes fiction worthwhile is reality. That's the trick, to be able to see people not on the surface but to see right through them. So stereotypes are pulp fiction. The "villain" and the "saint" are not real.

JORDAN: How would you define uses of history in your work?

PLAIN: I think you can't write without it because people exist in their time. For instance, if you take Romeo and Juliet out of Renaissance Italy and put them in twentieth-century America, the story would be different. You would have the same emotions, the infatuation of two adolescents for each other, but how differently it would need to be worked out!

JORDAN: Particularly in novels in which white female employers are portrayed with their black maids, do you think that ambiguity is a major device, among others, that black women use in relating to white women?

PLAIN: Well, not being a black woman, I don't know, but I would imagine, as I try to put myself in her place, that the black woman—partly because of the long history of racial relationships, and maybe to a greater degree the economic relationship—would be somewhat deferential. She wouldn't "tell the woman off," but then, the woman wouldn't do that to her either. Suppose the white woman has a problem with a child, for instance. The employee, whether black or white—maybe to a greater degree if black, but maybe not, would not say to the employer as she might to a friend, "You're a total jerk. I wouldn't allow that for a minute." She might give advice, but it would be politely tempered. I wouldn't call that ambiguity, rather a certain deference. It goes the other way too. If I have had the occasion to say to a woman who worked in my house, "Well, your son is just a bum, you should throw him out," I wouldn't say it. But then I wouldn't say that to a friend of mine either.

JORDAN: Finally, who or what inspired you to write *Crescent City*?

PLAIN: I was in New Orleans doing publicity for a previous book. There was a beautiful old house there, architecturally a gem. It was open to the public as a museum, maintained by some ladies' church guild. It was completely furnished in the period. The gardens were planted with the flowers popular during the nineteenth century. Very interesting. They gave out a brochure that had a brief history of the house. The opening sentences fascinated me. They told that the house had been built by a German immigrant before the Civil War; subsequently he went bankrupt and lost the house to foreclosure. That sparked an idea in my mind. I pictured this German immigrant, poverty stricken, traveling across the world for two months by sailing ship and making his way down the Mississippi to New Orleans and becoming rich. His was a glamorous, exciting story. It all came from that house.

JORDAN: When you look at Miriam and Fanny, would you describe them as friends?

PLAIN: I certainly would, within the limits that you see. Naturally Fanny, in a slave society, is not free. But yet there is an affection between them. A lot is unspoken. There is real trust there.

JORDAN: When your writing pulls you along a particular path and other responsibilities—speaking engagements, etc.—are pulling you in other directions, how do you resolve the conflict?

PLAIN: Well, I don't take many speaking engagements anymore, just a few that seem particularly important. When you get to be a best-selling writer, people call with many requests, and that's very nice. But I could spend half my time doing that so I have to be selective.

JORDAN: So you've never had this kind of conflict. When it comes time to write, you just write.

PLAIN: Oh yes, I do.

JORDAN: You just seem to have a sense of place and of the way things fit and I guess that's why you have been able to produce so many works.

PLAIN: You have to work on schedule. I think that's true of anything you do. If you're a pianist, you've got to spend a certain number of hours a day practicing. It's a question of self-discipline.

# EUGENIA PRICE

■

PHOTO BY GEORGE BENNETT

*Eugenia Price was born on June 22, 1916, in Charleston, West Virginia. At about the age of ten, she began entertaining the idea of becoming a writer. The first nudge in that direction came from her mother who, from her childhood, told her original stories were "better than those published in books." Her first published work was a poem written for a school literary magazine.*

*After three years at Ohio University, Price was accepted at Northwestern Dental School in Chicago, the only woman admitted. She applied herself diligently for three years, but she couldn't stay away from the typewriter. At last she made the decision that she would, indeed, be a writer.*

*She calls herself "an extremist by nature. I think you might say that I continually strive for balance in my life. I think about getting to the place where I don't always live between the covers of a book, but I doubt if I'd like it!"*

*Eugenia Price's fiction includes the St. Simons Trilogy (The Beloved Invader [1965], New Moon Rising [1969], and Lighthouse [1983]), the Florida Trilogy (Don Juan McQueen [1974], Maria [1977], and Margaret's Story [1980]), and the Savannah Quartet (Savannah [1983], To See Your Face Again [1985], Before the Darkness Falls [1987], and now Stranger in Savannah). She received the Distinguished Service Award from Georgia College; the Georgia Governor's Award in the Arts for Literature (for the St. Simons Trilogy); and the Matson Award from the Chicago Friends of Literature for Maria.*

**JORDAN:** Tell me about your latest book and work you're doing with black female characters.

**PRICE:** This book, *Bright Captivity,* is the one where I am going to be addressing these marvelous things you're addressing in your list of questions. I've always tried, and I've been very sincere about trying to make my black people whole, but truthfully felt timid about it. Timid isn't a word I think of in connection with myself very often. I spoke frankly with an African-American girl who had just entered Howard University about this book and my desire to make my black characters whole. She is the daughter of a good friend of mine and he said, "Call my daughter. You won't find a more adamant girl than she is. Call and talk to her about what you're going to do." I had just read Elizabeth Fox Genovese. You ask if I read black autobiography and biography. Yes I do! Every scrap and quote I can find. Well, I told this young lady at Howard University about my new book. In this book Anne, the protagonist, grew up with slavery and a half-white slave girl named Eve who had been her personal maid through both their lives. Eve, one year younger than Anne, seemed to sense the truth—they were friends, although Anne "tried to be the mistress." It is Eve I am trying to make whole and I'm also trying to lose my timidity with her. When I spoke to the student at Howard, I said to her, "I'm timid about doing it. I don't know what it felt like to be a slave." She said, "Neither do I. You have as much right to do such a character as I. I've talked to you long enough to know you're not pulling my leg." This girl somehow cracked my timidity. And I thought, "Well that's true." But if I really do feel skin color makes no difference, then why should I be timid?

What concerns me is putting down black speech on paper, and I would like your opinion on this. I have spent hours, days reading one of those WPA books called *Drums and Shadows*. It was transcribed back in the days when they had wire recorders. I remember wire recorders, and they were very bad. Anyway, they recorded black people, and tried to put the speech down the way the words sounded. But it is just very hard to read. Have you heard of a book of mine called *Lighthouse*? There was a man from New England named James Gould who came down here and built the first lighthouse on St. Simons. His idol was his preacher at church whose name was Lemuel Haynes. Lemuel Haynes was really loved by my white readers. He had been an indentured servant up North for seven years. He worked out his time and then he became a minister. James Gould idolized him and vowed he was not going to own slaves down here in the South. He and James Cowper, Anne's slave-owning father, became close friends when work brought Gould—an abolitionist—to St. Simons Island. That creates conflict in the work.

What concerns me most are the mechanics, not the conflicts. When I wrote my first novel in the early sixties, I didn't dare let my black people do more than drop a *g* now and then because that was when the civil rights movement was just starting and the libraries were adamant. I would have been taken apart. To me black speech is so colorful. It puts the writer in a box if she can't use it and yet I can't read this awful Brer Rabbit–type stuff. It seems overdone. I'm trying to come down the middle on this one, yet remain authentic.

My reward for finishing this book is that I finally get to read Toni Morrison's *Beloved*. She doesn't use it [black speech] at all. She does it all in structure. Tonight I can pick up *Beloved*. I really don't read many novels; I just like to write them. But what I have read of Morrison and Alice Walker, I like enormously. Both are far more talented writers than I.

JORDAN: I admire them too. Could you tell me more about Eve, the black female character in your latest work?

**PRICE:** Eve is very beautiful and the half-white daughter of the overseer on the adjoining plantation. She felt superior because of her half-white blood, but she hated her mother's allowing herself to have been coerced. She is an interesting study. To me, Martin Luther King was right. Integration is the answer. Intermarriage may be the ultimate answer. That's fine with me. We're people. We have so much to give each other. Eve's originality and character seem to prove that to me.

**JORDAN:** What specific conditions seem to be in place when black and white women become friends?

**PRICE:** That's a wonderful question, and I hope it means I can find a friend in you. In one sense, the specific conditions would have to be the same for both of us: We have to be open to each other; we have to trust each other, and we have to have a sense of humor about each of us. That's why Mabel Hillary and I were such close friends. I was also real close friends with Ethel Waters. She'd say, "Yes, white Baby. But Genie's not white—Genie's pink! I'm not black, I'm brown." And she was right.

**JORDAN:** We would probably look for a sense of humor in any person with whom we were going to be friends.

**PRICE:** Exactly. The same character conditions that exist for you and me would have to exist for Joyce Blackburn and me. We have to be open with each other and stop kidding around. All whites are not friends. All blacks are not friends.

**JORDAN:** Sometimes with black and white women we bring so much baggage that that's what keeps us from letting the sense of humor come through. In looking at novels, my research shows that white women have often written novels with black female protagonists. But the reverse happens less often. Could you comment on this phenomenon? Do you think this pattern will remain the same, or will black women start portraying the white female protagonists a bit more frequently?

**PRICE:** I shared this question with Tina [Tina McElroy Ansa, author of *Baby of the Family*]. I told her that white women write about black women because they think they know more. She laughed and said, "I might say that to Shirley [Jordan], but I'd never say it to you." I said, "Darn it, why wouldn't you say it to me? We're friends." As to whether or not this pattern will continue, I don't know. Tina doesn't think she will portray more white women. But I hope she will. I told her, "I'm going to just keep on being charming until someday you put a white woman in a novel." She laughed.

**JORDAN:** What kind of role does the black female play in white women's novels? What kind of role does the white female play in the black woman's novel?

**PRICE:** The black woman is almost always the servant. In my books, I'm blocked because of my writing in the mid-nineteenth century. People are crazy about the Civil War and the white South. I have a huge following in Great Britain, for example, and they're just carried away with it. Obviously, I'm also fascinated with this period.

**JORDAN:** Have you ever felt pressure from your publisher and/ or editor or audience to portray a particular kind of character or to treat a particular set of themes or have you remained free of such concerns?

**PRICE:** I had a sort of automatic 50,000 book sales with nonfiction books before I began to write novels, so I will have to say no. Publishers respect authors with followings. And I don't think that publishers do that generally. I've been at it thirty-five years and I've watched the publishing world change. It changes now from Friday to Monday. At times you don't know who the president of your company will be! When Tina came into publishing, at a risky time, I tried to shepherd her because I can do more for her personally by saying most publishing problems are "just par for the course. They're not neglecting you. This happens to everybody." The company president told me this morning, "Genie, you're our star. You don't need to worry." I laughed. He meant well, but I knew he knows how much I missed the previous president. But, no, I have never had any pressures from a publisher about my writing. Everyone has always shown respect. I am a Christian, a known Christian. I don't hide it. That, I find helps. I hope I never flaunt it, but being a Christian helps me control my sometimes strong opinions!

**JORDAN:** I was first introduced to your work through Billy Graham's *Decision* magazine, which my grandmother used to read.

**PRICE:** Oh really? I have a lot of inspirational books that Doubleday is bringing out again. Four of them when this novel comes out and four more when the next one comes out and then three more. I'm more surprised than anyone that everything I've written is either still in print or coming back in print, except two. I asked that they do not bring those two back because they're books for young people and quite dated now. They were written so long ago.

**JORDAN:** Exactly how many books have you written?

**PRICE:** I think *Bright Captivity* is book thirty-four. I'm in seventeen languages. That's a real kick when you get a copy of your own book and all you can read is your name. A lot of people think publishers want them to write very sexy books. There's a lot of sex in my books, but it is not overt. I have a big following in the religious world. I also have a big following among people who are trying to make up their minds about what they believe about God. I don't condemn them. I'm not affiliated with any church. I just try to follow Jesus Christ, and He did change my life, so things I used to cry about I can now laugh about and the things I used to laugh about I now want to cry about. I'm not, as you can see, a stuffy Christian but I am a believer and we are born to be mastered, though we'd better be darned careful of what or who masters us. Tina and I have our faith as a great common bond.

I have had no pressure to write explicitly. With the second novel, I went right to the best-seller list. I'm generally on for a couple of months. I haven't had any blockblusters like *Gone with the Wind*. I have a very loyal following, and my mail comes from bright ten-year-olds and dear, darling people in their nineties who have to use their magnifying glasses even to read the large print. Doubleday brings out all my novels in large print now. Each new book, thanks in part to my friends, the booksellers, sells more copies than the one before. All my mail is eventually answered. I'm fortunate to be at a place where I can afford someone full-time. Eileen Humphlett is my jewel. She pays my bills, she does my taxes, answers most letters. I used to do it all myself, plus I did all those autographing parties. I just got tired.

**JORDAN:** At age seventy, right?

**PRICE:** Seventy-six. I wouldn't have signed a three-novel contract without Eileen. I also have a friend who basically does most of my research for me. No one can read all the books for me, but Nancy Gashon handles all that comes out of archives in various places. She was my mother's neighbor, and they were bosom friends. I always knew she would be, as my father would have said, a crackerjack researcher. And she has turned out to be; she has a computer brain. And she knows what I want. She and Eileen know me like the inside of their own hands. And they both know they can take liberties with me that they might not take with anyone else. But they know me well enough to know I'd rather that they do it. And the other person that I couldn't get along without, Sarah Bell Edmond, helps keep the house clean and keeps us straight.

**JORDAN:** Do you work every morning?

**PRICE:** I work until three or four every day except Sunday. It used to be I wouldn't get started until 1:00 because the mail was so heavy. Now Eileen handles it except for letters from dear older people who've been writing to me twenty-five or thirty years. I have to write to them or they might think something is wrong with me.

**JORDAN:** What strategies do authors use to develop the characters' voices and to make them "real"? Sometimes the white women in black women's novels come off as stereotypes as much as the reverse is true in white women's novels. When the characters move beyond the stereotypes, what do the authors seem to have done that makes them seem real?

**PRICE:** Basically it is the answer I gave earlier. I think black people do know white people better than white people know black people. Not always, but often. Sarah Bell has worked for us and been with us more than any African-American friends, outside of Tina and Jonée. We ask her questions about her own life. She is a woman in control. She knows who she is, what her identity is, and no one diminishes her. Black people who work as servants for white people—which is not my main relationship to black people by any means—has to be the situation in my nineteenth-century novels because I'm writing about the slavery period. The only black person I've written about who was not a Southern slave was the Reverend Lemuel Haynes, the minister. I enjoyed that but I didn't think about his education when I wrote it. He was just an interesting man. I knew he was black.

When I was growing up, I escaped prejudice because of my parents. When my father could afford it, we had a cook but my mother helped her prepare dinner and she always had her place at the table. To me that was simply normal. I didn't know that it wasn't normal until I began to take speaking engagements in the South. Wealthy white Christians didn't want the maid who brought my breakfast up in the morning to sit down and talk with me in my room. I did. I was probably trying to pick her brain. It was the sixties.

**JORDAN:** I think a lot of times white employers never get to know their black employees very deeply because they don't inquire about the "little" things that do matter in relationships. That is so often the missing link.

**PRICE:** I agree wholly, and this is, in large part—class consciousness. Sarah Bell will tell us anything because we're all friends and we confide in her. She and Joyce run the house. And me.

**JORDAN:** Particularly in novels in which white female employers are portrayed interacting with their maids, but not necessarily limited to these situations, do you think ambiguity, among others, is a device black women use in relating to white women?

**PRICE:** I would imagine, yes. I'm sure you're right. I suspect that many black people are superior role players.

**JORDAN:** What can black and white women teach other about writing and about living?

**PRICE:** I think the biggest thing is to make room for each other. I'm not a converted white liberal. I happened to be born to a man and a woman who were really quite devoid of prejudice. I was born in 1916 and as I look back now I see the care they took with my brother and me, teaching us to be considerate of all people. We didn't have separate drinking fountains, restaurants, and parks, but we didn't go to school with blacks in my home state, and so I give my parents full credit.

When I think of black and white women writers, I think Tina and

I could learn a lot from each other. Tina has always done a lot for me. She wrote a superb article about me, and you wouldn't have known I was white except there was a picture of me. I think when Tina wrote that she was just writing about her friend Genie. So I think we can all make room for each other, accept each other as we are. We all have a lot to learn. I think my age helps because I've lived long enough and have had time to think more. I don't think there's a white person who has thought more about the race issue than I have and tried to be free of prejudice. The thing that I think is such a scourge is you thinking about us as they and me thinking about you as they. I can't tell you how much I want—I want as much as I ever wanted anything—to write my black people whole.

**JORDAN:** Is there ever a role for a stereotype in fiction—perhaps to introduce a character or to point out the danger of such attitudes?

**PRICE:** Yes. I think there is. I've done some white stereotypes, and I think I've done some black ones probably without realizing it and also deliberately. I haven't read my own novels for a long time, but yes, I would use a stereotype if I wanted quickly to drive a point. As long as the writer is aware of a stereotype, then it is all right.

**JORDAN:** Do you envision black women becoming more integrated into the women's movement as common concerns such as child care and abortion bring women of all races closer?

**PRICE:** I think so. I hope so. I'm sure there are a lot of us who had to be integrated into it. I've been liberated all my life, and I support the women's movement all the way, but I wouldn't say that I'm an activist because I've been single all my life, so have never been refused a credit card because my "husband" wouldn't sign. I built my house; it belongs to me. I earned the money that built the house. Surely black and white women know we need more women of all shades in Congress!

**JORDAN:** You really remain optimistic about all women coming together, don't you?

**PRICE:** Yes, but it takes time to make room for each other, Shirley. It takes time. But we have to do it. It's a gift, I think, when you want to make room for other people. If we can't write about each other, if you can't write about a white person and I can't write about a black person, we're both out of touch. I'm not talking about our talent. I can never write the way Toni Morrison does. I'm not Toni Morrison. No one writes for everybody, and that's probably the most important lesson I've learned. No one writes books for everyone. But if we can't make room for each other, we're sunk because we're all human.

# DORI SANDERS

■

PHOTO BY PAUL SHULMAN

*With the publication of her first novel,* Clover, *in early 1990, Dori Sanders became an overnight celebrity. Newspapers and magazines coast to coast praised its humor, pathos, and deft style. The novel and the author have been featured in* Time, Essence, *the* New Yorker, *the* Atlanta Journal/Constitution, *the* Washington Post, *the* New York Times, Vogue, McCall's, *and numerous other publications.* Clover, *which is being translated into Japanese, Danish,*

*German, and Dutch, recently received the Lillian Smith Award for
outstanding writing about the South.*

   *Sanders describes herself as a full-time farmer and a storyteller.
In the growing season she and her brother work the family land, one
of the oldest black-owned farms in York County, South Carolina. On
their farm they cultivate Georgia Belle and Alberta peaches, watermelons, and vegetables, which they sell at the Sanders's Peach Shed,
her family's open-air produce stand.*

**JORDAN:** What specific conditions seem to be in place when
black and white women become friends?

**SANDERS:** I think it's those little things that are so much a part
of us. We have our emotions that are common to women. We have
problems that are common to all of us. If you have children or if
it's just facing life in general, you have them. It isn't that one group
of women will have problems so far removed from yet another
group. There's that bond there that's between women everywhere,
but it also depends on the part of the country you're from. If you're
from the North, you doubtless won't get along well with me if you
don't like okra. It's those little kinds of things that once we get to
know and understand each other sort of pull us together. This is
something not to be overlooked from any group of women whether
they are all African-American, or if they are all white. It's that cultural difference—how you are raised is going to be a part of you. A
farmer will never ever feel at home in your [urban] environment.
Forget that you're African-American and I am too. We're coming
from different sides of the railroad track, so to speak. So often we
feel that it is prejudices that separate us, yet more than we acknowledge, it's common differences. If we spend our time addressing
those, I think we black and white women would become better
friends. For example, look at us. What are our differences? I like
grits, you don't. I'm from a farming community, you're afraid to
walk out there. You're afraid of snakes, I'm not. I think by the time
you wade through all of that, you begin to bond because you become real people, people with one outlook on life, and that is
just life.

**JORDAN:** So for you, Southern whites who had black maids
could move beyond the more superficial differences to see what
they have in common?

**SANDERS:** On that subject, let me tell you a little truth here. For the white women who had the black maids in their homes, based on some of my own little inside research, they were not nearly as divisive as it appeared from the outside. I know women who worked in their homes. I have never worked in a Southern white woman's home in that particular relationship. We had our own farm but sometimes in a little way I so envied their friendship because it was so real. Women have a caring about them that I think we've overcoated over the years, and we haven't pulled enough of the layers to find out how real so many women are, and a Southern white woman is not so far removed. They can be real. Imagine a white woman with a black maid in her home with a child who will go to the maid before they would come to her. You've got to develop a bond. And Shirley, that's the way I hear it happens. According to the maids, they talked about their problems, they shared their interests, their food, the caring, and their caretaking. Once you've talked to people who've worked in that environment, you'll find that they were deeper friends than we would assume.

**JORDAN:** I was wondering if you had seen *The Long Walk Home?*

**SANDERS:** No, I didn't see it. I don't get into film. I don't get into reading. While I'm doing this writing business I am so single vision I'm like a train inside a tunnel. I don't see anything except what's in front of me because I'm so impressionable. Everything that someone has said is so much better than everything I could ever say, so when I listen to all those profound things and the wonderful little nuggets that they drop, I go "I can't do anything to equal that," and it sort of gives me writer's block because it makes me think, "How can I try? They're so good." And then I'm impressionable to the point that if someone has done something and I'm fifty miles from it in resemblance, I think, "Oh I've got to pull that because they've already treated that." Case in point. I did a wonderful scene once. When I went into the lady's room at an airport, I overheard a conversation. Later on, I heard a woman read an excerpt from her work of the same kind of situation. I was ready to pull it. But then I thought, I had mine first. I didn't know she had hers at the same time. I kept it, and now it's in my upcoming novel. But I had been ready to pull it until I said, "No, I'm not. That was my own experience. I was writing from my own eye's view." And therefore I will not pull that because I have to remember there is not a monolithic experience in the entire world. Why don't I see too many movies? Because again I'm too impressionable. And then I think all those wonderful hours I could have spent getting my manuscript on my editor's desk. I'm always rushing toward a deadline, but as soon as the rough draft is on my editor's desk and he's said, "Okay," I'm watching movies and reading again.

**JORDAN:** From your reading and observation, what kind of role does the black female play in white women's novels and what kind of role does the white female play in black women's novels?

**SANDERS:** I think as far as we're concerned as black women, how can you possibly write a novel from any standpoint and not include us because we are a part of the American living scene, and if I may speak tongue in cheek, a very colorful part at that because we are women of color. But to the extent that we take them on I think we perhaps are not as inclined in some instances. I do not find that as a deliberate decision. I only consider that as your view. If they're not in your picture frame, I do not suggest that a writer bring them in just for the sake of bringing them in. But if they are there I see no reason to push them out of the picture or out of the camera's eye. In my work I look at it as people, women. I took them in segments as they would come to my farmstand on the side of the railroad. If they came in and were black and were fascinating, I pulled them into my little fictional world. If they were white, I pulled them in. I was writing from the observation of a world that was productive for my eyes, and I'm doing the same thing again because living in the new South today, there are not those black and white lines that divided us. Our kids go to school together. We do things together, and since we are enmeshed in all this togetherness, I think I would take them on just as quickly as they would choose to take me on. And I would hope that I would do that in a most realistic way because Dori Sanders does not have a bone to pick, and I'm not out there looking for a pawn to shred apart as a piranha would a piece of whale. I don't have that in my head to do. I'm a people person and I'm captivated by them.

**JORDAN:** So the fact that you include characters according to whether they enter your camera's eye is how you would answer this question probably? White women have often written novels with black female protagonists. But the reverse happens less often.

Could you comment on this phenomenon? And do you think this pattern will remain the same, or will black women start portraying white female protagonists a bit more frequently as white females enter their camera's view more naturally?

**SANDERS:** I think that will be true of the writer who follows the old staid advice, "Write what you know." And then the world will come to grips with what you have written because the work will come across as genuine and not contrived. I fear a writer's trying to address something simply because it's what they think people want to hear or because it's territory they feel they should invade. When you start doing that, I think you are working on a contrived plot. And I hate that. Sometimes a writer might think, "This will be more interesting, if I put the white woman as protagonist." However, I would never do that because then I'm trying to contrive a plot to suit some bias that I have in the back of my head. So often in writing, it comes across that way. I'm for real life as it really happens and you look at it and place it in its world of fiction. And then it doesn't become a categorized work when you say, "This belongs here and that belongs there." Women from across the country will find "oh that reminds me of" or "oh I can relate to that" because it becomes real. I don't know what the other writers might do because as you can see I'm not a today's writer. I'm from a different time frame; therefore, my thinking restricts me to a train of thought. Again as you may notice with the language, I was from a time where we didn't use all those four-letter words and let them fly. They're not in my head. They're not in my vocabulary. I guess I could do it if I listened to the right people but it would be contrived for me so I would not write along those lines. I'm not sure that would be true of most African-American women writers, but I'm sure it would be true of this one. I will not seek out to say "I'm invading their territory" just to pull them in for that reason because I need to address them with the wide angle of this camera I have in my mind. If they walk into it, I'm going to take their picture.

**JORDAN:** As you were drawing the character of Sarah Kate, you weren't concerned about her as a white female but just as a character that you wanted to flesh out? You weren't thinking this is a white person and how would this white person respond?

**SANDERS:** Shirley, that's the best question I have ever had asked of me in connection with Sarah Kate since I have been on book tour. You said it all. I was looking at that woman as a character that I needed to be fleshed out. I didn't look upon her as white or black or whatever. I looked upon her as a person needing to search herself to figure out "How will I get along with a little girl, a child that I only have two things in common with and that is my loss and my grief because she shares the same?" I set about with those two people first of all to write a story about a stepmother and child and their life and how they would set out on that life together. As the story continued, or as we would say in South Carolina, as we go on down and keep on going down, then you have to address the conflict. One reviewer said something quite interesting in one of the newspapers that it was obvious that Dori Sanders did not set out to write a story about race relations because she was a leisurely sixteen pages into the book before we even know the woman is white. So you get a stepmother and a child. Thank you for a question like that.

**JORDAN:** Who or what inspired you to write this novel?

**SANDERS:** I'm basically a storyteller. Stories go around and around in my head all the time. But I didn't get around to writing a novel because I wanted to be a writer. I started writing little blurbs and little things on pieces of paper lest I should forget. I have nieces and nephews who have no idea of how wonderful the farming life is. The freedom you have there. So much that can be said for physical work because it frees the mind, and I wanted them to know some of the wonderful things that had happened there. I was born and raised on the farm where I live now. So wanting them to keep in touch with all that, I started writing down little things. Everyone is aware that the people of South Carolina have had problems with their fruit crops because of cold weather. You end up losing it. I have a sister who lives in Maryland. During the winter months I'd go there to find something easy to do. Usually in hotels you can always find a job during the holiday season doing banquets and parties. I got a job there, and a woman, the owner of the hotel, caught me writing or found out that I had written on the back of one of those expensive banquet menus. An idea hit me. I needed it in the story I was writing for my nieces and nephews. And I wrote it all down. Maybe a paragraph, but it was just right. You may have noticed that when something hits me, I write it down immediately. I got caught up that day because I was waiting for a busboy to bring the glasses so I could pour the water.

The owner walked in and asked, "Who wrote on the back of these banquet menus? Don't people realize these things are expensive?" Well I'm from a family of ten and you don't own up to anything unless you have to. I didn't open my mouth. I just kept doing my work. Someone said, "I didn't." I didn't say anything. She picked it up, started to read. "Oh," she said, "this is good. Who did this?" Right away, I said, "I did." She said, "Dori Sanders, you are a wonderful writer! Why don't you try to get it published?" I said, "Published!" But she stayed behind me. She annoyed me. She was so insistent she made me angry. I can't stand someone pushing and pushing me so I said, "I'll show the woman I can't write. I'll send the thing in." It was rejected but with a letter saying, "Try writing what you know. We're impressed with what you've written, but it's melodramatic and contrived. Write what you know and we think you might turn out to be an all right writer." I wrote *Clover*. It was accepted. Dori Sanders is a writer. That's how it happened. In my book, here's what I say in my dedication: To my family for their patience and humor and to Nancy Shulman who saw something in me—that old worn cliché—I did not see in myself.

**JORDAN:** Was storytelling a part of your growing-up experience? If so, how has it affected your writing?

**SANDERS:** It was definitely part of my growing-up experience. We told stories about everything. Even to this day, if you were on my farm, my brother would be taking you maybe to a distant orchard to pick peaches but on the way over there he would tell you a story as you're riding on the tractor in the trailer behind him. He'd have a story going even while you are picking. We are storytellers. My father was a teacher, and he used to write plays for schools, and we'd have little roles in the plays. We've been storytelling and acting our entire lives. I think that sort of background definitely helps me in my writing because once the story is in my head it's easier for me to do the natural sequence of novel writing because that's just a story that branches out a little longer than an ordinary story. It also helps me in writing because of the style I write in. I am a totally unstructured person, and things will hit me as I see them, and I'll make a little note here, but as far as anything I do whether it be a novel or short story, I've already thought it out in my head exactly the way I want it to go and I've already written the ending. I write the ending first, and then I worry about how to get it in the story because the story's in my head so as I go about my day-to-day life, I think of the little things that will fit in and how it will build and shape the story. I make those little notes on pieces of paper. I will pick up one little piece of paper, I will state where I was, what day it was, and where I was going so that I can suddenly pull it up as if it were in a computer. I mentally pull up all the scenery around me and then I can go back and write whatever it was that was in my head. I can remember all of that by triggering the imagination. Nothing triggers where I left my glasses or where I put my keys though. But let me see a scene, write down where I was when I saw it, and the whole world opens up.

**JORDAN:** To what extent do you use sources such as biographies, autobiographies, and histories when you are developing your characters? It sounds like your sources seem to be snatches of scenes.

**SANDERS:** Of course, if I am going outside of an ordinary scene, it just means I have to truck down to the library and do a little bit of work there. For example, in writing *Clover*, most of it was visual. I looked at it and that's how I saw it and that's how I pulled it in. But that didn't help me get those people in and out of schools, and since I needed this woman from out of town—Sarah Kate—to meet Gaten Hill in South Carolina, I had to find a reason why a Northerner would come there to school in the first place and what would have pulled her there. We are well known for our textiles and designing industry surrounded by textile mills. They've actually upscaled and changed the entire landscape of the farming scene now in York County, at least. So I had my character in that field so to get her out of a design school in New York and have her come to Clemson University in South Carolina would be logical because it is one of the most prestigious schools for design. No one would question academically her reason for coming from that school to this school. Of course, it took a little time and help of wonderful librarians. I think for those kinds of things I'll have to put a small dedication in my next book saying, "Thank you, librarians. You people are wonderful." I must do that.

**JORDAN:** Have you noticed some subtle distinctions between the way black women authors portray characters and the way white women authors portray them?

**SANDERS:** I suppose our own cultural heritage would tend to make us have that because of who we are and where we are coming from. It again depends on your culture or environment. I feel that as a farmer I would portray or address a subject matter far differently than you, and we're both African-American, because I would have a decided insight that would be so different from you that you couldn't possibly approach it from the angle I would approach it from. If you were a kid who lived in the city, you would not have had the time to notice the little things of country life. I think it's where we are coming from that makes our writing different in that way. I don't think I could write successfully about a child that had a father who didn't care for it or about a person who didn't care for his family and didn't offer them the source of strength that my father did because there's no way I could get into their head. I only know it from one standpoint. Now in that way someone said I may be different because they say I wasn't addressing real life, but I was addressing real life for me. Every black person doesn't have the same experience. Every black farmer isn't destitute and wondering where he is going to get his next load of fertilizer. A lot of us have our farms. A lot of us are middle-class farmers, and we don't know what it means to be a sharecropper. I was privileged to not be from a sharecropper family, but all through my life I kind of wanted to be because they got to move ever so often. I was so envious of the girls I went to school with. They would say, "Oh Dori, we just moved to Mr. So and So's place and we got the best hiding places and blackberries are growing everywhere and we have plum trees." I wanted to be one. Here I was living in one house my whole life. I felt deprived and that is the truth, and I'm not trying to put on. So it's your view of where you're coming from.

**JORDAN:** What can black and white women teach each other about living and about writing?

**SANDERS:** I think our contemporary writers are beginning to address real life, and they are beginning to do an excellent job of it actually. It's not that I'm that much of a contemporary reader. I'm not. I am selective in my reading, and at my age I sort of narrow myself down in the things I read because my reading time is so limited. When I do read, I will go back to historical romances or historical drama. I enjoy the older stuff very much. I like Zora Neale Hurston, Eudora Welty, and others. I think they are dealing with life as they see it, and I think that so many of our young writers, white or black, have sort of stopped feeling that the only thing that matters is glitter and gold, what social party you went to or

New York's Park Avenue. I think that they're now able to see what it is that concerns a woman of today. Health is a concern. The problems that children face are also a great concern. Will they get mixed up with the wrong crowd and will they get mixed up with the social problems of today—the drugs, the abuse, and all those kinds of things? Will my children face that kind of society? What will we eat that won't throw our cholesterol balance out of sync and put too much fat into our system? I think they're coming down to real life and they're looking at it. If it's ordinary, I think they're beginning to address it and I admire that. If it is not ordinary and they still address it, I admire that also. There are people who live gilded and jaded lives because they are people that are in show business and the people who make all this money and they do all of that. I'm fascinated by their lives but won't try to write about that just because I think that is what someone wants to read. I think, sit on your own doorstep. See what you see from there, and I think people will be interested in that too. We want to be able to identify with what goes on around us. That's what I think a lot of the young women writers are addressing today, and I commend them for it.

JORDAN: You just mentioned women being concerned about their children and the kind of world that they're going to grow up in. Do you envision black women becoming more integrated into the women's movement as common concerns such as child care and abortion bring women of all races closer?

SANDERS: I think they're going to be forced to if they're going to become that integrated part of that integral working society. Black women are out there working too, so the same problems that concern other women concern them as well. They also have to worry about what kind of day care they're going to give their kid. No working woman is left scot-free. Although on a scale of one to ten down through the years, we have had an advantage on that because we've had moms, and we've always counted on them, but with the younger group of women, their mothers are out there also in the work force. In the old days when a woman did leave the home to work, nine times out of ten her mother was there to help her out with the children. Mothers today are becoming mothers earlier, and there are younger grandmothers, and they're in the work force too, so therefore, the child-care issue will surface there. And the abortion issue will also pull in the reins and have its place there as well, and I say that without offering my own views because I don't tend to get into anything that does not actually concern me at this time in my life. I leave a person's own decision on that because it's kind of hard for a woman my age to try to set guidelines for someone else. Now one of my greatest concerns centers around the care of our senior citizens: nursing homes. With the high cost of medicine and hospitals, it saddens me. How in the world will they be able to make it? I was in the drugstore and a woman was buying medicine and her pills cost $47.00. I asked, "How long will they last?" and she said, "These will last one month." Those are the things that begin to concern me. I'm sad that they often have to go into the grocery store and buy the wrong things just to get full. That saddens me. It's those things that are a part of my concern and that I do address in my next work of fiction.

**JORDAN:** There was a time in the black community where just as your mother would take care of the children when you went to work, you could also depend on your children, your daughter or your son, or your daughter-in-law to take you in when you couldn't do for yourself.

**SANDERS:** Also, Shirley, you could depend on not necessarily a relative but a stranger in the community. Miss Ann, Miss Margaret, Miss Susie would take you in because they knew who your people were. The first thing they want to know is, who are your people, and if they know your people, they have an obligation, but you see we are getting away from that sort of feeling. No one today feels responsible for anyone anymore and that sort of callous feeling is beginning to invade the farming community. That pains me. It distresses me to see it begin to happen all over even though it's not to the same degree in the country. You still occasionally have that woman sitting on her front porch and saying to some child, "If I see you doing this or that, you're going to have to answer to me." That still happens but on a limited scale. And still you hear, "I'm going to tell your mama." But it's very, very rare because the young people will say, "You tell her, you pay." We even used to hide from a person who was not our mother, our father. You couldn't do anything wrong in front of anyone that knew you. You'd better not get caught doing anything you did not want your mother to know. Everybody's eyes were watching you. That's gone today. You were afraid to sass someone.

Our latch-key kids are there today, but it's because we have made it so. Older women are afraid to take on the care of a small child for fear it might fall down, then it would be said, "You've neglected my child." But I feel for the children today. I sometimes look at them and think, "Who will take care of our children?" I feel for our children, Shirley, who are not even deprived. I feel for the children whose parents so want them to have it all that the little children get up on a rainy day with a scratchy throat, and their mama has to drive them out to some day-care center because she has a corporate meeting. I want to say, "Take care of your child. You'll never have that child as a one year and three day old—or whatever—again. The child will never be that age again. Treasure the moment. Savor that little bit of time," I want to say. "And don't stress them out. Don't feel that they have to be a ballet dancer and a violinist all at the same time. Let them play." In my own little subtle way, after seeing how so many little children are being pushed today, I addressed it in my book *Clover*. Little Clover said, "I don't want to be a gifted, talented child," so she hides the elephant she drew because her aunt will push her, and she'll show it, and the next thing you know she'll be sending her to art school and she likes to play. Don't deprive them of advancing but don't push them too much. Give them a chance to be little children. There's plenty of time down the road to be gifted. But then I'm not a mother so they'd shoot me down in a minute. Never had any children, but I care for the children. I worry for them. I love the children so when you have that love, naturally you're going to zero into that. I do.

JORDAN: When you look at young children and teenagers who often do not know their own family histories and do not have or know the words to voice their experiences or what they see, what kinds of things do you think ought to be done to help them gain control over their own voices to appreciate their stories and their personal histories?

SANDERS: Since childhood can only be interpreted from a distance of the years, that puts it right into our laps. As adults we have to try to instill in them a sense of pride and a sense of stability. Writers have the opportunity to tour schools and to be around people. Use those opportunities to talk to young people. And I think I'm in a good position to do that because I'm a farmer. When most of the high-school kids meet me, they say, "You aren't a farmer." In other words, if you're a farmer, how in the world did you end up writing a book? And then I say, I AM a farmer." "You mean, you farm?" "Yes," I tell them. "I drive a Massey Ferguson tractor every day." I try to encourage them to use their experience, have their voice. I tell them, "Do not feel that someone else's life out there is better than yours. You bring your life up and you will find that your life is just as important." I want children to remember something that a young man from a little, little, little town in South Carolina faced when he went away to an Ivy League school. He was there among the country's elite, won a wonderful scholarship, and the young people there wanted to know if he'd been to Paris, if he'd been to Rome, if he'd been to England. Of course, the young man hadn't so he had to say, "No." They embarrassed him by saying, they had traveled to Spain and to here and there, and been on cruises. The young man looked at them, studied them, and then he asked the question, "Have you ever been to Walnut, South Carolina?" The guys exchanged looks. "Walnut, South Carolina? We don't know where that is. No," they answered, "we haven't been there." "Then if you haven't been to Walnut, South Carolina, you're going to have to do a lot of traveling to come up to me." That is the story. I thought what a wonderful way to do someone who is putting you down. Young people need to remember that. Be yourself. Be proud of yourself as an individual. And then others will see you as someone worthwhile because you feel that you are worthwhile. And it rubs off. That's it.

**JORDAN:** So many of our young people feel so lost, though.

**SANDERS:** Yes, they feel that way because we have made them feel that unless you are this, unless you are that, you are no one. Unless you copy all of those people out there, have the shoes that cost so much money, have an expensive everything, you are no one. And that's how we've lulled ourselves into thinking that we only become someone by how someone looks at us, and we think that amounts to what we're wearing or what we can afford, the cars we drive. And it is so sad. So sad. But I think older people are much more aware of that feeling than someone else. You make them feel that that is what success is all about rather than that creative voice, that creative ability that could be yours, and no one else in the world can take it away from you or copy you. It takes a lot of doing though to get it done. And I don't have wild hopes that it will ever be done. But I think it's doable if we ourselves as older people stop putting emphasis on what you are wearing. Forget the latest style, what it costs, the designer everything. Be yourself and be secure in that. However, peer pressure is very strong when you're young and I'm aware of that too.

**JORDAN:** In part you wanted to write the stories down to pass on to your nieces and nephews.

**SANDERS:** Only to encourage them to keep the farm going. That was my reason for that. Stories about the farm that would make them think. Actually, stories about the farm that would make them love it as much as I did. I wanted to create a richness of place and to make them always feel that no matter how old they would become, they would always want their children to come back to that land and would say, "This is home, this is where your grandparents lived." Then they would remember the things that they wouldn't have known about. I suppose I was trying to preserve an oral history. So many wonderful things happened there. I think about the watermelons. We still grow the best ones. I don't care what anyone says. I think of how we would have family reunions, and all the relatives would come in. And we'd cut those wonderful melons. Oh what a time! What a life! Just all so grand. And I wanted them to know about that and the stories my grandfather used to tell us. I figure if we keep on going and no one is remembering, we'll all be gone, and no one will know those stories.

**JORDAN:** Do you see literary critics, particularly black ones, as having a special role in shaping how stories of black women's lives are read, assessed, and taught?

**SANDERS:** I suppose in the many ways, as it has always been in the opinion of many people, critics included, they somehow try to prescribe or establish how they think a black woman should write. If I go back to some of the things that I've heard expressed early on in my writing career that I absolutely did not do and have no desire to do, but I've heard the opinion that because I am a black woman, there are issues that I should address and am required to address because I have established a voice. Some people have labeled me as escapist because I have not as yet in my writing established a platform where I'm going to speak out for this issue, speak out for that issue. Do this and do that. There are those who feel that there is no place for fiction. Every word should make some sort of statement. No, I do not agree with that. If I am labeled as escapist because I do not address issues that people think I should, then so be it because perhaps then I will be different. There is a place for fiction that does not have to address the controversial or even the political issues. I feel we have so many wonderful writers who are more prepared and certainly more qualified than I am to address them. I also feel fiction has a place. I think that just because a rabbit does not fly does not mean he is not as beautiful as a dove. So if fiction does not take on the political world, I feel that is all right too. It has its own bright spot of beauty in the sun. So my personal works of fiction will not be fiction that I will so contrive to address some issue just because I have a voice. I will not venture out and do that. I will write fiction as I have in the past, purely and solely for my enjoyment. When I have a story in my head, I would hope that through fiction I can tell it. I have no ulterior motive, Shirley, that I must address this and I must address that. If those issues crop up and they come within my writing, I will not sidetrack them. I will address them, but I will not go find them to bring them in just for the purpose of saying, "I have a voice so let the world know how I feel about this." I will not do that. I think it would take away my joy of storytelling, and I think it would make writing laborious for me instead of the pleasure I now find. Now I'm free in my own little world and I love it that way. I think that's the joy of being a writer of fiction.

**JORDAN:** Have you ever felt pressure from your publisher and/ or editor or audience to portray a particular kind of character or to treat a particular set of themes, or have you remained free of such concerns?

**SANDERS:** Well, I certainly had no pressure from my publisher. I had no pressure from my editor. There wasn't any pressure on me to slant my writing to address any issues. "Write what you know," was the advice from the editorial department. "Write what you know. Write what sounds right to you and then leave it." I was privileged in that way because it gave me all the freedom I ever needed in the world. I've received most favorable reviews, and let me tell you, it's a wonderful feeling, yet it makes me wonder, can I do it again? It also exposes me too. Before the novel, no one knew who I was. Now I am there. But again I will not try to write what I think people will want to read. I will just take a deep breath and write the way that I wrote before. Only this time I will not remember when I was younger. I will remember what I see today and as you know from a much older viewpoint.

**JORDAN:** What is the responsibility of the reader, if any, in the creative process?

**SANDERS:** I think you can't have one without the other. I really sincerely believe that it would be very difficult for a creative writer to write if she didn't believe readers would view the work as one of fiction, and that conclusions reached by the author might differ sharply from their own.

**JORDAN:** Is there ever a role or function for a stereotype in fiction? Perhaps to introduce the reader to a character or to expose the danger of such attitudes?

**SANDERS:** I personally think that as a writer that role would have to surface. If in using people, those people happen to fall into a stereotypical role, then so be it. I think that whosoever we are we have our own function in life, be it the town drunk or the town crazy. A writer will bring them into fiction because they are a part of the territory. Believe you me, real life offers enough variety of all sorts without your trying to bring in someone just to set up some scene.

**JORDAN:** So you don't worry about the reader in that regard?

**SANDERS:** Well, maybe I do, but I try not to. If you do that, then you're not writing for yourself. You're writing for the reader, and you're really supposed to tell a story rather than to try and reach out and find one you think the reader may like. Then it becomes contrived, and you start to dream up a plot and may be missing out on the best possible fiction you could find. Write what's there, and then if it sounds right to you, you'll say that's the story I sort of had in my head. How can you possibly know what someone else would like anyway? People think that if I don't put in some sexy situation then the reader won't read it. *Clover* was on the *Washington Post* hard-cover best-selling list, and had no sex and no dirty words. You can't second-guess what someone else will want to read.

**JORDAN:** In writing *Clover*, was one character more difficult to write than another for any reason other than race, class, sex, or age?

**SANDERS:** In this case, it didn't happen that way because it just all flowed in because I really was viewing life from my farm stand and I'd come across such a wide group of people every day, and I had all those wonderful farmers who sit by and talk and tell their stories. I didn't have to search for characters.

# OUIDA SEBESTYEN

■

*Ouida Sebestyen's* Words by Heart *chronicles the life of a black family that settles in an all-white town somewhere in the Texas, Missouri, Colorado region at the turn of the century. At the heart of the novel is the family's struggle to adjust to unfamiliar territory amid opposition from some of the town's whites. The novel became an instant success and later was made into a movie.*

*Born February 13, 1924, Sebestyen had been writing thirty-five years before* Words by Heart *was published in 1979. In its sequel,*

On Fire *(1985), Sebestyen takes the reader into the world of the white family whose son had killed the black father in* Words by Heart *in which we see the family struggle to gain control over their lives.*

*Sebestyen has written several other young adult works, all published by Little, Brown:* Far from Home *(1980),* IOU's *(1982), and* The Girl in the Box *(1988). All Sebestyen's books have been well received, but* Words by Heart *remains her most popular work. It was selected as a* New York Times *Best Book of 1979, a* School Library Journal *Best Book of 1979, one of* Learning Magazine's *Year's Ten Best, an American Library Association Notable Children's Book, and an American Library Association Best Book for young adults and received the International Reading Association Children's Book Award for 1979.*

*The mother of one son, Sebestyen lives in Boulder, Colorado.*

**JORDAN:** What specific conditions seem to be in place when black and white women become friends, whether in literature or in life?

**SEBESTYEN:** I can only speak from my own limited point of view. I guess in the back of my mind, I'm always thinking, "What if I should say something, just dashing along the way I'm used to, that this friend might be sensitive to? Something that smacks of that 'us versus you' and might be hurtful?" But I worry about that with anyone of a different race, culture, or age, and try for empathy. My worry may stem from growing up in Texas knowing so few black people except someone coming in to help my mother.

**JORDAN:** As you were drawing the characters of Lena and Claudie, were there particular concerns you had about the portraits you wanted to produce? What do you think of them now?

**SEBESTYEN:** Well, I like them both. I think they've come across the way I meant them to. It's a funny thing. I didn't realize that I was doing something unusual in choosing a black family. It seemed right for the situation, and I was mighty surprised later to find I had done something one doesn't do. Kids ask me why I wrote about a black family, and I ask, "Why did you decide to wear your red sweater this morning?" It just felt right. I needed people who had a whole history of enduring and being hopeful. And for the father especially, I needed someone who went through a terrible, terrible disappointment and still didn't become a bitter person. One who had just escaped being a slave and still dared to have high hopes for his children. Instead of having a Lithuanian family, for instance, and having to explain to readers why these foreigners suggest a threat to the town, it just seemed like everyone would say, "I see." I thought a black family would represent exactly what I was trying to say in the story. Of course, I was writing from inside me—that's all you can write from. And I was able to use things that my parents had told me about their childhoods. Otherwise I wouldn't have dared to write about that part of the country at that time. I remember being very concerned, as I was writing, about getting 1910 correct!

**JORDAN:** One of my later questions concerned that very point. Your description of poor, rural life was excellent. How were you able to take your imagination back in time to create such a realistic depiction of life at the turn of the century?

**SEBESTYEN:** Most of that came from my parents' stories. They were both poor. My mother's father was a Methodist circuit rider who went around preaching, and marrying, and baptizing people; he didn't have a home and wasn't ever paid money. And when he died, he left my grandmother with seven kids to raise without a home or any cash or anything—those stories stuck with me, the things that she had to do, the ways the children helped, and the way they were put down.

**JORDAN:** You also capture the speech of the characters really well. How did you train your ear to hear the characters speak so naturally?

**SEBESTYEN:** I don't know if it's a gift writers have or whether it is something that interests them so much that they work at it. Of course, I heard Southern speech even though I lived in that western part of Texas. My parents were from Alabama and Louisiana originally, or their parents were, and a lot of people in my part of Texas have a Southern way of saying things. We had Southern food, because that's what they knew how to cook. That part seemed to come naturally. Of course, I was worried about the father's dialect. I decided *this* man especially would be very proud of passing on pure English to his children. I'm sure his speech was influenced by the Bible. And, of course, he liked Whitman.

**JORDAN:** Was storytelling a part of your growing-up experience, and how has it affected your writing?

**SEBESTYEN:** I guess that's a Southern sort of thing, especially when relatives get together: Great-aunt So and So and Cousin So and So by the third marriage. Yes, *that* I loved being in on, hiding under the bed. But I couldn't tell a story to save my life. A lot of writers talk about making up stories and telling them to other kids. I couldn't even tell my son stories. [*Laughs*]

**JORDAN:** I take it you had to read them to him. [*Laughter*] Who or what inspired you to write *Words by Heart*?

**SEBESTYEN:** I guess the person who most influenced me was my aunt. She was the oldest of the seven kids who helped my grandmother after my grandfather died. She was thirteen then, and they both went to work doing everything that they possibly could do, like helping people butcher hogs, to get the other kids through college. That just amazed me. She wanted to be a writer but was so busy helping everybody that she didn't pursue it. One of her own reminiscences became the beginning [of *Words by Heart*]. She said when she was young, she was in a contest—I can't remember if it was for spelling or Bible-reading—but she won it and got the prize that was meant for a boy. And I thought, "That's something to put in my little cigar box to keep," and I wrote it down one day in a story.

**JORDAN:** Did she get a chance to read the story or the novel?

**SEBESTYEN:** No. No, but she knows.

**JORDAN:** Yes, she knows. To what extent do you use sources such as autobiographies, biographies, or histories to develop your characters?

**SEBESTYEN:** Lots and lots of research. That's a process that could go on and on. Sometimes you have to stop yourself. After I've puttered with plot long enough to know it's going to be in a specific time period and why I'm setting it there, I go to the library and bring home armloads of things—just general history first, who was president at the time, and then books on the slang, the music, the heroes, the jokes—all sorts of picture books, like *Time* and *Life*. Even though it may be a picture of a gathering of mayors, I get to see what the different cars are like, the people, the sidewalk, the women, what they are wearing, how they do their hair and that sort of thing. I also go through the replicas of catalogs like the Sears 1897 to find furnishings for people's homes. And, of course, the more personal things like biographies, journals, autobiographies, letters tell me what the people talked about and how they expressed themselves—what was happening, things that were on their minds in general.

**JORDAN:** What were some of the research pieces you used in writing *Words by Heart*?

**SEBESTYEN:** Anything I could find in the Boulder Library about that period, from the Civil War up to 1910, so I could see what the parents must have felt and what their concerns were even before the story started. I remember *Time* and *Life* because they have lots of pictures. And then this wonderful book on slang gave me help with a lot of words that I wanted to be sure were in use at that time. I read turn-of-the-century histories and general outlines and Du Bois and Douglass and some books just on black history, which had pictures. I depend a lot on pictures. I remember I wouldn't write about Colorado until I had lived here fifteen years for fear I would put the wrong insect on the wrong flower. It terrified me to think that I might say something was in use in this book when it hadn't even been invented yet, so a lot of the research was just technical.

I knew what it was like to be a little girl. I could remember that, and I knew about the experiences of my parents—of course, that's vicarious but pretty close in terms of feelings and emotions. Still I was worried about a lot of that, which is good I guess too.

**JORDAN:** Were you a student of literature in college?

**SEBESTYEN:** I didn't go to college. I just went during the summers. My father was still working on his masters and came up from Texas to Colorado in the summer, so we would combine his studying with a little vacation, and I took some courses then. When

World War II started and I decided I'd rather paint airplanes and be patriotic, I never got back to school. I just had to keep learning on my own. Of course, literature has always been wonderful to me. I was an only child, so books really opened the world to me, and I'm still fascinated by everything that's going on.

JORDAN: You have such a strong sense of interactions between siblings, I would not have guessed you were an only child.

SEBESTYEN: Oh, you have to fake a lot of things. You search for some other emotion that would be suitable and exchange it and *feel*. And maybe I know more about having brothers and sisters from being outside looking in than I would know being in the midst of it all. At least I have a certain objectivity.

JORDAN: White women often portray black female protagonists or main characters, but the reverse happens less often. Could you comment on this? Do you think this pattern will remain the same, or will black women start to portray white female protagonists a bit more frequently?

SEBESTYEN: I hope they do. We all benefit from insights from all points of view. I don't know why this is a pattern. Do white women just feel that they can speak about whatever they like? Do you have an opinion about that?

JORDAN: When I started looking at this subject not so much to interview writers but to select novels, it just turned out that I could find more novels that white women had written with black characters than the reverse. And even now, that's the case in contemporary fiction as well.

SEBESTYEN: That's strange. Maybe white women just don't think they can't. They think, "Being black is something I can look upon and grasp and write about." And maybe a black woman writer simply thinks the same thing. When I'm writing a novel for people my age, I think, "Gosh, my readers know so much more than I do. Anything I say, somebody is going to know more about it." Maybe I started to write for young people because I felt fear [of writing adult fiction]—not because I think it's less complex or I look down on it—but I felt that I've been through that age so maybe

I know it. But I hesitate to write about adults who are richer or adults more experienced than I am.

**JORDAN:** I would think though that black women have been writing for a long time true, but when they get published—granted it's hard for anyone to get published—when they see the opportunity to be published, they publish their own experiences. It's important to have their own experiences in writing. We write about what we know and care about.

**SEBESTYEN:** That seems strange and technically reasonable. But if we write only about what we know we can only write about ourselves. Nobody can write fiction without putting their characters in a social setting, a world.

**JORDAN:** I think that most black women writers are probably so interested in and intrigued by the range of their own experiences as told from their own point of view that they don't feel the need to explore white female characters as much. When I taught a class on the novel last spring, we somehow started to talk about the development of the black novel, especially the black female novel. I told the students that probably in ten years, we'd start to see some very different kinds of novels from black writers—it's already happening—with more diversity. Perhaps then we might naturally see more depictions of scenes between black and white women because the writers themselves will have been born in the seventies and eighties, and their experiences are just going to be very different and their imaginations will go in directions that have not been explored as fully.

**SEBESTYEN:** It's going to be exciting.

**JORDAN:** Yes, it already is. I feel so comfortable talking with you that I was about to ask if you were a feminist before I move to this next question.

**SEBESTYEN:** Go on feeling comfortable. I think I was the luckiest girl alive. Nobody ever told me that I wasn't a boy. Being an only child, I did things with my mother, of course, but then I was also with my father, so I got to be the boy too. I helped him fix the car and build things and put new shingles on the roof, and I didn't know there were certain things girls did and certain things boys did until it was too late. It didn't warp me at all. I've always been independent and didn't think of myself primarily as a woman—so not being girly cute didn't bother me. Well, it bothered me at one time that I wasn't pretty or beautiful, but peripherally, I think. I figured it could only get better, so I was spared all the stress and it was wonderful. And then when people began to say, "Look, women are doing things that they haven't been doing all these years!" I went, "Okay."

I admit a lot of the inequities and the conditioning makes me angry. But then I also think, "Why can't you just be like me?" [*Laughs*] We start out conditioning children at such young ages and that makes me sad. We're coming, though. When you get to be as old as I am and have a history, you see the changes. I know it must be frustrating and hard for young people to see the changes, but we're becoming a lot more aware, in all things, I hope.

**JORDAN:** You sound like you really had special parents though.

**SEBESTYEN:** Oh, I did. My mother would yell at radio announcers and later television, "Don't tell me what I want, what I am, what I'm thinking!"

**JORDAN:** That's a struggle for so many women now as they seem to come into their own. It's like the fight with "mother and what she told me" and what I now believe I want to be.

**SEBESTYEN:** That's sad.

**JORDAN:** It is sad. I went to a conference once where a woman said—I'm sure she had to be at least forty—that she did not know any strong women growing up.

**SEBESTYEN:** That's sad!

**JORDAN:** Yes. That meant she didn't see her mother as strong or whoever was the female in her life as strong. I couldn't get that thought out of my head.

**SEBESTYEN:** Maybe she meant that in the sense of domineering or aggressive.

**JORDAN:** But she never said that, so I have to assume she really didn't know any strong women, however she defined strength. I wondered if she had finally seen some having clearly been in the process of examining her past, but she didn't say that either.

Do you envision black women becoming more integrated into the women's movement as common concerns such as child care and abortion bring women of all races closer?

**SEBESTYEN:** I should hope so. All those things women have in common and that humanity has in common all over the world. I can hope so.

**JORDAN:** What can black and white women teach each other about living and about writing?

**SEBESTYEN:** First, we can remind each other to concentrate on the universals that make us all human, to rejoice in our individuality, and to get out of the habit of labeling and comparing and other insidious divisions. Then we can share our differences in ways that enlarge us: "Now I know how you feel about that. Now I understand your background, or your history, or how to cook black-eyed peas." Enjoy each other in that way. As for writing, I think white writers tend to think black writers, black women writers especially, are closer to the heart of things, with a kind of intuitive largeness. A lot of white writers almost finger things to death, overmanipulating, trying to process life mentally instead of through feeling. We don't like to think a black writer might be closer to the realities. There are things we can learn from this. What can black writers learn from white women? [*Laughs*]

**JORDAN:** This question focuses on children and young people. When you see teenagers and children who do not know their own family histories, what kind of things ought to be done so that they gain control over their own voices to tell their stories? In other words, what can be done to help our children?

**SEBESTYEN:** I think we're on track with a lot of the creative writing that's going on now. It is so much more widely used than when I was growing up or even when my son was in school. That's if it is channeled wisely, a creative writing program can give everybody a chance to express feelings in a safe atmosphere. I see it around here—it's done beautifully—and it encourages students and their teachers. Now this may not be encouraged everywhere, and that can be devastating if it isn't done with pride and full acceptance. We need more television dramas, too, more movies, more historical things like *The Autobiography of Miss Jane Pittman* and *Roots*. We're hungry, the whole country is hungry for that sort of background. I always tell kids to seek out their grandparents, their uncles and aunts, elderly friends, and capture some of their stories before they're all gone. I beg them to put those reminiscences on tape, or listen and write them down, or have their grandparents write them down, because their stories are our roots. Parts of their backgrounds make up who we are, they formed us, so I hope oral histories are encouraged. We should be saving anything we can about our backgrounds.

**JORDAN:** It's not that children don't have stories, but sometimes we don't encourage them to say what they want to say.

**SEBESTYEN:** Yes, that's true. At school, I know it's hard. Teachers are rushed so that things that are artfully done by some talented students get the most attention; and when the other children don't, they may feel discouraged after trying so hard. I remind teachers it may not be the fluent ones or the ones who can dash off something in the twenty minutes you give them who are going to be writers someday and knock your socks off.

**JORDAN:** I suppose parents could tell more stories too and have the children tell more.

**SEBESTYEN:** Yes, just sit down and ask questions. My son keeps begging his dad who is Hungarian, "Make me tapes, tell me about the war and all the things about your past that I won't know when you die." It's sad because all of that will be lost. I wish kids could force their parents to sit down and talk to them. I'm trying to get my French neighbor to write the story of her life. She went through the occupation of Paris and she had the most exciting and horrifying adventures. She'd have a best-seller if she'd write it. At least a great gift for her children and grandchildren. It's a pity that stories of our past aren't told and treasured and valued. There is something that teachers could say to kids: "Please go home and find out from your parents."

**JORDAN:** When I supervise student teachers, I could encourage them to do that more too. Then they would go into their first teaching experience encouraging students to just write and, as you said, not to be worried about the writing being perfectly fluid, but just write it down.

**SEBESTYEN:** I tell kids: write it down on scratch paper, junk mail, anything, so you can think "I know I can throw this out. I can throw out two hundred pages like this if I don't like it," instead of being intimidated by that beautiful white page.

**JORDAN:** Have you ever felt pressure from your publisher, editor, or audience to portray a particular character or to treat a special set of themes or have you remained free of such pressures?

**SEBESTYEN:** I have the most wonderful editor who says, "Do whatever feels right. Take your time and let it grow until it feels right." She's never pressured me, and I'm so shy that I don't show her anything. I don't even talk about what I'm working on until I'm almost finished or am finished. Then she sees it, so I don't feel pressure from anybody. She does say, "You do historical books so well." Maybe she's hinting.

**JORDAN:** I need to be reminded that you don't necessarily get the writing right the first or second time.

**SEBESTYEN:** Oh heavens, no! I'm so bad at that. I make a terrible mess the first two or three times. I rewrote my last book three times. It gets harder. The last book was about a girl in a cellar, and I said if I had known I was going to be in the cellar with her for three years, I would have had her marooned on some tropical isle. [*Laughs*] But it's okay. If it doesn't work out the first time, it's all right. I'd like to have the kind of mind that's clear and serene so that I could sit down and write something beautiful in one draft. Maybe that will come.

**JORDAN:** Well, I needed to hear that because I get impatient and I then become frustrated and might stop for a while.

**SEBESTYEN:** Always think, about whatever you put down whether it turns out to be right or not, that you have a crystal now to begin to grow from and without that you wouldn't have anything. Whatever you have done is worthwhile and important. If it turns out not to be the final thing you want to say, that's still okay. It's coming.

**JORDAN:** What's the responsibility of the reader in the creative process?

**SEBESTYEN:** I think it's about half and half. I think a writer has to be a juggler or game player who puts down certain words and triggers a response and hopes that each word will trigger the response he or she wants. Then the reader brings his or her half— the experiences and memories and emotions the writer aroused— and together they've made the book.

**JORDAN:** Are there ever uses for stereotypes in fiction—perhaps to introduce a character to the reader or to point out the dangers of such attitudes?

**SEBESTYEN:** [*Pauses*] If it's a very minor character, someone that you just need for technical reasons to move the plot, a stereotype . . . well, even that's scary. But I'm thinking of a character that you can describe quickly in a line, and people will think, "Okay, I know that." In other words, the stereotype is more like shorthand, and you're not going to use it except to get someone on the train or something like that. A stereotype has more ramifications for me. As a writer—it can mean I'm being trite or using clichés. But to use it in a belittling way, I don't think there's ever an excuse for that. But in the sense of, "Oh yeah, I got a picture of that guy in those three words," that's okay. When it is someone you're hurrying through the plot, that's okay. You understand what I mean?

**JORDAN:** But you don't want a central character to be one or one who plays a major role in the novel to be one?

**SEBESTYEN:** If they're important enough to use in your book, they're important enough to be individuals who are as unique and detailed and wonderful and special in their living and breathing as you can possibly make them.

**JORDAN:** In writing *Words by Heart* and *On Fire,* was one character more difficult to develop than another for reasons other than race, sex, class, or age?

**SEBESTYEN:** I guess Miss Chism was a little difficult because she's ambivalent herself. At the time, I was also cleaning house for a Miss Chism, and I didn't want to bodily put her into my book, but I needed a character somewhat like her. So I was trying to be careful not to just pick her up and put her in because real people never fit. And the father of the boys—I couldn't kill him off because you can't do that to people you don't know what to do with. It's not allowed. [*Laughs*] I had to stop that book and grow a little before I knew what to say about him. But the others just seemed to come. It's wonderful. Sometimes the characters flow into your head and you know who they are and what they're like. Do your writers ever tell you that something is working through them instead of from them?

**JORDAN:** Oh yes, yes.

**SEBESTYEN:** It's kind of mystic. It's exciting and it's scary.

**JORDAN:** One writer said sometimes you don't know exactly where a character is going to take you, but it's always rewarding and fun to have gone with the character.

**SEBESTYEN:** I hear that a lot from writers. I'm always afraid to start out that way. Some writers say, "Hey, wonder what's going to happen today." I need to know from the beginning what's at the end so I can write toward it. Otherwise I wander too far off. But I think it would be kind of exhilarating to just take off after a character.

**JORDAN:** How would you define uses of memory in either novel? The two young men in *On Fire* do quite a bit of remembering.

**SEBESTYEN:** I think all characters come alive as we know more about them. Anything they can tell us without bringing the plot to a halt makes them more sympathetic. If I'm writing about the universal themes that we all share—fears and concerns about growing up, losing loved ones, self-worth—then I try to put in as much as I can without slowing things down.

**JORDAN:** When your writing pulls you in one direction and speaking engagements pull you in another, how do you resolve the conflict?

**SEBESTYEN:** First of all, I lead as simple a life as I possibly can. I can cut out a lot of things when I'm writing. I can tell people I don't speak unless my publisher actually sends me off to something fancy, a convention or something. In that case, I drop the book, write a speech, press my clothes, and go.

I try to keep a lot of notes so that after the interruption, I can go back and gather my thoughts. Also I can reread if I've been away from the book, go back several pages to get the tone and the speed and the mood in mind again. I spread my notes all around. Sometimes I can grasp it again and sometimes I can't, so I do something else: walk, read, work in the garden, do the dishes. I get wonderful ideas doing the dishes. Finally, I'm back into it.

**JORDAN:** Despite the murder of Ben Sills at the end of *Words by Heart*, the novel ends on an optimistic note. Have you considered going back and writing another novel to see what happens to Lena or some of her offspring later in life?

**SEBESTYEN:** A lot of kids ask me that, and adults do too. Right now, I don't know what happens to her. It's a fascinating idea, but I don't know where to put her next. Do I make her twenty? Then she's not the same little girl everybody's read about. Anybody reading the first book and then saying, "Hey, I'll get the sequel," would have such a leap to take. But if I had her only one year older, I really don't know of anything large enough she could be doing at that time that wouldn't be anticlimactic. Someone else would have to die, or something else very important would have to happen. Technically, I just can't see what to do or what age to make her. But occasionally I think about it.

**JORDAN:** Telling the story, however, though the eyes of Lena and then those of Sammy was particularly effective. Did you ever think of telling the story from an omniscient narrative point of view or first-person point of view rather than limited omniscient?

**SEBESTYEN:** Not for either of these two books. I thought I could get inside the characters even though I wasn't using first person. I could get into their minds if I would ask myself, "Would they say this? Would they use that word?" I was always trying to talk for them even though I was in the third person. In both cases these two characters seemed to be the ones feeling the most emotions, having the most things happen to them to react to, and were the ones creating answers to or solutions for the problems that the world heaped on them. And they seemed to be the ones who spoke from a kind of innocence about something that wasn't innocent. I think that kind of juxtaposition makes a book strong and striking, but it couldn't have been done in first person because they wouldn't have known they were innocent.

JORDAN: I just thought about if *On Fire* had been told from Tater's point of view, what a wicked, violent novel!

SEBESTYEN: Yes. After I got the reviews from *Words by Heart,* many reviewers went right along with me calling the Haneys: shiftless, vengeful, ignorant sharecroppers. And I said, "Wait a minute. They had a life too, even if I just snatched them out of the air to be my villains." I was startled that everybody agreed with me without wondering how these people became who they were. I had to write *On Fire* to get to know them and find out what happened to them.

JORDAN: As I was reading *On Fire,* I found myself thinking in relation to Tater, "Why am I so concerned about this boy? This is not right!" But I couldn't help myself.

SEBESTYEN: I felt the same way. I thought, "I'm switching loyalties from the first wonderful family that I felt deeply about."

JORDAN: Once you get to know the person, there's a way in which just knowing them makes them human in a way that they hadn't been, so you just care.

SEBESTYEN: Of course, that's the whole point. That happens to all of us. Once we understand, we care.

JORDAN: I guess that's what Ben Sills would say too.

SEBESTYEN: Yes, I think so.

JORDAN: I also thought that the setting was one of the distinctive features of the work because you explored black life in a particular region of the country that had not been examined—the move West rather than North, particularly in 1910. What determined your selection of this setting?

**SEBESTYEN:** The West is really the only part of the country that I know. I knew that I could be comfortable writing about it. It's interesting that people have set the book everywhere from Kansas, to Oklahoma, and eastern Colorado. I wanted them to put it where they wanted it to be. In fact, when they did the television drama, they called it Missouri, and that's fine with me. But in my mind, it's set in and around where I grew up in Texas. I wanted to use familiar surroundings so I could be accurate about what was growing, and so I put in some little knolls and hills from my childhood because I had seen snakes there and I knew snakes could scare Lena. Drawing from memory makes the plot move because if you are sure of something you're not afraid to use it.

**JORDAN:** When Lena learned that the gift for the contest winner had been preselected, Ben Sills handles what is probably Lena's first recognizable bout with racism very well. And even though Lena doesn't fully understand the racism involved, she has a wise, supportive father who will guide her through her problems. For too many children today, this is not the case. Do you have any thought on how parents today, regardless of color, may help children deal with prejudices concerning, for example, race, sex, weight?

**SEBESTYEN:** Parents have to teach by example, and if they haven't learned it themselves, you've got a losing case. It's pathetic that we move on from generation to generation permitting this lack of concern and lack of awareness. I think we have to somehow bring up sensitive, empathetic children who can reach out into another person's feelings and think, "Wait! That could hurt so I won't say it or do it." Now a lot of us just are too busy or self-centered, too worried about material things, or we don't know what to say. It's never been said to us, so how can we know? It's a dilemma. I don't know how we can turn things around.

**JORDAN:** Well, they need to read your books for one thing. That would help.

**SEBESTYEN:** Well, writers do help, I think. I know children often read a certain book, and carry some part of it on through their lives, but even an inspiring example or idea can be dislodged by somebody's putting it down. I do hope we're coming into some wider understanding of our common humanness. We are one family, and people aren't all that different in their basic needs, wants, and emotions, but that when we are different, that's exciting and fun.

**JORDAN:** I think *On Fire* would be such a great novel to teach because in terms of prejudices there are several different groups that are discriminated against. This group is fighting for this and another for that. In some ways—at least for Tater and probably for Sammy—these different groups start to become people in their own right. The book goes far beyond the black/white conflict— which people do at least recognize—and looks at a number of forms of prejudice whites heap upon each other.

**SEBESTYEN:** I hope teachers will use it that way.

**JORDAN:** After the contest and the return home, Claudie tells Ben, "Tonight she pushed a white town too fast. She overstepped herself just like you're always doing." I admire Ben Sills's courage, but at times I, like Claudie, feel afraid for the Ben Sillses of the world. Would you describe Ben Sills as in any way an idealist, or is his philosophy of living one that is practical and realistic?

**SEBESTYEN:** I think he is an idealist, a too-good-to-be-true sort of person who probably would be ineffectual in any place except that small place where he is. He thinks everyone in the world ought to be living by high ideals. I know he's exaggerated, but I think people are hungry for him. Some even seem to regret that his philosophy is too difficult for real life. They accept him as an ideal father figure—maybe the father they would like to have. Or they see something of their father or grandfather or somebody that they love in him so they accept him.

**JORDAN:** Well, I thought that as a father figure, he was wonderful and that he was the kind of father that if you had him for twelve years of your life, you'd really be ready to deal with the world in a way that you might not if you had had a bad father for fifty years.

**SEBESTYEN:** Well, I wanted him to be special, and as you were saying, I did have a wonderful father—a very kind and gentle sort of person. I may have been making a kind of memorial to him. He had died about ten years before I started the book. Since I didn't get to say last things to him, I guess I made an idealized father in memoriam.

**JORDAN:** I just left the novel feeling that Lena will be just fine for the rest of her life because she was Ben Sills's daughter.

**SEBESTYEN:** At the end, I tried to leave my characters in a state of balance so a reader knows at this point they've changed and are strong enough to go on no matter what happens. Kids need to have upbeat endings and hope because they've vulnerable and a lot of them haven't experienced much in their own lives. Sometimes they have to be shown in an obvious way that in spite of all the tragedies of life, wonderful things will balance them out.

**JORDAN:** But the endings aren't sentimentalized. You know that the characters are going to be all right. They still have problems, but it's okay.

**SEBESTYEN:** At this point, we see that they've just reached the top of one mountain with other mountains all around them, but still they're higher.

**JORDAN:** Lena goes to Miss Chism's home to "cheer her up" when she learns her dinner party failed. How would you describe both characters as they interact in this scene?

**SEBESTYEN:** Miss Chism is probably sorry, bitter, and thinking in terms of "Look at all this food that's wasted and all the cleaning up we did and nobody came." I think she was feeling so sorry for herself that Lena's efforts at kindness seemed like a rebuff. I hope she reacted like a child.

**JORDAN:** She did.

**SEBESTYEN:** Poor Miss Chism. Like a lot of people, her first reaction is to be paternalistic toward these somehow inferior people she doesn't quite know what to do with—now that they have invaded her world. And she is a naturally gregarious old lady who likes to have Lena's company, and yet she has to consider what the rest of the town will think of her.

**JORDAN:** I thought that in a number of ways, little Lena understood Miss Chism better than Miss Chism understood herself and anybody else.

**SEBESTYEN:** Oh yes. I think so. Being an outsider gave Lena a larger view in a sense. Miss Chism was beginning to like this child and yet knew she wasn't supposed to like this child.

**JORDAN:** Do you think she changes even a little by the end of the novel?

**SEBESTYEN:** Yes, she's softened up, but she doesn't want anybody to know it. She's much more aware of the Sillses as people, but she still doesn't know what to do with them and she tells them, "You people make me so mad." She means "perplexed" because she realizes she is on their side now.

**JORDAN:** Mrs. Haney had a haunting silence for me. One line says, "She watched in silence honing what energy she had for growing babies." She doesn't speak much, but when Sammy says he is going to find Tater, she does finally tell him to go on. In some ways she seems like a woman who wants to make herself invisible. I'm not sure if she is an abused wife, but she certainly is neglected and in that sense is abused. How did this silent, yet powerfully drawn character evolve?

**SEBESTYEN:** Probably I saw her face in one of Dorothea Lange's photographs. She looks like one of those women. And I knew women like her. You hear about them in little towns, always on the edge somewhere, having to move and you never see them again. Probably she was just someone out of my memory or a composite of people I knew or had seen on the street. There is no reason for her to speak. She's not carrying the plot. She's just carrying it in the sense that her shadow is there, suggesting what they all feel: that they are of no importance.

**JORDAN:** She is just such a contrast to her husband when he's drinking. He strikes me as loud only when he has had some help from the bottle. He probably could have been a nice person if it had not been for lack of money.

**SEBESTYEN:** All the characters could have been wonderful with help. They try hard, and I hope I give them a little core of something beyond the ordinary, something spiritual.

**JORDAN:** That's true even of Mr. Haney. It really didn't surprise me that he killed himself.

**SEBESTYEN:** It really was a surprise to me. I didn't know it until I heard about it from his family. [*Laughs*]

**JORDAN:** I usually get upset over suicide, but the boys had my attention. At that point, suicide was a relief from the other emotional dramas of the story. I was so concerned that Tater was really going to kill Mr. Stoker because he clearly was not thinking and he was not exactly in control of his feelings. Therefore, he had the perfect excuse to vent his frustrations on some innocent person. At that point, the father was dead. There was nothing else he could do, so finally the mother was able to move on. I was just pleased they [the boys] didn't kill Mr. Stoker.

**SEBESTYEN:** You sound like the ideal reader.

**JORDAN:** Well, I try to get into the work and go with it. Thank you. This has been wonderful.

# CYNTHIA VOIGT

■

PHOTO BY WALTER VOIGT

*Cynthia Voigt was a high-school English teacher for nearly twenty years before she published her first young adult novel,* Homecoming, *in 1981. Within five years, she had published nine other young adult novels, several of which trace the lives of the Till-ermans, four fatherless children, aged six through thirteen, who are eventually abandoned by their mentally unstable mother. In* Dicey's Song, *which received the Newberry Award in 1987, Voigt explores the life of the oldest child, Dicey Tillerman, and "her emerging un-derstanding of her new life and her relationship with her siblings and grandmother."*

*Voigt's other young adult novels include:* Tell Me If the Lovers Are Losers *(1982),* The Callendar Papers *(1983),* A Solitary Blue *(1983),* Building Blocks *(1984),* The Runner *(1985),* Jackeroo *(1985),* Izzy-Willy Nilly *(1986), and* Come a Stranger *(1987).*

*No longer a full-time teacher, Voigt lives in Maine where she devotes her time to her family and writing.*

**JORDAN:** What specific conditions seem to be in place when black and white women become friends?

**VOIGT:** Here's what has been crossing my mind, and I think it's black and white; I don't know if it's peculiar to women. Although I think women are more resilient than men about these things, it has to do with being involved in a common endeavor. When you're working with someone, you work with them regardless of race, color, or creed, and they are there as people in the same field or with the same objectives or whatever that you have. As I was thinking, of course, of Dicey and Mina, I realized they were in school together, and I consider a classroom a common endeavor.

**JORDAN:** What do you think it is about the two people once they're involved in that common endeavor that allows them to become closer?

**VOIGT:** I think a common endeavor probably means you're going to be exposed to one another: you're going to simply see one another. One often tends to become friendly and chatty. If you're going to become friends, you become friendly with neighbors because you see one another, and it's not entirely one's personality or character. I think it's the same reason why it's harder to become friends once you're out of school. Most people will say that the time when they made friends with the most various kinds is when they were in school together because there they had this common endeavor, whereas when I meet people now—especially since I'm not teaching—I feel as if I only have myself to bring to the occasion. You invite people to dinner, or you run into them, or you make a point of seeing them, and there's no common ground. Somehow you have to construct it, and it's harder, I think, to make friends when you have to set up bridge-gates, which we don't do, in order to achieve the exposure that'll enable us to know one another. It's knowing one another and having the occasion to know one another. Having worked with my second husband before I took up with him, I think it's all very revealing. You really know the people you work with, so that's why I think it goes that way.

**JORDAN:** What kind of role does the black female play in white women's novels? What kind of role does the white female play in the black woman's novel?

**VOIGT:** The only white woman's novels that I have read of late is that wonderful woman who's seventy-two years old in England, Mary Wesley. Part of my problem is that I think books that are good are good regardless of race, gender, whatever categories you can put them into. I don't have in my memory any novels where black women appear. . . . I don't think they do appear in one another's books that much.

**JORDAN:** Not often.

**VOIGT:** That seems to me to be the role of absence. *The Women of Brewster Place*—I don't think there are any white characters in there.

**JORDAN:** No, I can't think of any.

**VOIGT:** So I would say absence or unimportance when we talk about friendship. Well that's interesting, isn't it?

**JORDAN:** Yes, especially the notion of the role of absence, which I hadn't thought about as much as I have what the actual presence might signify. It's easier to find white women novelists who will have black female characters. Maybe they aren't protagonists but they are semi-important in the work.

**VOIGT:** Or they are real people in the work.

**JORDAN:** Right. They play a special role in the work nevertheless. But it is harder to find white female characters in black women's novels.

**VOIGT:** But there's something exclusionary about it.

**JORDAN:** Yes. Do you think that this kind of pattern will change in which black female novelists portray white females more frequently?

**VOIGT:** I would certainly hope so. When it does happen, I will take that as a sign because seeing one another as "woman beings" for good or ill seems to me to be what all of us need more practice in. But I wonder how much of it is the publishing tradition. Are there any black characters in Judith Krantz and Janet Daly? I can't think of any. I'm thinking in terms of Harlequin romances and Sweet Valley Highs. I don't know how low your reading sinks. The Society of American Murder Mystery tends to be more inclusive in terms of color. And in kids' literature a greater variety of characters appear. It's almost as if it [race] is only a question of interest to younger people, as if it's something schoolchildren are supposed to wrestle down—all our theories and feelings about blacks and whites and race. And then when they get out of school—like so many other things—they get into the real world like nothing matters.

**JORDAN:** I had not thought about the murder mystery connection. I had thought, of course, about young adult novelists because both black and white women seem to cross over in terms of exploring race relations more frequently than "adult" novelists do.

**VOIGT:** Well, the children's field, which includes young adults, is always much more generous than the adult publishers seem in terms of categorizing. If Stephen King, for example, wanted to write *Moby Dick* or a reasonable facsimile, they wouldn't let him. I don't think it's a good thing. I know that Judy Blume published *Tiger Eyes*, which is unlike all her other children's books, and the kids let her do it—the kids read it in the same fierce numbers, and the publisher let her. But I'm not sure if Stephen King's readership would allow him. So the publisher clearly—what they perceive the market to be has something to do with what in fact gets published.

**JORDAN:** Have you ever felt pressure from your publisher and/ or audience to portray a particular kind of character or to treat a particular set of themes, or have you remained free of such concerns?

**VOIGT:** I am very much free to write in whatever genre, and I hope that I've said it often enough that everyone knows I'm grateful because both publisher and readership get credit for that. Every now and then someone will suggest a book that needs to be written and will say, "Do this one next." That's the closest thing to anybody putting pressure on me, and that's just sort of a suggestion. It's always interesting to hear suggestions because they're very revealing, and over and over again I've heard one of my books should have a sequel, which I originally thought didn't have one. But pressure in terms of "should I write something that will enable or improve race relations?" for example? Never, never at all.

**JORDAN:** As you were drawing the character of Mina, were there particular concerns you had about the portrait you wanted to produce? In other words, how was this figure born? What do you think of her?

**VOIGT:** I think she's terrific. She was actually born in *Dicey's Song*, and she was so clearly the most vigorous, the strongest person in Dicey's peer group—I hate that phrase—that to earn her friendship was proof that my character was working in a sense . . . which is a horrible way to say it. When I first thought of her, it was necessary that she be vivid and strong and at ease with herself in ways that Dicey wasn't, partly for contrast and for some reason, it never crossed my mind that she would not be black. In my imagination she is a strong, dark figure, and the dark skin seems to breathe with a sense of vitality and strength. Isn't that wild? That's a stereotype of a different kind. It's still a stereotype, isn't it?

**JORDAN:** It is. I have a follow-up question on that comment, but do go on.

**VOIGT:** And then of course she was so wonderful in *Dicey's Song* that it seemed to me because she was female and strong and black in that order probably, she was bound to get herself into trouble because the world is not well suited to such people. And so, of course, I wanted to write a book about her. It seemed to me that this is the kind of character that was interesting and surprising and one could love. A heroic character—that's what she is.

**JORDAN:** Are there ever uses for stereotypes—perhaps to introduce a character or to point out the danger of such thinking?

**VOIGT:** I would think so. I don't think things get to be stereotypes or clichés without somehow or other touching a standard response in a whole mess of people. As a teacher, I've never gone through and said, "This is a cliché, this is a cliché, take it out!" It's not a kind of critical reading I've ever done well. Maybe archetype is what I mean. That phrase stereotype implies two-dimensionality. An archetype defines a kind of mythic truth to the characters. The ones that really live in my memory are what they are in themselves in their particular details—but somehow they are also all the rest of us.

JORDAN: Or what all the rest of us want to be.

VOIGT: Yes. Well, that's what all the rest of us are in a funny way. Never mind all the constant failure. So maybe a stereotype is just when an archetype doesn't succeed. An archetype like Ahab.

JORDAN: To what extent do you use sources, such as histories, biographies, or autobiographies, when you are developing a black female character? Is Mina straight from the imagination, or is she from some figure that you've known?

VOIGT: I'm not sure. I would say she's from the imagination because she's not anybody in particular. Although when I thought of her, I did as I often do for my own sense of visual reality. The person who was in my mind was a black girl I taught when she was in fourth grade, and I think fifth and sixth as well, who was large. When she was in fourth grade, she could pick me up and turn me around in circles. And she had that vibrant presence. She wasn't as bright and she wasn't as ambitious as Mina, but she was clearly strong and stable so that she was the first glimpse, and then I took that glimpse over and hopefully made it my own. I'm not sure. I know I don't do much research reading. I read as voluminously as the impulse strikes me. The only black biography of any sort I've read is Zora Neale Hurston's. However, you do run into things in reading anything that catches and hooks your imagination and stays in there.

JORDAN: What can black and white women teach each other about living and about writing?

VOIGT: The same thing any writer can teach: the art of being human. This character, Bullet, in *The Runner* whose attitude toward race certainly from the beginning is not what any liberal would approve of says at one point you have to honor the differences before you can use the similarities, and I think he's sort of my "spokescharacter" in this respect. I think because we are all human beings—and especially women—and women have much less trouble I think because everybody menstruates, which is a great equalizer. I've never had a female student terrified of me the way a female student might be of a male teacher or the way a male student might be fearful of a female teacher, but I don't know about that from my own experience. There's some basic thing that happens and you're not afraid of a female person. I think black and white women are aware of this, and I think—for myself at least—one of the things I realize is that because their experience has not been favored sociologically and socially speaking—black women have a lot more of the characteristics that I admire in people: a certain amount of fortitude, sturdiness, and grit. One author quoted Toni Morrison as saying that black women know so much more about how to be aggressive than white women do. That kind of thing strikes me as extremely correct—that they are more aware of how women can be and are victimized by individuals or society and have been wrestling with that for longer and understand the terms of the battle more clearly than do white women, who are barely able to sometimes admit that this victimization exists. Whether or not white women have anything to offer black women writers? [*Pauses*] I don't know. I'm thinking and I can't think of anything. . . .

**JORDAN:** Maybe this next question will help there. Assuming that there still is a women's movement, do you envision black women becoming more integrated into the women's movement as common concerns such as child care and abortion bring women of all races closer?

**VOIGT:** Now what was in my mind as an area of my own ignorance is the assumption that black women are not involved with the women's movement, which I don't know. It is probably more of a matter of class than color. The women's movement comes out of the middle class I would think, and it's economically based with so many single parents, so that I can see a middle-class black woman with the education and the training and the profession being more aware of the issues of the women's movement than a black woman who hasn't had the advantages of education, profession, whatever it is. I wonder how much that has to do with it. I love these ideas because I learn from them. In *The Women of Brewster Place* only one of them is at all issue oriented. And that's the girl who has moved from Linden Hills. The rest are survival oriented.

JORDAN: When you look at young children and teenagers who often do not know their own family histories and do not have or know the words to voice their experiences or what they see, what kinds of things do you think ought to be done to help them gain control over their own voices to appreciate their stories and their personal histories?

VOIGT: [Pauses] Again I know where it ought to come from. It ought to come from education, and it ought to come from the family, and it ought to come from the society as a whole. And I have to admit that numbers one and three are extremely hypocritical. What they say they want is one thing, but what they in fact do seems to work against children growing up to be themselves first and, to fit in, second. And part of being yourself is to know your own story. Now the family seems, to me, under attack.

I had an argument over lunch with my daughter and a friend of mine. When my daughter was in middle adolescence, our house rule was that the ground floor is the public place and the upstairs is the private part, and she was not supposed to have gentlemen callers upstairs. And all her friends were appalled by that, as was my friend, as was my daughter feeling that that was the only place a child could have to herself. Now I knock on my kids' doors before I go into their room. I am allowed in, however, and that was compared to my study where people can knock on the door and come in and do often come in without my permission. But it was as if I should not have this inviolable sense of space of my own, that kids couldn't have it because they were powerless. That whole family structure was a power question. Based on power and not on love was what I was thinking at the end of the whole thing. There's something screwy in that because it seems to me that the family unit is the one that should be the safe place for people. And, of course, so often it isn't. And the most stunning example, of course, is abused children. But there are seventy-eight flavors of abuse, and some of them wear very pleasant faces. So here I am thinking, "Wait a minute. Wait a minute. Privacy is important. Mine is important. Yours is important. It's not inviolable. It's not a terrible thing I'm doing to you. As an adult, I'm supposed to make the decisions partly because I pay the bills and partly because I'm the grown-up." And yet that was interpreted by the other two as being a question of not giving the kids power, depriving them of self-governing or whatever. But as a teacher and a parent you're supposed to train people to be able to grow up and be independent. They aren't born knowing it, and we don't train them to be independent at seven or two or whatever. And it's a great shuffling off of responsibility to do it because, of course, responsibility hurts so that whole question in my mind is what is it exactly that we expect the family to do. And what do we hope for from it, and to what extent are adults refusing to honor their obligations and responsibilities? The notion of any number of men not making child-support payments, or the notion of the way a single woman's income falls to 23 percent of what it was whereas the man's falls to 79 percent of what it was in the case of divorce is just one little bit of it. And you know what else throws me on the same subject are things like that *Doogie Howser, M.D.*, show because here's a kid who's supposed to be a grown-up and better than the grown-ups. It just drives me crazy. All those things work against kids learning their own stories, their own selves, and they're the very things that are supposed to work for it. End of that little speech. That one touched a nerve, didn't it?

**JORDAN:** The thing is you and your daughter could talk about these things, and for so many children they wouldn't have the opportunity. Or maybe they have the opportunity but their parents aren't open to talking with them about what they think of the rules, so that silence stifles the child's ability or willingness to speak at all, I suppose, until much later.

**VOIGT:** Well, my daughter is nineteen, and she feels that she was stifled. And here we thought we were doing good responsible things. All of her friends had no curfews—came in any time of the day or night, had anyone sleeping in their bed for as long as they wanted. Is it necessary for kids to feel stifled? She did turn around and yell at us (which she only did once), and she feels it was quite late. I think it was wonderful that she did it because she's the oldest child and she's female, which mitigates against her in that respect. It's important for kids to feel rebellious and to be able to enact their rebellion, and if you have strict rules, of course, they can do themselves less damage and still be effectively rebellious. It's the kind of thing you can only discover in hindsight. I don't know.

**JORDAN:** Probably, and for some people the hindsight comes at forty, some at fifty.

VOIGT: Some at fifteen, and some never. That was interesting.

JORDAN: Do you see literary critics, particularly black ones, having a special role in shaping how stories of black women's lives are read, assessed, and taught?

VOIGT: Obviously. You can see it in the reviews of a book. A book that's uncomfortable takes a while. The first couple of reviews are sort of tenuous—most of them in the *Booklist*—until they [the critics] see how people are going to roll on it. And then they become clearer. I'd love to see a whole new school of critics come up. The difference between British and American reviews at their very best is very interesting. I'd like to see critics deal with the substance of a piece of work—what the argument of a work is. And I think if they would then they would enable better teaching. I think in certain colleges, there's a sort of canon literary approach.

JORDAN: Very much so.

VOIGT: Very much so, and I think James Baldwin may now be on it, and I suppose Toni Morrison probably is, and Alice Walker maybe in some areas, but I would imagine that's about it. Langston Hughes occasionally.

JORDAN: Yes. Maybe *Native Son* sometimes gets read.

VOIGT: But *Native Son* is so uncomfortable. I read it as a young person, and then my daughter read it when she was a junior, and I picked it up and read over the first chapter, and it knocked me out. I remembered the scene but not how vivid it was, and then I saw the movie and that was good too. So yes, maybe *Native Son*, although Richard Wright lost face quarreling with James Baldwin. . . . But that's not a very representative number, and how many of those come under the category black or female as a course heading? But critics seem to be more interested in their own ideas than in making successes. They're looking to make a discovery like art critics. But the point is all that playing it safe makes for worse criticism. Critics are probably the first step because they are the line between the individual book and the public, and I don't know how many black critics there are.

**JORDAN:** Not enough, of course.

**VOIGT:** There are some?

**JORDAN:** There are some.

**VOIGT:** And do they publish in black-only publications?

**JORDAN:** Sometimes, but they publish in very well known publications too.

**VOIGT:** Yes, name brands.

**JORDAN:** Generally that's true, and they are people who've published quite a bit already, so the name is already well known.

**VOIGT:** Like the *New York Times*, where you can tell you're in a certain professional status if they ask you to write a review.

**JORDAN:** Yes, that's usually right. Let me ask more specific questions about the texts. Was one character more difficult to develop for any reason other than age, race, or sex?

**VOIGT:** I can name some that were harder to construct rather than easier. Alice was hard to construct. Tamer appears in an earlier book as well. I think he's just a wonderful man, so I had to be careful not to sort of wallow. He was wonderful because everything he came into I enjoyed. I seem to have trouble with the vapid, bad-mother female type, but I don't remember any of them being particularly hard.

**JORDAN:** Was there anything Mina's parents could have done differently to soften the blow of racism during her second summer?

**VOIGT:** I think there are things you can't protect your children against. And I think what you do is just make sure that they know that they can come home and tell you the truth. Then you really have ultimately protected them because they won't then be destroyed by it. If they told her ahead of time—and her father hinted at it a couple of times—that there was something dubious about her presence there. For the first summer the information she got told her her father was wrong, and she can only work with the information she gets. So I don't think there's anything they could have done except to make sure it didn't turn out to be a body blow to her and to destroy her.

JORDAN: Does it matter that Mina and Dicey—not as much Mina—are both outsiders in terms of their being able to find each other?

VOIGT: Yes, I think so. That's a question that's been raised about my work frequently, and it's time for me to address it. Mina is an extraordinary person. She has more talent and more life and more ability than most of her classmates. Dicey also has more talent and more life and more ability, but it doesn't come out the same way that Mina's does, so she doesn't have the same easy social go. But I would think that's one of the things they recognize in one another. Both of them are in danger of getting their own way for the wrong reason. Either one of them could turn into a real bully. People of more than usual strength have to recognize that it's a danger as well as a strength and to seek out friends who will not let them bully them, who can stand up to them and knock them down occasionally. And I think both Mina and Dicey have that so in a sense they are outsiders. Mina, of course, is an outsider whom everyone else wants to be like—the Queen or something. Classes have queens, and I sort of think of her as the queen of her class, and Dicey is the one whom nobody wants to be but no one is surprised to see on the cover of *Time* magazine in later years. But none of them is really mainstream in that limited sense—although my theory is that no one is mainstream in that limited sense. That's one thing that my teaching taught me.

JORDAN: I do have one question about Mina in terms of conformity. Does her wanting to be accepted by the white girls at camp also suggest that to some degree she is experiencing some feelings of inferiority to them—whether it's in terms of not having as much money as well as in terms of skin color?

VOIGT: If we talk about the second summer—the first summer she sort of gets by with the grace that children have—I'm not sure she wants to conform or that she has a sense of inferiority or whether she has a sense that there are measures that you want to be measured with. For example, take a woman in a man's world. Now do women look for success because they feel inferior or maybe they value or overvalue success and that's why they look for it? I suspect that anywhere the difference is so immediate, as in male/female, black/white, young/old relations—sometimes I'm not sure how I would understand the desire to be honored by the other group—could it be a question of conformity or a sense of your own inferiority or is it a sense of superiority that you can in fact stand up and do well by anybody's measures? It could be any one. And in Mina's case, she doesn't think of herself as inferior. What she runs into that summer is a fire-engine hose of the society's perception of things that she has luckily been innocent of until then. It's confusing and it's distressing, but I don't think she takes it in that sense personally. I could be kidding myself.

**JORDAN:** Is Mrs. Maddington right in suggesting that perhaps Mina should not have been allowed to attend camp without the presence of other blacks? Would such a strategy perhaps lessen Mina's initial feeling that she'd only been chosen as a token rather than on the basis of her talent? Would it have mattered really to have had another black or two around?

**VOIGT:** That I don't know because I'm not sure she would work herself past that "the only reason you. . . ." She was certainly surprised when the tennis coach told her that she had natural coordination and grace because she had taken the woman's word for it, which is not like her. I did that on purpose because I think it's important when someone does something that is not like her. But would she have? It's the minority question, isn't it? What are we supposed to want to do with minorities? The Jews certainly—many of them—do not feel assimilation is any good. The American Indian is raising that question. The blacks must certainly feel that way, and then an equal number seem to feel assimilation is desirable because of the quality of life you achieve. And certainly it seems to me that if I were an Indian parent, I would move my family to the city or somewhere off the reservation simply because that's the life [life on the reservation] that is going to get in the way of my children growing into what they can be. Not that it's not good and not that you want to give anything up but that you don't want to not take something. So if there's one black girl there—I'm trying to think of this as the administrator of this dance camp—if there's a black girl there she will have a better chance of making one-on-one relationships with the white kids because she will be there on her own, which in a way makes it more possible for her to be herself in a funny way. It's like when you go to a dance with your girlfriend, you're more likely to meet people than when you go on your own. I'm not sure of the answer. There should have been more black kids there, I would think, but not one or three and not so that they would be isolated to themselves, which of course is the other danger of integration. People tend to cluster. . . .

JORDAN: I just thought that the observation on Mrs. Maddington's part showed a different side to her and that she perhaps was aware of how Mina was feeling. Maybe she had thought through some things but simply didn't have the answer.

VOIGT: Maybe that is her answer. I figured she had the wrong answers for things. She was not a reliable witness; that was my feeling because she would never talk to me the way she talked to a kid. I wouldn't anyway. You can think what you want to, but you don't say things like that to a kid. I don't know. You would certainly probably know a great deal more about this and what would work. The desired end is that people should be able to function totally within the society without losing this sense of self. Bring the best of what their background is into a position that everybody accepts and honors. How do you get there?

JORDAN: I don't know if the outcome was going to be that different for Mina, given her situation. She just simply was not the dancer that she was first year, and there's no getting around that either. Even if there were other blacks there, she still was going to have to deal with that question of whether or not she was a token.

VOIGT: Right. And if there had been other blacks there . . . then at least . . .

JORDAN: And even if there were other blacks there, there was no guarantee that they would have necessarily befriended her anyway, or that she would have befriended them.

VOIGT: Right, or that they would have shown her that it was in fact her own growth pattern, not her color. One of the titles I thought of for this book had to do with the W. B. Yeats line about the chestnut tree, "How can you tell the dancer from the dance?" separating herself from the dance. That is one of the errors that I think Mrs. Maddington made somehow or other. If Mina has to leave because she can't dance, that should be one clear thing, but if her color gets brought into it, then suddenly it is not possible for it to be something you can grasp and understand and accept for the dancer.

**JORDAN:** That's another tough question.

**VOIGT:** I think she's faced the question of blackness—her own and of her people—her family, her friends, and all blacks. She's faced it, and she's integrated it, which means that she hasn't been knocked down by it. She hasn't wrestled it down but it's because it's part of her character. And I think everybody has to face that question—not always about the same subjects, and every group has their own particular things they have to face and integrate. Even white macho men have that, and every individual I think does. I think it's a good growth thing. It's one of the things you hope will happen when people grow up. The kid who is never going to get an A in your course even though he may like it and may be one of your most enthusiastic students and the most rewarding student and a student you really would like to know for the rest of his life, he's still never going to get an A, and he has to somehow integrate that. That [integration] is what I think she's done.

**JORDAN:** And she still likes herself.

**VOIGT:** And she still likes herself and still has it be an enabling, not a limiting, experience.

**JORDAN:** Is it not downright prejudice that keeps the Smiths and the church from accepting Maybeth into the choir? I was a bit disappointed in them.

**VOIGT:** Well, of course, but you couldn't have them be too heavenly, could you? One of the things that I wanted to do with this story—and I may be wrong but I like to think in part I achieved this—is to point out that we all have our prejudices. And it seemed to me quite reasonable that the parents certainly would be more aware of racial differences than the kids were. This is something I think is happening in America—that my daughter is much less aware of them [racial prejudices] than I am, and I than my parents, and one hopes that things will get better and better for everybody as things go on. Only time will do some of the work for us. With the best of intentions, only time can do it, and it seemed to me the Smiths had come pretty far along. It wasn't that they themselves didn't want her there. It was that they recognized the social situation made it impossible for them [to accept her in the church]. The church unit—the black unit—would not be able to accept her. And I must admit I rather liked that because otherwise blacks are just always the victims of it, and I can't believe that.

**JORDAN:** Well, the rejection of Maybeth was realistic but nevertheless disappointing.

**VOIGT:** I'm glad it was realistic. My working premise is that we're all pretty much alike. When I was growing up in Fairfield, Connecticut, there was a small residual problem with Catholics. Never mind Jews and blacks. They weren't even considered, right? So I know something of which I speak.

**JORDAN:** I wasn't surprised by their excluding Maybeth because I had some indication from the father's reaction to Dicey's grandmother already—that there were probably some prejudices there.

**VOIGT:** And mistrust.

**JORDAN:** Definitely mistrust, and it wasn't just because the grandmother had all these eccentricities. I knew that it was a little more than that.

**VOIGT:** So I foreshadowed okay?

**JORDAN:** Oh yes. Very much.

**VOIGT:** My theory, of course, is that that's why this is not a tragedy, but that's how tragedy works. The reader's will or hope goes in one direction, and the story goes where it has to go, which is in another direction. And that makes for a kind of tension that makes the story linger somehow. I love happy endings but most of them I forget . . . I can't recall the lines or the scenes.

**JORDAN:** What responsibility do readers have, if any, in the creative process?

**VOIGT:** I don't know if responsibility is the word. Sometimes I get letters from responsive readers who are able to let the story come to life. Maybe just to lay off and let it be is what I would call their responsibility. I think of it as a gift—you're lucky if you have it. In terms of teaching the books that I like to teach, I would put into a curriculum the ones that make that happen for the majority of the people in the class. You don't have to worry about the ready readers. They're going to fall in with all of it. It's the reluctant ones where you can have a book doing its part of the job—just luring them however unwillingly into it until they really care. I think it's the book's job to lure them, and the teacher's job to find the book. Once the book has taken a reluctant reader and made him ready, his chances for the next book are improved. But those readers for whom it just comes, I think a writer can only be grateful for readers like that.

**JORDAN:** When your writing pulls you in one direction and other concerns pull you in another, how do you resolve the conflict?

**VOIGT:** Badly. I don't know. I try to claim and own a part of my day in which I am supposed to be sitting down and writing, and after that time it can no longer be a first priority. It's a negotiated-settlement kind of approach. When they all went to school and I was home alone, that was fine. Then I simply had to stop at an appointed time and go out and teach my own class. Sometimes that was very easy to do. Once I even went to class and called a student by the name of my character, which wasn't his name. But that only happened once. I don't know that anybody follows those things well. It's always seemed to me that as long as I'm not greedy, I haven't had to give up being a mother or a teacher or a writer or a wife. And part of that is because I was willing to go on a part-time teaching schedule, and the school let me bring my kids with me when they were small, which is harder on me. It would have been fun to teach as many classes as I could, but you give up part of one thing to get the other. I was alone for six days this spring. They went south to settle on a house, and I was here all alone with the animals, and I realized that I could wake up in the morning and I could work. Then when my best working energies had faded I would do something else, and then I could go back to it all day long back and forth, and it was so conducive. My God! But you can't do that if you want to have a family. You can't ask them to do that for you. I don't think a family should be entirely subservient to any one member of it.

**JORDAN:** You've said a great deal just then. You have your priorities in order is what you are saying.

**VOIGT:** Well, it says that, and on paper I think I do, but you have to remember every day falls apart in its own way. It sounds good, and the occasions when it works it's wonderful. But sometimes it doesn't.

**JORDAN:** But you don't allow it to frustrate you either when it falls apart?

**VOIGT:** Well, no more than I can help. Of course, sometimes you can help more than you do. But I try not to. One of the things I try to be aware of is that as a child of my parents—who are not perfect unlike me—I have been lucky. I have been very fortunate, and I'm not even talking materially. I've never had to go to a job I didn't like. If people were treating me badly, I've always been free by circumstances and character to quit. I was a single parent, and we had very little money but we had enough to see us through. And I like my work, and I like my children. This is really lucky and to be ungrateful and greedy seems to me foolish.

**JORDAN:** You have been such a help to me in putting things in the proper perspective.

**VOIGT:** I like my writing . . . the ideas are interesting. Women. The issues that women face are worth thinking about. I think women should be starting up industries. Enough of this stuff where industries say we can't afford to do day care, and we can't afford to do flex time, and we can't afford to do maternity leave. I think that's a bunch of garbage, and I think women should simply start their own industries. Make their own cars. That's been going through my mind for the past couple of years. Let's just get on with it. It's going to have to happen anyway. I don't know why they're dragging their heels. So to think about women and then to think about black women who face the same problems intensified in many ways but in many ways they bring more abilities to them, it's very interesting.

# MILDRED PITTS
# WALTER

■

*A native of Louisiana, Mildred Pitts Walter taught in the Los An-*
*geles schools in the 1960s, and her husband, the late Earl Walter,*
*was that city's chairman of the Congress of Racial Equality*
*[CORE]. As members of CORE, they worked with the American*
*Civil Liberties Union and the NAACP to file* Crawford *versus the*
Los Angeles Board of Education *in 1968, a case they hoped would*
*end segregation in their public school system.*

*Mildred Walter's activism and her novel* The Girl on the Outside *were inspired by Grace Larch's courageous actions during the 1957 desegregation crisis in Little Rock, Arkansas.* The Girl on the Outside, *the focus of this interview, was chosen as a Notable Children's Trade Book in the field of Social Studies in 1982 and as the* Christian Science Monitor Best Book of 1982.

*Though very active in political causes during the sixties, Walter, born in 1924, is now a full-time writer and educational consultant. Urged to write so that her students might have books that reflect their own experiences and history, Walter has produced over a dozen books for young adults. Her first,* Lillie of Watts: A Birthday Discovery *(1969), and her second,* Lillie of Watts Takes a Giant Step *(1971), were published by Lothrop, Lee, and Shepard. Since that time she has produced a steady flow of well-received works among which are* Ty's One-Man Band *(1979),* Because We Are *(1983),* Justin and the Best Biscuits in the World *(1986), and* Mariah Keeps Cool *(1990).*

*Mildred Pitts Walter now lives in Denver, Colorado, where she continues to write.*

**JORDAN:** How did your involvement in the civil rights movement influence your writing?

**WALTER:** My involvement in the civil rights movement came about through the work my husband and I were doing before we got into the civil rights movement. Everything that one does and who one is influences greatly her writing. Our writing is a part of us. It comes out of all that you have done and all that you are, so the civil rights movement, of course, affected my work, too. The civil rights movement made me aware of how tenuous and how precarious life is. When I saw so many people give their lives for this movement, I recognized that we have to do what we have to do. What I have to do is write. So the civil rights movement and the death of my husband gave me a different perspective on life. Suddenly I knew what I must do, when I must do it, and how I must do it.

**JORDAN:** Each person has to figure out what he or she has to do in the fight for equal rights. Sometimes we professors don't see our students as active and as vocal and are somewhat disappointed when we compare students of the eighties to those of the sixties. But you wouldn't share that same kind of disappointment?

**WALTER:** Well, I'm not sure that I wouldn't be disappointed, but I think what I would see is that we have to take students from where they are.

**JORDAN:** How do we do that?

**WALTER:** First, you have to understand where these young people have come from. Then get them to understand where they have come from. Discuss with them and try to ascertain why they are the way they are and get them to know why they are the way they are. Then take them from where they are. You cannot take them from any place but where they are. You must know where it is you want them to go and in the process of knowing where they have come from then you can ascertain how far they can go. You set your goals according to how far they can probably go at a given length of time. Set goals with them, and then you'll not be disappointed because you will understand how far they can go, how far they *want* to go. You set and reset goals to avoid disappointing them also. Sometimes I think teachers have *their* goals and not the students' goals. Teacher and student must set the goals together.

That is the way I feel about my characters when I'm writing a story. I like to equate teaching with writing. The teacher is not the creator; the writer is a creator. The teacher is *not* a creator. The teacher can only set the environment in which the child/student can create him/herself. That's the best we can do as teachers, to set the environment so that the student can learn to do what comes natural for that child to do in terms of his or her pace of learning. For the writer, of course, the characters set the environment for the writer, and the writer creates. In fact, the writer creates those characters out of the material that the characters bring to her. The knowledge that the writer has of the character, the character opens up and gives the writer, and the writer creates. But the teacher cannot create the pupil, and if she knows this, she doesn't become disappointed. She sees students unfolding in front of her, creating in front of her, and that's how I feel about any work I do.

**JORDAN:** That also leads to patience with students if we understand that students must move at their own pace.

**WALTER:** So does the character.

**JORDAN:** You wrote a story about black and white relations in *Girl on the Outside*. Is it perhaps easier for black and white girls to be friends than it is for women because as girls they are "equals" and they don't bring the same kind of baggage to a relationship?

**WALTER:** It depends on where and who they are. I think that children who are innocent and in the process of forming friendships if left alone and not prejudiced could become friends. But usually—and I see this all the time in the high schools—by the time they're beginning in high school, they're beginning to separate. They don't play together, they don't eat together. You go into schools and all the blacks are together and all the whites are together and there's a reason for that. They are beginning to select the people they really want to relate to, and in this country, it is very difficult for people to buck the patterns of racial separation and be true friends. So I think that as long as there is this kind of ingrained racism, it is very difficult for black and white people to become true friends.

**JORDAN:** In a way, they can be sociable then.

**WALTER:** They can be sociable, and some can be friends. I don't doubt that there are some who are but it's very few and far between.

**JORDAN:** As you were drawing the portrait of the white female in *The Girl on the Outside*, were there particular concerns you had? In other words, how was she born and what do you think of her?

**WALTER:** My first idea for the book was to have had Sophia an adult. The very first draft was to try to show the life of the woman who really helped Eva, and her name is in the back of the book, Grace Larch. I had wanted to tell her story as an adult and the kinds of problems she had in this town with her children. I had wanted to draw the character with one of her daughters being anti-black. This would have been strictly fictional, but I do know Mrs. Larch had been down South and had worked at a black college just outside of Little Rock, Arkansas. She had also been active in the theater. I wanted to tell her story, but nobody wanted to buy that kind of story. They said they would be interested if I wrote about two teenagers or young adults. So I set out to make Sophia the antagonist rather than the daughter of Grace Larch. I knew Sophia's character very well because I had worked in and around white people since I was seven years old. I knew the environment; I knew the house; I knew the people; I knew her mother; I knew her brother. I knew her father. I knew them all, so I had no problem with her character and her development. One reviewer criticized me saying that I seemed to have put more emphasis on the white girl than the black girl, but it was the white girl's story. Eva was the catalyst for Sophia's attitude and her development. I feel that I knew Eva's parents, and I knew all the people around her, and I wanted her to be lesser but equal. I think they were both equal, but it was Sophia's story and I had no qualms about doing it that way. If there was anything in the story that was stereotypical of Sophia, I knew it. I knew that I was not capable of drawing her fully, but I also knew I was more capable of drawing her than she or any other white person would have been of drawing me.

**JORDAN:** So you didn't find it more difficult to draw one character than another? They both [Sophia and Eva] seem to be so real.

**WALTER:** I had no problems drawing Sophia because I knew her. She was as much a part of my experience as Eva was, a part of my experience in the light that I showed her.

**JORDAN:** In reference to your comment that parts of Sophia are stereotypical, do you think that in general stereotypes can be useful?

**WALTER:** Oh yes. They can be very useful, and they can be dangerous, however, if writers aren't aware that they are stereotyping. I don't think that many white writers are aware that they are stereotyping us when they write and think that they are doing us as we are. I think Faulkner thought he had a good picture of Dilsey and that he was doing a really magnanimous kind of character, but I think he didn't know her at all. He had not seen any one of the characters in their homes. I think it's fine if you are aware that you don't know all the ramifications of your character, but you have to know more than Faulkner knew about Dilsey. You have to know more in order to make the character provoke memory in the people who are like the person portrayed.

**JORDAN:** To what extent do you use sources such as biographies, autobiographies, or histories when developing characters?

**WALTER:** Of course, I used history for *The Girl on the Outside.* I often use history in developing my stories and my characters. I think of the problems that we've had historically with teachers in *Because We Are.* It's a story of a black girl—Emma—that involved a white teacher and how this teacher wanted Emma not to relate to black people. The teacher had the idea that if given an opportunity, Emma could move up into the mainstream. However, in order to move up into the mainstream, she had to leave all other black people behind. We can't relate to our people and move up into the mainstream, so there was conflict with the white teacher. Emma got put out of the integrated school and had to go to an all-black school in her neighborhood. That's part of history and the integration movement. The white English teacher had the class scrambling for books reminiscent of the time when blacks were in a boxing ring made to fight each other as they scrambled for coins.

In the book *Justin and the Best Biscuits in the World,* I used a lot of history. I talked about black cowboys, and I also talked about the exodus to the West. I went to the source, *The Exodus,* the scholarly work by Nell Irvin Painter, and *Exodus: Stories of the Black Migration to Kansas after Reconstruction.* Then I fictionalized it. Of course, I got a lot of criticism for telling how white people cut off the hands of a black man and threw them in his wife's lap. Yes, I use a lot of history in my work. I haven't done anybody's biography. I want to do a work on the Mississippi Freedom Democratic Party [MFDP] to tell the story of the Mississippi Challenge as nonfiction. I want to tell Fannie Lou Hamer's and others' stories. I want to show how the Student Nonviolent Coordinating Committee [SNCC] started that project and worked it through with the MFDP.

**JORDAN:** It is easier to find white women writers who have portrayed black female protagonists or main characters than it is to find the reverse. Could you comment on this phenomenon? Do you think this will remain a pattern, or will black women start to portray white female characters a bit more frequently?

**WALTER:** I won't. I think that there is so much to write about our own people. There is so little known about us and our relationship to each other and our ability to survive the hostility in the white world. *Trouble's Child* is a book about black people. No white people in it at all. None. The only time I have white people in my books is to show how racism has affected us. Sophia came around to saving Eva—she could not have been human had she not. She could not have been human if she had not changed and grown. Her growth was sudden! It was like Paul going to Damascus and being blinded with the light.

JORDAN: I noticed that; she wasn't even aware of what was going to happen.

WALTER: She wasn't aware. It was like someone who sees someone drowning and jumps into the water to save her, but can't swim.

JORDAN: You just do it!

WALTER: Yes! You just do it because that is part of human nature. It is part of our wanting to protect life. We cannot afford to see life extinguished if we are at all human and that's what I was trying to show. The heroism came out without her even being aware of what she was doing. She did it because deep down under she was human.

JORDAN: As I read the novel, I knew something had to happen, but Sophia didn't give me a clue. I noticed when she became angry with Ida that something was really wrong. She was uneasy, and she had not been mistreating Ida before.

WALTER: Ida had been her friend, her loyal servant. Then all of a sudden she realized: this woman knows everything about me, and I don't know a thing about her. Why? I don't want her in my life this way. Sophia was beginning to get a glimpse of how she was being cheated. Ida knew everything about her and was in her life so deeply that Sophia was totally dependent upon her. Ida had always been there: ironing her clothes, selecting her clothes, doing everything for her. Yet she knew absolutely nothing about Ida and this upset her and that's the way she felt about this whole problem of integration. Black people had always been in her life like Rob, the groom, was in her life at the stables. She knew nothing about him, and yet he was everything to her. He knew when she was coming to the stables, had her horse ready, everything. And that can be disconcerting to have someone anticipate your every wish, and you have no indication whether or not this person is friend or foe. And she was beginning to see and sense that black people in her life were human. She was a decent girl, had always been loved by her family, had always been taken care of by black people, and she had this wonderful brother who was not prejudiced.

**JORDAN:** Those kind of characters—like her brother—intrigue me because they make me wonder how they become as they are given their surroundings.

**WALTER:** Well, there were conditions that made him be that way. Early in his life he had gone with his parents to many black functions, and he was bright. Both of the men—her boyfriend and her brother—saw through prejudice. Her brother had also been away to war and lost an arm. I'm sure he had come in contact with black soldiers who had probably been helpful to him.

Sophia's boyfriend had been to Princeton—not that that would have helped him a lot—and had seen people reacting in different ways. There were some whites in the South who were more considerate of black people. Now I think Lillian Smith was truly a kind woman who tried hard to end racism, who worked against it, and who suffered greatly for it.

**JORDAN:** That takes a lot of courage.

**WALTER:** Oh yes! Well, it didn't take courage for Sophia because she didn't know what she was doing until afterward, and then she found out she had jumped into the fire.

**JORDAN:** You depict several scenes in *The Girl on the Outside* between each girl and her grandmother. Would you comment on the way in which you incorporate family history or history into the novel itself?

**WALTER:** Sophia's grandmother [Mrs. Stewart] was the one who instilled in Sophia the fact that she was different and better than black people. Eva remembers her grandmother telling her how great she was without comparing her to any other race or color. Eva was good because she was human, normal, and it was natural for her to be a good person, and she did not have to worry about going to places where she was not welcome. She could find things that were equally good within her own home and with her own people. And she remembered her grandmother sharing things with her that were important, like the newspapers. But Sophia's grandmother had to impress upon her that she was good if she put someone else down. They can only be good if somebody else is of less value—comparison and competition—whereas we are good if we cooperate, if we share, if we are part of a whole rather than separate from the whole as individualists. When Mrs. Stewart takes Sophia to pick up the wash and Sophia wants to know why she can't play, one of the lines from Mrs. Stewart to Sophia is, "They're not our kind."

There's also a juxtaposition between Arnold and Sophia and Eva and Cecil, the two boyfriends. It's an interesting contrast because in some ways the men are supportive, but they don't see things in the same way. Cecil felt that for Eva to be protected, she had to refuse to risk going to Central High. He had a different sense of self. He had a sense that he wouldn't want to be a part of white people simply because they didn't want any part of him, and it was dangerous to be around people who didn't care about you. Cecil tried to show Eva the nonintegrationist point of view. Integrationists thought if they went to white schools, everything would be all right. Cecil saw that was not the answer. Did you get that?

**JORDAN:** Oh yes. In fact, the father very much kept talking about integration, and Cecil kept saying that separation may be better.

**WALTER:** Yes, Sophia's boyfriend saw the strength and spirituality of black people. He went to their churches and listened to them. He sensed that blacks had something of value to him and to her, whereas Cecil saw nothing of value in white people.

**JORDAN:** What did you see as the key motivation behind Eva's behavior? Is it that she really does buy into the notion that if she were able to go the same school, then she really would have a chance to make her life much better?

**WALTER:** Yes, she believed that white schools had everything that black schools didn't have. They had science labs. They had heat! Their schools were warm; they were clean. They had new books. They had good books. They had all of the things that implied good education. There was no such thing as separate but equal. Eva represented that group of black people who really believed there was no such thing as separate but equal. And she was influenced by this idea. She felt she could get a better education; and she truly believed that once blacks were integrated they could prove that they were as capable and as good and as smart and as clean.

**JORDAN:** How do you personally view the effects of integration on black children? Has it been basically positive as opposed to negative?

**WALTER:** Now in the eighties I think for the black child most of the outcomes have been negative—especially where they have been placed in schools where they were pretty much isolated from other black people. I think the idea of integration in this country is not the idea that integration is becoming a part of the whole. When a thing is integrated, it is no longer in parts. You don't lose your identity completely. You gain a lot when something becomes integrated; there is an enhancement of the whole part. The whole becomes greater; everything is evened out, molded, and shaped. White people saw integration as black people losing their total identity and becoming the same as they are. They wanted sameness for equality, and they felt that if black people can become us, then we can absorb them into our schools. They were not going to take anything from us. We had to give up everything, and our children lost. They lost a great deal because in black schools blacks had an identity. They had clubs they belonged to. When they went to white schools, they could not belong to clubs; they could not participate except in basketball or sports, and then only the very best could participate. Those who were ordinary could not get on the team because they had too many ordinary players and only the stars could get on. Girls couldn't be on the cheering squads or in the drama club because there was not room for them.

Students hardly remember the reading, writing, arithmetic in schools. It's the extra things you do that are remembered: the plays you're in, the glee club, the drama club, the extracurricular activities that enhance you and make you think of school as important and valid. Our children didn't get that when they went into the so-called integrated system. Our teachers, too, lost because many were not absorbed into those schools. The actual benefits, I think, were negative for us in terms of the things that were lost when we integrated.

**JORDAN:** But we felt we had no choice though except to fight.

**WALTER:** We felt we had no other choice but to try to become a part of the total system. We tried and saw that it just was not working for us even though we tried. Our children took the brunt of a lot of mental abuse to make this nation whole. The nation didn't want to be whole. And it still doesn't want to be whole.

**JORDAN:** When you look at young children and teenagers who do not know their family histories or have not developed the voices to tell their own stories, what kinds of things ought to be done so that they gain control over their own voices to tell their own stories?

**WALTER:** I think we need to utilize the churches in our community more than on Sunday. We have these big churches with all these rooms that are closed at least six days out of the week, and on the seventh day people go to church. What we need to do as I see it is to provide activities that are geared toward teaching our heritage. Our children need to participate every day after school. Somebody should be there to guide them into knowing who they are, what our history is. I know no other people in this country who do not have some kind of education for their children; the Jews do, the Japanese. White people don't have to because all the institutions belong to them. We must learn that the institutions in this country will not serve all of our needs, and create institutions for ourselves. We will have to have clinics in the churches or somewhere in the community where our children can come and learn good health habits, cleanliness, and how to prepare simple meals that are nutritious.

When I say children, I mean these children with children. We will have to open up churches so these young people can come and learn about themselves and their history. I think dance and music for us is highly therapeutic. I see no better way to reach us and to get us relaxed than through our music. I'm talking about music that can be channeled into methods of relaxation. I feel that in a tutoring hall, music and dance could be used for releasing tensions before children sit to their studies. Then teachers and tutors may find it easier to get the work done that needs doing. And there's another thing: We like pomp and ceremony. We like wearing uniforms. We love parades; we love getting together. Marcus Garvey understood this and used it to great advantage. We could now utilize his methods to organize our communities to see what organizations can tutor more children, have the cleanest blocks, safest streets, etc.

We don't utilize that anymore. That's part of our heritage, and I think we will have to do these kinds of things to get our children to know who they are and where they have come from and to know the greatness of our heritage.

**JORDAN:** There is a church scene that Sophia remembers in the first chapter and then Eva remembers a church scene in the second chapter. We're very aware of the black church's role in the civil rights movement, but is this juxtaposition also to point out the use of the white church during the movement?

**WALTER:** Southern churches did not do much. Most were very much opposed to the civil rights movement.

**JORDAN:** Sophia remembers that her brother was thinking what peace the church should bring and, of course, that's not the case. The church is about something different.

**WALTER:** Yes, Sophia's church was very much against integrating Central High. The minister encouraged his parishioners not to become involved. [According to him] Scripture showed that it was not the thing to do.

**JORDAN:** Even though the story is that of Sophia, both girls are still on the outside of "something."

**WALTER:** Yes. Yes. Eva is more on the inside than Sophia. Sophia is the girl who is truly left outside because she had violated the rules of her house when she came to the aid of a black person at that particular time in history. It was not considered good. You just didn't because "they were not her kind," but she found that for her it was the right thing to have done.

Eva was on the outside as far as Sophia and her friends were concerned. But as far as her family, she was protected, loved. I don't think that Sophia's family protected her. They were very much afraid. They couldn't protect her.

**JORDAN:** At the end of the novel, I sometimes wonder what Sophia's life would be like and I wondered if you find yourself wondering where she might be twenty years later?

**WALTER:** Sophia's parents were ostracized. They were put down, and her boyfriend's parents probably forbade him to see her. Although he may have loved her very much, it would have been very hard for him to continue seeing her. I think in the long run she would still feel she had done what was the best thing. In the end I think she like many Southern women will feel a kind of maternal attitude toward black people with some bitterness toward them for having wrecked her life.

**JORDAN:** Have you ever felt pressure from your publisher and/ or editor or audience to portray a particular kind of character or to treat a particular set of themes?

**WALTER:** I am not pressured by publishers. They will say to me, "We'd like another Justin or another Mariah," or something like that but as far as pressuring me about what I write, they don't do that. I felt the need to write a lighter fun book when I did Mariah. I felt I should appeal to the interests of young girls who are in love, and who are frivolous in a way, yet, have serious problems within the family.

**JORDAN:** What started you to write professionally? Did you always write?

**WALTER:** No. No. I never thought I'd become a writer because I didn't know any writers. Contrary to those people who always had books, we didn't have books in our house. I had the Bible, and I read the Bible over and over and over. In our school we had very few books, and we could only read them at school. We couldn't take them out. In the summer we had no books at all because we couldn't go to the public library. So I didn't grow up with books. Therefore, I didn't know much about writing. I wanted to be a schoolteacher because I knew a lot of great teachers and they were highly influential in my life. That's what I wanted to be and that's what I became.

I taught in Los Angeles where all the children were black and there were so few books for and about them. I knew a person who was in the publishing business, and I asked him to publish some books for my children and he said, "Write them." I got upset because I knew I was not a writer, and I felt that he was passing the buck, and I told him that. Anyway he insisted, and I wrote this book, *Lillie of Watts*. It got good reviews, and I started writing. I got a lot of rejection slips. Finally I met a young black man at Scholastic who was in the Sprint Books section. He asked me to do a book for him. I did a book called, *The Liquid Trap*. He liked it and introduced me to another editor in the house. She did a book of mine, *Ty's One-Man Band*, and that's how I became a writer.

**JORDAN:** Rejection slips are just a part of the process, huh?

**WALTER:** Oh yes. It takes time to build a craft, and writing is very definitely a craft that takes a lot of time and a lot of doing to get it done.

**JORDAN:** When your writing is pulling you in one direction and other obligations pull you in another, how do you keep yourself on track?

**WALTER:** The other things I do are subordinate to the main work. I know if I want to keep writing I had better stay on the main track.

# SHERLEY ANNE WILLIAMS

■

*Sherley Anne Williams is a novelist, poet, playwright, and scholar. Born August 25, 1944, in Bakersfield, California, Williams first published a collection of essays,* Give Birth to Brightness: A Thematic Study in Neo-Black Literature, *in 1972. Her first book of poetry,* The Peacock Poems *(1975), received a National Book Award nomination in 1976; her second book of poetry,* SomeOne Sweet Angel

*Chile, was published in 1982. Williams received an Emmy award for a televised reading of poems selected from* SomeOne Sweet Angel Chile. Dessa Rose, *the focus of this interview, was named a notable book in 1986 by the* New York Times. *Based in part on an actual slave revolt led by a pregnant slave,* Dessa Rose *is a fictionalized account of a thwarted uprising and the ex-slaves' refuge on the plantation of a slave mistress. Williams wrote* Dessa Rose *in part out of a deep sense of dissatisfaction with William Styron's* Confessions of Nat Turner. *Mona Gable writes in a* Los Angeles Times Magazine *interview that Williams "not only wanted to challenge Styron's view of slavery . . . , which she believes dismissed the brutal social and political conditions that led to Turner's revolt, but to show up the 'hypocrisy of the literary tradition' by detailing the strengths of black culture."*

*Currently a professor of English at the University of California, San Diego, La Jolla, Williams has also taught at Miles College in Birmingham, Alabama, and the California State University at Fresno. In 1984, she was selected as a Fulbright lecturer at the University of Ghana.*

**JORDAN:** You stated in the author's note to *Dessa Rose* that you had once read historical accounts of a slave woman who had led an uprising and of a white woman who had offered refuge to slaves. You then wondered if these two women could have met. Once this topic had "selected" you, what determined the terms on which they should meet?

**WILLIAMS:** I guess that realism determined it because I knew that, despite the facts, the institution of slavery offered chances for interactions between black women and white women. These interactions were always set and defined within the context of a master/ slave relationship, and I wanted some way for them to meet outside of that set so the women could actually get to know each other. Part of what I wanted to explore in the novel was the basis on which black women and white women, despite their differences— the justifiable accusations that black women might be able to make against white women—that they, despite all these things, might come together and then find a basis for mutual respect.

These two things really determined the situation in which I placed the two women and how they met.

**JORDAN:** Could a novel set during the same time period have a black woman be the equal of a white woman?

**WILLIAMS:** Well, you know you can do anything in a novel. [*Laughs*] Of course, it is entirely possible, as I said, but one of the things that was guiding me was realism. I wanted people to believe that this could actually have happened because I felt what I had to say not only about relations between black women and white women but also between black women and black men really had some very real applications for today. I felt it had to be a realistic situation in order for people to draw the parallels. If I created something that was totally idealistic—which I think, just off the top of my head, would be true of a situation in which they were not employer and employee or master and slave, but were actually meeting each other as social equals—it would have seemed like a romantic ideal, so "reality" or credibility set the bounds for the situation itself.

**JORDAN:** I ask that question because it reminded me of a workshop I once did on black women writers in which one woman spoke out that she didn't feel that the protagonist of Harriet Wilson's *Our Nig* was realistic because there were not any other black women around. But then everybody said, "Yes, but this is in the North, and she is very isolated, so perhaps there weren't any other black women around she could have talked to. Therefore, maybe this was perfectly realistic that the only other contact she would have had was with white women."

Did you know immediately that Dessa Rose should be the narrator, for instance, or that parts of Rufel's story would be told from a limited omniscient point of view?

**WILLIAMS:** Well, the telling of the story was kind of interesting because, in part, the novel was derived from an earlier short story called "Meditations on History," which is told out of Nehemiah's journal entries. And when I came to do the novel, I really just wanted to have that story as the opening section and then I would do a couple of other sections and that would be the novel. Then I had planned to do some minor revisions on the short story. But once I got into it, I could see that just in terms of what I knew was

going to happen at the end that I could not have a white man telling even part of the story, because I didn't want to give him that
much importance or that much control. Once I had subsumed his
voice, it was the most natural thing to subsume Rufel's also under
the omniscient narrator. But when it came to the third section of
the novel, which I had always planned would be from Dessa's point
of view, I could really see that something else was needed. At first
I kind of toyed with the idea of doing something that was more in
keeping with the original slave narratives, that is, having Dessa's
story told from birth to maturity, but I decided that I couldn't do
that—I really didn't want to. I wanted to have Dessa speak. I was
also, I think, very much influenced by Robert Steptoe's criticism
of Zora Neale Hurston's *Their Eyes Were Watching God* in his *From
Behind the Veil*, in which he says that Hurston's use of the third-
person voice really shows her distrust of the character's ability to
tell her own story. Well, I think I am one of these people—and
maybe in some way we all are—who has known a host of very fine
female storytellers, so I knew there was nothing inherently wrong
with the character's ability to tell the story. If there was any question about ability, it would be my ability to find a way in which
she could tell the story. So having thought about these things, I just
set out to have Dessa tell the story, and the point at which I break
the manuscript seemed like a natural place to keep the momentum
going but at the same time offer some real surprises to the reader.

**JORDAN:** You mention in the author's note William Styron's
version of *The As-Told-To Memoirs of Nat Turner*. I wondered if that
had in any way influenced you to allow Dessa to tell her story?

**WILLIAMS:** Well, I think Styron's influence on this manuscript
was pretty much confined to the original short story. The short
story was begun in a time when many, many black intellectuals
were still incensed about Styron's portrayal of Nat Turner. I think
that book *Ten Black Writers Respond* had recently been published.
As I said, the short story is told through the journal entries of Nehemiah, and I took great delight in finding ways for Dessa's true
story to come through to the reader without Nehemiah, in fact,
being aware of what was going on and being truly ignorant of what
was being said. I felt that that was also a possibility with Thomas
Gray [the white man who actually wrote down and published the
"Confessions" of Nat Turner], and Nat Turner, or with anybody
who was in that kind of situation who was trying to act as an

amanuensis for somebody over whom they really have quite a bit of control in professing to tell their stories. Whatever else the slaves were—that they were, for the most part, uneducated and unlettered—did not mean that they were unintelligent. Certainly, they had a lot of mother wit about them, so that the idea of setting up that situation was my way of saying to Styron "See what you missed. You went for the easy thing—the stereotyped thing. This is the real story that you missed." Once I had gotten that off my mind, I was through with Styron, and I actually wrote the introduction or that preface because of some questions that the editor had. They kept coming back to me about the story with "Is this a real story? Did this really happen?" "No," I'd reply. "It didn't happen; it was this and this." "As a foreword," she [the editor] said, "I think we ought to say that up front—that it's not a historical incident." This is at the end of the writing, and the writing in many ways was very difficult and very painful, and the process of copyediting I had some real thoughts and real feelings about. I was just tired of people coming to me and saying "Do this with the manuscript, do that with the manuscript." So when they said, "Tell me the circumstances of whatever," then I said, "All right, I'll tell you. There it is, so now, take that to the bank. Publish that! Leave me alone." So that [the foreword] was really more or less an afterthought to the novel. It was not the original plan.

**JORDAN:** That leads me to my next question. By fictionalizing about the lives of these women, you control another way of interpreting history. How would you define uses of history in your work?

**WILLIAMS:** That's kind of a big question because I guess in one way or another you're always dealing with history. And to a large extent I would have to say what I said in the preface, which was that another part of the reason I did this book, was for that child that I was thirty or forty years ago whose imagination came up against the institution of slavery and was stopped. And I had felt so strongly that young black women and young girls *now* not have to go through the same kind of experience I did, that they understand that whatever our historical circumstances that those circumstances had never barred us from heroic action. And whatever our present circumstances, the possibility of heroic action is still here, and I think that it is very, very important that children—that black children—be able to imagine themselves in heroic roles in history without having to imagine themselves as white. I am just livid about that idea that so much of our culture is presented to us in such a way—and I am talking about us now as Americans—that so much of our culture is presented to us in such a way that young black children, young Hispanic children, young Asian children have to say "Well if I'm not going to be a coolie or a servant or a slave then when we play this game, I have to be the white man." It is still a very painful idea to me that this is what we continue to do to our children.

And I just also happen to think that that era in American history—and there are three or four eras that I would talk about in American history as being truly heroic and heroic in the sense that what happens there is within keeping with the highest political ideals of the country, and the era of slavery is truly one. It is one of those eras in which blacks and whites begin to say, "This institution is wrong and it has got to be abolished," and that movement gathered strength from that. To me, it's one the most exciting periods of all, and I wanted to share that sense of excitement. And also I believe that until we as a people are able to look history in the face and not flinch—that until that happens we are always going to be at the mercy of that history and at the mercy of white people. Dealing with history, whether it's a very recent past or something that happened a hundred or two hundred years ago, is the kind of thing that makes people stop and look and rethink, and by so doing, see that there are other possibilities for looking at the world. Of course, one is an academic. I've been teaching at UCSD [University of California at San Diego] going on twenty years now, so of course I have been influenced to some extent by the kind of debates that are going on in literary circles about the uses of history, deconstruction, and other aspects of contemporary critical theory. That is part of what I'm trying to do. And I'm responding to some of those arguments when I am writing. But because I'm a writer who began by wanting to talk, not to academics, but to people who are pretty much like myself, and to people who ordinarily might not pick up a book, it is obvious that I can't talk about it in a way that destroys traditional story and traditional narrative. I wasn't going to get—I might get a host of white readers by going out and destroying a narrative line and doing all that kind of stuff—but it didn't seem to me valuable if black people were not going to be reading it and praising it.

JORDAN: I have been thinking about Harriet Wilson's portrayal of her protagonist of *Our Nig* and your portrayal of Dessa Rose a

great deal. Wilson's preface suggests a number of extraliterary concerns that shape the novel. She is clearly concerned about abolition
and would like to use the book in the service of that movement. Yet
she is aware that she cannot alienate her readers to the point that
they do not buy the book. Writing almost 150 years after Wilson,
does a concern for audience ever become a consideration as you
are writing?

**WILLIAMS:** Not as I am actually writing. But, generally, I'm primarily concerned about the reaction of black readers because I see
them as my primary audience. It's like knowing the people who are
most fitted and capable of judging whether this is good or bad. And
in a very great way because I used black vernacular speech, "dialect," a great deal—at least I used to—I am aware of the kind of
stereotypes and images that most readers, whether black or white,
have about those uses, and I'm also aware of a lot of white critics'
impatience with the use of black speech. Being just the kind of
person I am, the kind of writer that I am, there is that concern but
as far as it being a kind of conscious thing in my mind as I write,
no. That [being consciously aware of audience as I'm writing] is
not true because I am also aware that a good deal of what I say may
escape readers maybe on the first or second reading. But I want to
create something that is going to draw readers back again and
again, so that you read first for the story but even as you are reading you say, "Ah, I notice something going on here. I need to go
back here." And the story pulls you along, pulls you along. It's that
kind of thing that I always want to create when I'm writing. And
in that sense you're aware of an audience, but I really have to say,
too, once you are into the story, the poem, or whatever it is, it has
its own momentum and pulls you pretty much in the same way
you want the reader to be pulled. The real consideration is getting
the story out; nothing else is really important at that moment.

**JORDAN:** Do you ever have to fight with yourself, so to speak,
as writing is pulling you in one direction and perhaps something
else is pulling you in another? Or does the work always take
precedence?

**WILLIAMS:** [*Pauses*] Well, yes. I guess I'm ashamed to say it, but
I guess that [the work takes precedence] is really true.

**JORDAN:** Barbara Christian notes in her criticism on early
black women novelists that in their concern for combatting nega-

tive stereotypes of black women in literature often they really didn't seem to give as much attention to their art. They seemed very concerned about controlling the images by which they would be viewed, and therefore they felt the need to present alternative images. Do you think that concern remains for women writers, even though they are clearly not so limited in their portrayals that they merely counter negative stereotypes?

**WILLIAMS:** I think that certainly is a concern of mine, but I happen to be fortunate to live in an era where there is not any need to separate the need for positive images from art itself. Those things come to us inextricably tied together so that we are much, much freer than any other group of writers in our history. We are able to construe our message of racial uplift, if you will, in such a way that the art can always be seen to, or can be construed to be taking precedence over everything else because we, to a large extent, understand that just the telling of the story itself is in fact a blow against stereotype. But I don't think that was a luxury that earlier writers could afford—or that they could see. They didn't write historical novels then because they didn't have the money that would give them the leisure to do the kind of research that is open to most of us.

**JORDAN:** I have been reading novels by white women in which black and white females interact, and I found myself trying to define sometimes where the stereotype ends and where the multidimensional character begins. And sometimes I'm not quite sure. But I'm particularly fascinated by how you portrayed Rufel. The Southern white woman as well as the black woman was often stereotyped in fiction, and she was often very much a flat character. But you humanized Rufel—at least for me—as much as you did Dessa Rose. Did you find yourself very drawn into this character as you got to know her? Or was some of the initial conflict Dessa had with Rufel also there for you as a writer?

**WILLIAMS:** Well, I thought that the initial portrait of Rufel, of course, partook of a good deal of stereotype. But the character of Rufel for me was—especially compared to the character of Dessa—a kind of fun thing to do. You know what I mean? I knew here was a character that you had to start out in one way or another as something of a stereotype because if she comes on at the very beginning as this great-hearted liberal, there is really no story and

Dessa looks like a dog for being so ungrateful to her, right? She couldn't come out so perfect, but at the same time there had to be enough of a circumstance so that she could believably move from stereotype to full character. So, as I say, it was comparatively fun doing that. You say that I humanized her, but it's not the writer that does that. It is really her contact primarily with Dessa and the other runaways that does that. When she takes that baby in her arms, I mean, she is a person. She is a human being because that baby is a human being, and whatever her conflicts about it—and despite the fact that she is shown as this kind of silly, stereotyped white woman—she had to have at least that much initial humanity in order for me to even work with her at all. And once she had allowed herself to be human on that level, then she is open to all the other lessons that Dessa and the other runaways had to teach her.

**JORDAN:** In terms of just looking at the various dimensions to Rufel's character, you examined her sexual identity among other things, and to me that is something of an unexamined aspect of white female identity in fiction during slavery. They were there to procreate and little else. Was this also a part of your fleshing out this character to give her different sides?

**WILLIAMS:** I have to admit that there was a less literary and artistic reason. I wanted to do something very startling and shocking. It was also true at the time when I was thinking about doing this novel—and I thought about doing this novel for many years before I actually sat down to write it—that one of the sore points in relations between black women and white women was black men and white women and the sexual relationships between those two. And I wanted to explore the situation, not from the point of view of the black man and the white woman, but from the point of view of the black woman who is watching and who is involved in some way with the black man. The biggest stumbling block to any kind of coalition between black women and white women was the idea that white women were stealing our men or something like that, so I wanted to see if despite that this basis for mutual respect could develop. It hadn't occurred to me that in putting her in this situation or in having this situation develop that I was breaking new ground. It just really had not occurred to me consciously. I knew in a sense; I had read no historical accounts of affairs between black men in slavery and white women, though in fact Harriet Jacobs's *Incidents in the Life of a Slave Girl* suggests that kind of thing. I understand that recently, more historical evidence has been uncovered and historians have begun to write about some of these situations, but back then, I felt that in proposing that romance I was doing something out of the ordinary rather than "breaking new ground." And I wanted to do it, and I wanted to startle. Writing is a means or a form of communication, and if you don't sell those books you are not communicating, so there that was. But, as I say, exploring the sexual identity of Southern white women and slaves was an idea that had not occurred to me.

**JORDAN:** Is Dessa Rose's concern with Nathan sleeping with Rufel that she really does feel for him and, therefore, loving a white woman is somehow an insult to her as a black woman? Or was it something else?

**WILLIAMS:** Everybody wants to make Dessa into this jealous woman, and that, to me, I just have to tell you the truth—that is beside the point. It is as though black women can't have any other feeling for a male except sexual ones. It seems to me that circumstances in the novel perfectly justify Dessa's attitude. Why would you want somebody whom you love whether it is sexual or platonic or whatever way, intimately involved with somebody you hate and think is no good? Would you want your brother? Would you want your uncle? Would you want your son? Would you want your friend? That seems to me perfectly legitimate and reasonable, and she doesn't have to get in bed with Nathan herself in order to feel that way. I think I was getting pretty upset with some people who want to suggest that or who want to see it exclusively that way. Yes, sure she might have felt some attraction for him, but that's not ever the main thing.

**JORDAN:** Harker does ask her though at one point, "Are you willing to lose the friendship over a white woman?" and I thought that was very striking. In other words, was she really willing to go that far?

**WILLIAMS:** I believe she was not. She is shocked that there is a possibility Nathan would choose Rufel over her, but in fact it seems to me that if it had come to that, it wouldn't be Nathan choosing this white woman over the friendship of Dessa Rose. But what he is saying is "Listen, you are my friend and we are equals. This is my life. This is my life." As he says to her, "I was bred in slavery and people told me who to sleep with in slavery and now you are going to do the same thing to me?" And she has to understand that. But you notice that finally when he understands how deeply she really feels about it, he doesn't try to keep denigrating her for feeling the way she does. He understands the legitimacy of her feelings, and she finally comes to understand the legitimacy of his. It's not that she likes it any better. No! But she says, "He has a life—that is his life, and in this instance he should be able to lead it as he sees fit."

JORDAN: Now that brings me back to Rufel and Dessa Rose. What keeps black women and white women from developing the kind of trust that leads to genuine friendship? Is history so embedded in our memory that we can not move beyond that pain? Do we simply not allow ourselves to be close enough to each other to know each other intimately? Once these two women are in such constant contact, close contact—for instance, the attempted rape is so close to them both—that they start to see each other as having common concerns.

WILLIAMS: I think that as you say the fact remains that there are so few opportunities to meet on equal footing. I think that that's a large part of it. We are both victims of stereotypes, and in order to come to any true understanding of each other we have to be able to move beyond that. Now, I will say that in looking at the kind of woman that Rufel becomes, it is as though I took the white women that I know and that I am friends with and said to myself "How would it be possible for someone like you to get to this point? How would you have gotten to this point of being able to be my friend if you had lived back in those days?" Rufel, in a sense, becomes very much like the white women I know today. It was that kind of journey for the character and for myself. Of course, I think there can be far more possibilities for black and white women to meet on equal terms today than there were in the nineteenth century, so we have in a way a greater freedom but we also have a greater responsibility. And it seems to me we keep shirking that responsibility, and I think it is also true that over the last ten or twenty years there haven't been those great issues that would bring us together. I think today pro choice is a very definite common ground for us to meet on and to begin building the kind of coalitions that would finally free women from the kind of domination that has been so much a part of history.

JORDAN: That was my next question. Do you envision black women becoming more integrated into the women's movement as common concerns such as pro choice, move to the forefront?

WILLIAMS: I think that there ought to be all possibilities open to us. Some black women would see themselves doing greater work or better work as part of the women's movement. Other women see themselves doing greater work or better work by joining with the white women on specific issues as opposed to working with them all the time. But, however one chooses to do that, it seems to me it is valuable and something that we need. I think that there are very real concerns that black women have as women that white women don't necessarily share. They started striving to enter the work force and to be treated as equals at a time when black women were largely confined to lower-level and lower-paying jobs, and that entrance [white women's] has in fact been of benefit to all of us. At the same time I think that insofar as the women's movement is concerned, it has been, I think, erroneously construed as a power play—not as a move to be equals in terms of economic opportunity and those things, but to dominate men in some kind of way. I guess if you have been doing wrong to somebody, you automatically assume that that person wants to do wrong to you. I think that part of what has kept black women ambivalent about or keeps us ambivalent about the women's movement, aside from the black man/white woman issue, is that so much of our struggle was tied up in allowing our men—in finding ways that would enable our men—to take their place as men in society with all that that meant. As people have said over and over again, we [black women] are not necessarily wanting to move into the executive boardroom but to have our men in the executive boardroom. It seems like a real adventure for a white woman to go out and work every day. And what we have been wanting was to see our men with enough economic opportunity so that they could allow us to be solely the homemaker, the nurturer, care provider; and I still think that that is a legitimate aspiration on the part of black women.

JORDAN: The narrator frequently questions the power of the word and who controls it. Is the writing of the novel itself a kind of triumph in which the story and the word belong to a woman?

**WILLIAMS:** Yes. What originally enabled me to talk about wanting to be a writer was the fact that I wanted to tell the lives or talk about the lives of women characters who were like the women I had grown up with—lower-income women who were going through the normal difficulties in trying to raise families. Most of them had been abandoned by the fathers of their children and were having to deal with the welfare system, which was very treacherous. It is destructive not only of family life but of the individuals who are supposed to be its charge, in its care. And I saw these lives as ones of tremendous value. The women themselves were waging very heroic struggles, and they were doing so with a good deal of humor, dignity, and grace. And I thought that these stories, these women, ought to be better known by the reading public. And certainly we, as black people, ought to know their stories, ought to know and appreciate their lives and their struggles. Yes, this novel, even though it is about a slave woman as opposed to a welfare mother, certainly is in line with the kind of thing I wanted to do when I started writing twenty years ago. It would be a story that would illuminate some things for us and allow us to see ourselves in new ways, different ways, and in more constructive ways.

**JORDAN:** When you look at young blacks who often do not know their own history and who often do not have the words to voice their own experiences, what kinds of things should we as adults be doing to help them gain control over their own voices so that they appreciate the stories they have to tell?

**WILLIAMS:** First of all, we have just got to see that they learn how to read. I think that that is the biggest failure of my generation of black people. We were handed a mission, which was to go out and educate and better ourselves, and from what I see we have failed to pass on that mission to our children. And I think that that is the biggest contemporary tragedy, that so many of our children can construe being smart in school as being white. That, to me, is almost criminal that twenty years after the civil rights movement black children can say that and not look at this proliferation or comparative proliferation of middle-class blacks as a model to be followed. Instead, they see us as something to be shunned, or certainly they don't want their lives to be our lives. I think that what is going on now—from the drugs to the dropout rate to the early and continuous pregnancies—our children are saying to us you have to show us some way to be successful and to be black at the same time, and you have not done that thus far. You have shown us ways to be successful like white people, and this is not what we want to be.

JORDAN: Do you think that having more black producers like Spike Lee and Oprah Winfrey will help?

WILLIAMS: I think all of that helps and that it is good, but the sad truth of the matter is middle-class blacks have deserted black communities. We no longer live in the communities about which we write so lovingly and elegantly. Our children don't attend those schools. We don't go to those churches. We don't frequent those places of business. Until we go back and do that, the children who are left there are going to continue to see us as white people and not at all like them.

JORDAN: Yes, that does sound tragic.

WILLIAMS: It is, it is! And maybe it is not the whole of the problem, but certainly I think it is some part of the problem. When we tell our children that they, in order to have any kind of education at all—that we can't provide them with a decent education in their neighborhood; they have to go outside of their neighborhood; they have to go to white people in order to get a decent education. What are we telling them about our lives? We are saying first of all, we have no control over our neighborhoods or our schools, or whatever. White people have all of the control, and we have to go to them. I have had students who were in that cut-off between the days of the segregated schools and the integrated schools who have talked to me about the differences in going to the segregated schools—dilapidated and rundown as they were, with books that had been all marked up by white children and stuff like that—and their integrated school. They knew that the next year they would pass to Miss Dempsey's class, and Miss Dempsey lived right down the street, and they knew that Miss Dempsey was going to tell their mother about them in school. And Mr. Jacobson went to the same church, and while they were in Mr. Jacobson's class if they didn't act right and get their lesson, Mr. Jacobson would be on the phone to their father. When they went off to these white schools, they were in a totally hostile environment where they were not protected from racist epithets—where other students could call them "nigger" and all sorts of bad names and not be disciplined in any kind of way. Where if they retaliated, they were disciplined. Where they cannot become involved in the social activities; where the teacher has no connection with their parents. Nobody is going to tell them [the parents] about it [their behavior]. These kids can be gone for three months and not go to school, and the damn school is not going to say a fucking word to the parents. Do you understand what I am saying? That is the damnable part of it. Shit!

We are told we have no control over it. Nothing. Go to the white man. The white man will take care of you.

JORDAN: [Pauses] I have just one or two more questions. I have read novels in which a white woman has depicted a black female protagonist. Do you know of any black women novelists who have depicted a white female protagonist?

WILLIAMS: Ann Petry, in A Country Place or The Narrows. I'm not sure which one. Alice Walker and Toni Morrison have also depicted major, white female characters. No others come to mind offhand. We really need to do that [portray whites] so that white people know not only how we look to ourselves but how they look to us. You're not going to bring about racial harmony and understanding by talking about only one side of the equation. We have some real thoughts, some real feelings, and some real ideas about white people in this country, and they need to know what those things are. James Baldwin said years and years ago that, in a lot of ways, we know these people better than they know themselves. Until they know what we know about them they are going to continue to rape the goddamn world and we can't afford that. We have got to force them to look into the mirror of our faces and to see themselves.

JORDAN: Which brings me to my next question, which you probably just answered. What do you think about the particular responsibilities of the black critic in shaping the ways our literature is read, assessed, and taught?

WILLIAMS: That is an interesting question because I know that there is that responsibility, but I hadn't thought about it in its particulars. I think—for me—that a lot of what's happening with the criticism—what blacks are doing with Afro-American literature—is a most exciting thing. I continue to feel very lucky to be alive at this moment and to be a writer at this moment because I think

it's the first time in our history that we really have had the opportunity to develop a real criticism that talks specifically about the
aesthetics and dynamics of our work. And I think that is very important. But I think there is a very real danger that our criticism
will become so academically inclined that instead of leading black
readers to us, it in fact shuts them out. Most black academic critics
are trying to perform in the same way that other, mainly white,
academic critics perform. White people have layered criticism so
that it doesn't matter in any real way because it doesn't reach, because it turns off, the mass audience in its original form. The impact of academic criticism has been mediated by the newspapers,
television, and film so that the current stress is on philosophy and
linguistics, and not on aesthetics or dynamics. The academic critics are not concerned with contemporary literature. So, if they
want to go and use all these Frenchmen who want to take language
out there and all that kind of stuff, that is fine for them, but we
need a criticism that shows you can do the same thing with black
literature as you can do with that old seventeenth-century stuff
(and have a lot more fun because it's about today and what's going
on now), and we also need to be developing a kind of popular criticism, that in fact is intended for the masses of black people. And
when I say that, I mean for black people yes who are literate but
who don't really care whether the narrative has been deconstructed
or reconstructed, but who are interested in the story and what it
means for their lives. And part of the difficulty is that we just don't
have the kinds of outlets for the kinds of criticism that are available
up and down that critical ladder to white people. We have few
newspapers. By and large we have very, very few journals and certainly only one or two of national distribution. We just don't have
those kinds of outlets, so when you go to conferences, the people in
the audience are primarily white. So, again, despite the fact that
we finally have a criticism, we are talking or we seem to be talking
primarily to white people. I think that the real thing is to have a
criticism or at least have a part of the general criticism that is di-
rected very specifically toward black people to let them know what
the literature is and to encourage them to read it so that they can
understand that these people are in fact talking about their lives
and that it is not something that—because it is in a book—has no
relationship to them.

**JORDAN:** How do you draw upon our oral tradition in your
work—the blues, folk tales, folk sayings?

**WILLIAMS:** A writer draws upon the tradition of storytelling, of sounds, of words, and people playing with words, and all of that. That is still going on today, showing a continuity that in fact it's a part of our lives, and it is so intrinsic that you can't get away from it. I think that when black people see that in a work they are seeing themselves in a way that they haven't before and that they come to value about themselves these things. It's not some strand that is going to pass out of fashion after one or two years and stuff like that. It's an abiding part of our lives.

**JORDAN:** It is so difficult to help students understand that black dialect should be appreciated. They are extremely ashamed. As soon as you mention Black English, they say immediately "I don't speak that way."

**WILLIAMS:** In some ways I do understand. I've been working with black speech, and I've been trying to work with that consciously for a long time. When I first started out in teaching, it seemed to me that if, for example, I could get people to see or to look at their own speech and to see what they were doing, it would help them to learn Standard English much better. I had an experience while I was working at Miles College in Birmingham, Alabama, with an adult education class. I was there in the mid-sixties, and I had a little adult education class and these people could do wonders on those form tests where you fill in the blanks and all that kind of stuff. They had that stuff down pat but ask them to write a sentence, not even a paragraph. It was really bad so I started trying to work with their own speech, taking paragraphs from what they had actually said and reproducing them and then asked them to write those same paragraphs in Standard English. And these grown people tried to get me fired. They complained that I was not teaching them English; I was trying to teach them how to speak broken English. And I kept saying "But look! you seem to do well on these little form tests, but you cannot write and the reason you cannot write is because you don't pay any attention to the way you speak." So it is not just the children that you are working against but the grown-ups as well who have said, "I didn't come here to learn that. I come to learn the good stuff, the right stuff. So I have, by law, stopped speaking about "black dialect." I talk about black *speech*.

# RITA WILLIAMS-
# GARCIA

■

*Rita Williams-Garcia wrote her first novel,* Blue Tights *(1988), in 1979 when working with a sorority reading project for girls fourteen to sixteen who were reading below the fourth-grade level. Her second novel,* Fast Talk on a Slow Track *(1991), has received several citations and awards; most notably a PEN Literary Citation for realistic portrayal of African-American teen experiences, the 1991 Parents' Choice Award, and a recommendation by the National Council of*

*Christians and Jews. Her third novel,* Like Sisters on the Home-front, *is currently in press.*

*Rita Williams-Garcia is currently at work on her first adult novel and a biography of Queen Latifah, perhaps the best-known female rap artist in the music industry. She lives in Jamaica, New York, with her husband and two daughters.*

**JORDAN:** What specific conditions seem to be in place when black and white women become friends?

**WILLIAMS-GARCIA:** I can only speak personally. Though I am friendly by nature, I have an innate suspicion of white people. I listen sometimes too carefully. Though I have many relationships both working and social with white women, I put my trust on reserve. It takes a lot for me to be friends. For me, trust and a willingness to share and respect must be mutual. My friendship with Antonia, a white woman on my job, is a joy and a sanctum because of our openness. We definitely do not see things the same—how can we?—but we listen to each other. Our openness and friendship comes out of shared oppression: We want to quit our jobs and do our artistic thang. We grew up during the same times and remember the same things, so we're always witnessing and referencing when we talk, which can be for hours. We don't agree on many things, but we remain open. She has become a very real person to me. Racist of me, isn't it? Intellectually and morally I know that we are all people, but my instinct does not naturally relate to them as real red-blooded spiritual beings. My Christian background tells me we're all God's children, but my immediate perception of them is as types. They don't become real people until I get past the superficial relationship. Antonia is real to me. She forces me, just in the nature of her being, to open my eyes. We break through the barriers and find that we have things in common. Real things.

**JORDAN:** It's working through the barriers to see commonalities. What kind of role does the black female play in white women's novels? What kind of role does the white female play in black women's novels?

**WILLIAMS-GARCIA:** From the books I've read, the black woman is usually supportive in some way to the white woman or the white girl. No matter how the black character is presented in those instances I still see shades of Mammy. The subordinate. I'm especially concerned about this in young adult literature.

**JORDAN:** But what kind of role does the white female play in black women's novels?

**WILLIAMS-GARCIA:** It depends upon the time period of the novel. Right now I'm reading a lot of early American fiction—which for us is the nineteenth century. In those novels the white woman is portrayed in one of two roles. She is either helpless and powerless in a white man's world, or she is blinded by her own racist cruelty. In both portrayals, the white woman is someone who is served by the black woman or black child. In contemporary literature, however, the superior/subordinate roles are confronted, like in Morrison's *Tar Baby*. You're seeing more reversals and deeper character exploration of both sides, as in Walker's *Meridian*.

Interestingly enough, there is very little fiction—from either black or white women authors—about the status of white women and blacks during colonial and precolonial America. Many white women were indentured servants, and their whiteness did not save them from being oppressed by their male counterparts. Dig, John Q. Pilgrim had no problem sprinkling a little salt over Jane Q. Pilgrim and having him some salted wife during Starving Time. So, in the beginning, gender and not race was more of an issue. In early America you had a lot of intermarrying of white and black indentured servants. There was a commonality among indentured servants who lived together, worked side by side, were of the same class. But once race was used to justify slavery, and slaves were not of a "human" class but deemed property, the white woman, regardless of class, had to be protected against the black beast. When the indentured class was phased out, that bond between the two races of that class was phased out as well.

**JORDAN:** To what extent does class make a difference in relationships?

**WILLIAMS-GARCIA:** Class has a tremendous effect on relationships. People of the same class tend to have similar backgrounds, experiences, priorities. I think women seek others with similar educational background, family structures, parenting styles, goals, and interests to form their social and friendship bonds. Exchange is spontaneous and varied when you speak the same language through shared experiences. I don't have too much in common with the women I work with. They're younger, they're marketing execs, they read bodice-rippers or horror novels, they're into their single lives, and are mostly white. Besides that superficial blasé blasé, what do we have in common? Well, there's this white woman on my job who never says a non-work-related word to anyone, black, white, or green. Systems analyst. She's real intense. One day she saw my books and my posters in my office on medieval poetry—I'm really getting into Spenser—and now we have this connection. We can talk pastorals and epics till we lose our jobs! I'm sure economically we're not in the same class. In the forties her mother was an advertising exec, and mine was a domestic. But education and a shared interest in poetry made a bridge.

JORDAN: Have you noticed some subtle distinctions between the way black women authors portray characters and the way white women portray them?

WILLIAMS-GARCIA: I think black women authors accept ugly as a necessary shading on character. Ever see a baby being born? Blood, slime, sac, feces. I think black women authors treat characters starting with that reality. I think white women authors start with the character cleaned up, still needing to crawl, but nonetheless cleaned up. I think black women authors can appreciate ugly. Philosophers say truth is beauty. No, no. Truth is ugly; it is hard to look at. You know black women authors always got their eye on what you don't want to see. When I see the picture of Toni Morrison in *I Dream a World*, I see the eye of a storm, which reminds me that Morrison finds beauty in the most ugly, wrenching things. She does not spare us in taking us into that truth. I think that's how black women authors portray our characters. The women do not fare well. Neither do the men.

I remember reading *The Awakening* when I was in high school. I didn't want to hear all that white stuff. Besides, I couldn't believe this Edna person was in pain, because there were no guts lying on the floor. It sounded like a lot of whining to me, a fifteen-year-old with an attitude. And then, it [the novel] was very civil, which was boring. I judge everything by my mama. When Miss Essie is up against it, the whole world knows! Anyway, this Edna person was just whining in my ear. I could barely sit through another fifty pages of "Jane doing Jane's thing" : "Oh, what shall I do? What shall I do?" Now, however, as a woman with children, who does not own herself fully, I respect *The Awakening*. I treasure it. *Mrs. Dalloway* struck the same nerve. It was Jane having too much leisure time on her hands. When I read those books back in 1973, I couldn't respect them because they were about women who didn't know what to do with themselves. Women with relative comfort, no less. So, when my teacher told the girls in the class, "This is going to be a very important book for you one day" I knew she wasn't talking to me. She told me, "Keep this book," anticipating that I would change my mind. *The Awakening* isn't as high up on my shelf as *Their Eyes Were Watching God*, but it's up there.

**JORDAN:** But now we're back to the commonalities in experience that bind us regardless of color. We all make choices and we understand what that process entails and can mean in how we live our lives. To what extent do you use sources such as biographies, autobiographies, or histories in developing your characters?

**WILLIAMS-GARCIA:** Initially, to very little extent do I use source materials. The characters always get born before the story. The character will, when I'm least prepared, shout something in my ear and that's that. I have to follow whatever they've revealed to me. I do use source material more for supporting characters, who must leave strong impressions in little time. For example, Denzel's father in *Fast Talk* is not someone I have immediate access to. I went back twenty-five years to see what kind of eighteen-year-old he was. I read magazines, and newspapers. Reread *Soul on Ice*. Listened to music. I looked for written materials that might have the flavor or feel of how people spoke. Not to mimic, but to understand. I may not directly use 95 percent of what I've compiled, but it all goes into building the character from the soul on up.

**JORDAN:** White women have often written novels with black female protagonists or certainly major characters. But the reverse happens less often. Would you comment on this phenomenon? Do you think this pattern will remain the same, or will black women start portraying white female protagonists a bit more frequently?

**WILLIAMS-GARCIA:** Black women are not writing about Jane in the first person because the urgency is not there. I get this surge of energy just after I have my characters down, and their purpose is apparent. That energy comes from urgency. I'm just dying to tell my story. Can't wait to put it down on paper and watch it take shape. Got something to say and the right somebody to tell it to. Pen gonna be smoking 'cause it's time this story gets told. I get excited because of the creative aspect, and mainly because I'm telling a piece of our story. Mind you, just a piece of it. There's so much out there that must be told. Explored. Too many emerging black women's voices, forgotten voices, suppressed voices out there.

Now, you can pick up a book, any book, and find Jane. Jane is everywhere. I remember, as a sixth grader, reading *Mary Ellis, Student Nurse* about fifteen times because that was the only book in the library that had a black female protagonist besides Harriet Tubman. I asked the library for a book with some color. After all, it was 1968, the school was 98 percent black. She gave me a book about a black protagonist from Africa. A girl who would rather go out and hunt with her father than tend the garden with her mother. That book became my Bible. Then in 1970, I graduated to *Soul Brothers and Sister Lou*. Had to read that every day too. Now, there's a whole resurgence in black literature. Lost treasures are being rediscovered. More black women writers are coming forth in a variety of voices. Everyone from grandma to homegirl is reading.

I just don't have the urgency to sing Jane's song. That might change. For me, no time soon.

Though, I can see why the reverse is happening. White women writers are intrigued by women outside of their class and culture. I think white women are looking for themselves in other women and finding there's something that they can connect with. I think that's mainly because their images have been controlled and shaped by their white male counterparts. They do not accept those sexist types. I think when they see women who are not so bound by those images they see resilience. Little do they know. . . . Take birthing. White women are fascinated by women's attitudes on sex, and giving birth outside of Puritanistic male-dominated society. They go off and get renewed by some basic woman grunting in the bush pointing their bellies to the moon, and Jane's got a new craze. I think the same thing happens when they write through a black character. They're trying to find parts of themselves in other women.

**JORDAN:** We will follow up a little later on the character of Joyce. Let's continue with a more general question. What can black and white women teach each other about living and about writing?

**WILLIAMS-GARCIA:** We can start by being open for the learning experience. "That's not Jane, Rita. Like you, she has a name, a mind, a past, and a few good ideas."

Now see, I'm saying that, but I'm struggling with believing that fully. Nobody wants to admit their biases, but I grew up with them ground in. You know the right answer, but true change is no easy trick.

My impressions of black women grow out of what I observe within my family, in my neighborhood, on the job. There is something about us that is different than other women. I have always felt that black women have a competency issue. A common-sense issue. No one applauds when you look up childrearing strategy in a book or call the pediatrician every five minutes. But you get that nod when you use some common sense and do what you know better. Being helpless, needing much assistance, and being in a panic are not respected. Even today, a career woman is only fully respected when she's got her domestic routine together. An incompetent woman is not cute. Woman is a badge of honor. A woman is supposed to be competent in all domestic and social arenas. She don't have to be correct, but as long as she moves on some common sense, she is respected. Woman is a title to aspire to. A mother is always quick to remind her daughter "There's only one woman in this house," but in the same breath, expect daughter to perform womanly duties in the household. A lot of thirteen-year-old girls wanting to stretch their wombs into forever to jump into the role of woman.

I will never forget this scene I observed. I was standing in line at KFC because it was too hot to cook. The mother was in line ahead of me and her daughter who had to be four years old—she could not have been five—was sitting at a table feeding her baby brother out of a jar. She held that baby expertly and was working that spoon and dribble cloth with precision. You could tell she was not feeding her doll, she was not having fun or enjoying this little treat of "I'm playing Mommy." She was Mama, and that's the problem: girls with no childhood being competent women before they're girls. And if we can learn something from Jane, it's to let our girls be girls. Let's encourage them to discover themselves, to have childish dreams.

**JORDAN:** I see women reach back after the fact to try and recapture that girlhood when I would think it's much too late to recapture it.

**WILLIAMS-GARCIA:** My five-year-old daughter invents mousetraps, has a kid husband, and wants to be a policeman, a nurse, and a writer. She's curious about everything, giggles about everything, is afraid of everything. Every day is a new adventure. She's a girl. A kid. Now, the kids in her class are more mature, if you want to call the absence of wonder maturity. Sometimes I have to tell her to leave her fantasies and inventions at home so the other kids will not make fun of her. We encourage her imagination but sometimes I have to break her heart before they do it. As black parents living in a black community, we have to give her a little armor. I want her to have all the stages. Not just be a baby woman, a grown woman with something missing. We cheat ourselves out of our girlhood. We cheat ourselves out of developing into wholes. You really can't go back. See, people really missed *For Colored Girls*, entirely. Really missed the point. Shange tells you right from the start. "Visions of never having been a girl . . . scattered half notes." Why do you think it's *For Colored Girls* and not *For Black Women*? One is whole and one is missing something. Girlhood. When we force our daughters to jump those stages we are contributing to their underdevelopment.

**JORDAN:** It's breaking my heart, but I also know that that's the reality. Do you envision black women becoming more integrated into the women's movement as common concerns such as child care and abortion bring women of all races closer?

**WILLIAMS-GARCIA:** All women must unite. As long as women and children are second-class citizens, we have to unite. We may not be heads of corporations, the majority on the Supreme Court, the majority of the Senate. What we do have is our bodies. What we better start exercising is our voices. We have to vote. Men will shoot off missiles for freedom, justice, and the pursuit of happiness; the least we can do is vote for ours. Freedom, justice, pursuit of happiness. Sounds pro-choice to me. If the women's movement offers the opportunity to present a united front in terms of numbers—that's what they respect—they'll kiss toes and make all kinds of pro-choice noises for votes—then we all must come together so that our issues are addressed.

I was never really much for the feminist movement when it started jumping off at the tail end of the sixties. To me, it didn't seem like it was about women of all classes and races, circumstances coming together for women's rights. It sounded like Jane wanting the privilege to work, ho' around with reputation intact, wanting to be more than secretary and have the right to wear pants in the office. I saw black women sneaking to their night jobs to keep up the pretense of "my man won't let me work." I saw black women who didn't want to wear the pants in the family, but [were] unable to take them off. Jane was looking for fulfillment beyond wife, mother, and office wife. But the black woman's struggle for place and fulfillment was different because her family structure and relationship with her man was different.

I'm looking at the women's movement twenty years later and what I'm seeing is women concerned about the planet. Making sure there is an earth, and that we're here, sane, and whole for the twenty-first century. Got to be the women, because the men of power aren't really looking to the earth's future. No capital gain in that. But women, on the whole, are concerned that humankind has a home. I think women have a different view of legacy for future generations.

**JORDAN:** When you look at young children and teenagers who often do not know their own family histories and do not have or know the words to voice their experiences or what they see, what kinds of things ought to be done to help them gain control over their own voices to appreciate their stories and their personal histories?

**WILLIAMS-GARCIA:** As mothers, aunts, grandmothers, we must take the time to pass on stories and remembrances of kin. It's so simple. We, my generation, must sit down and relate the past to our children, by first touching the past. Talking to our mothers, grandmothers, older people in the neighborhood. Then sharing with our children. Little ears and eyes become so fascinated with family history, trivia, and family traditions. They're at that age. The schools can help by bringing grandparents and great-grandparents into the classrooms, particularly in kindergarten classes, while that child-grandparent bond is special. Black children need to hear about black traditions and historical contributions firsthand from sources of love and wisdom.

Adolescents have different needs. They really don't want to be told. They know. Therefore, they need to express themselves. Here's some Jesse for ya: They need more forms of expression and less forms of oppression. [*Laughs*] All of these little acts of hostility you see around you—the graffiti, the cussing, the obnoxious behavior—come from a need for self-expression. When I went to Ohio, the kids there were involved in a writing program where they were the authors of their own books, telling their own experiences. I hope the books were not censored. The kids tried to clothe the works with pseudonyms, but the stories were their own. Self-revelations emerged from their works. Revelations that would have remained submerged had the students not been forced to sit down and write. They wrote everything from rap, poetry, fiction, soap operas, comic books—you name it. They were proud authors. Guardians. Some of them truly brave. Their tough little faces would soften when that bound portfolio was placed in their hands with their byline on the cover. "Did I write that? Is that me?" Then they read it. Confronted themselves. It's very difficult to go back and do all those negative things that you've been doing when you have this little bit of control. Writing helps put these kids in touch with what they feel and with what they have the potential to control.

**JORDAN:** Do you see literary critics, particularly black ones, as having a special role in the ways stories of black women's lives are read, assessed, and taught?

**WILLIAMS-GARCIA:** You better believe it. All I ask of critics of adult literature is to remember your role: *literary* critic. Respect the literature. The work of black women writers is not just "womb letting," and superwoman cape-flagging. Trace the literary root of the work. Throw out some references so that a non-black educator will have a framework to build a lesson on other than, "My, what strong women they are." Then maybe more than the six black novels that teachers are comfortable with will be taught, if the critics would toss a literary bone to those who respect their opinions.

With black young adult books, critics want to know two things only: is it a positive little story and is the character a positive little role model. Tell you what . . . my newspaper and my window says young people are in a crisis. What they read must be commensurate with their lives. The kids that I write for listen to rap music. That hard-core stuff. Tiptoeing around sex is ridiculous when fourteen-year-old girls deliver their own babies and stuff them into garbage cans. I believe the homegirls can handle a little prose in the "for real" tense. See, I love the kids I write for. As they are. Not how I'd like to package them up.

I try not to read too many reviews. Those critics don't understand who I'm writing for. But you know, they decide whether the librarians are going to buy my hardcovers or not. Kids don't take their hang-out money to buy hardcovers. It's frightening that someone who does not know my audience has so much say.

**JORDAN:** What is the responsibility of the reader, if any, in the creative process?

**WILLIAMS-GARCIA:** Think! Think! Please think! That's all I ask. Don't come to my books in a catatonic state anticipating formula teen sap. I don't do those series. You know. The captain of the team likes the popular rich girl but then the "substantial" gets him anyway and that makes her life wonderful. I don't do those, and I don't do the wronged black child who rises above her/his racist tormentors to gain a greater triumph. Shades of William Blake. No thank you. I write about real kids who must face themselves. All I ask of my readers is that they be open and think. That's basically it. Bring something to it.

I think we're going back to the critics question. This is what happens with *Blue Tights*. My editor is a white woman. She conferred with one of her black colleagues on an issue because she was uncertain about it. Joyce is in honors classes but Joyce doesn't feel comfortable there. The black editor says, "My kids are in honors classes; they've not had a problem." I thought to myself, "No? How can you miss the fact that Joyce does not feel comfortable anywhere?" Joyce's self-esteem is so low that when she gets the part for the African dance queen, she thinks: "Oh, they're not going to like me." Joyce will take anything positive and turn it into a negative because she feels ugly about herself. Now why is she going to all of a sudden feel wonderful about being in classes that are predominately white and predominately Jewish, where the kids talk about what went down at the B'Nai Brith meeting? Please don't walk away from the characters because you think it's more important to make a general statement about black intelligence. That's disrespecting the character. Joyce is simply a person with very low self-esteem, and her behavior is always consistent with her self-perception. Why would it all of a sudden be something else? I got reviewed by someone who felt that there was too much attention being paid to Joyce's sexuality. Too much gratuitous sex, especially when she gets into the car with the older man. After all, girls don't go through those kinds of things. Well, Joyce is so starved for any kind of love that she'll take it from whoever, even when she knows better. She's learned that her body has value. Men tell her this when she walks down the street. She figures "I know I'll have to do this someday so I might as well get it over with." This is her attitude. Her self-imposed reality.

I have a lot of faith in readers. I'm not going to throw in a guidance-counselor-type character to narrate Joyce's bad choices for the readers. They are smart enough to pick them out as they read along. Just because I write in simple terms and simple images doesn't mean I want to write down for my reader.

**JORDAN:** Have you ever felt pressure from your publisher and/or editor or audience to portray a particular kind of character or to treat a particular set of themes or have you remained free of such concerns?

**WILLIAMS-GARCIA:** My editor is very concerned about the way that my books are perceived. Of course, she is. If my books are not perceived well, they don't sell. But if I come up with that NAACP Image Award equivalent, or that Coretta Scott King Award then I will have more rope. I won't have to fight so hard for this little raw thing Joyce says. Well, I've already told my editor, "I will not be winning any Corettas." I do feel pressure in having to prove myself. "Okay, Rita, we gave you your chance with these 'no apologies' characters and they're just not selling." When books are returned, I worry.

Then I go to schools and meet these kids. "How do you know this?" The girls all think they're Joyce. Yes. Even the white ones. They scribble little notes to me because they're too embarrassed to say "This really happened to me." That's all I need to keep going. I suppose I could write through a more admirable character, but I don't think kids learn from people who aren't involved in self-struggle. My characters will always be involved in self-struggle, as opposed to external struggle. Now, my character Denzel doesn't think he's engaged in self-struggle. He's too full of himself to see this. But you know, he's as commonplace as the mailman. We know him when we see him. We just don't see enough of him, or other complex characterizations in novels aimed at black teens. It's a shame. When you ask young people why they don't read, they shrug. That shrug says the books are not hitting on the true experiences of young black people. I think my window is my saving grace. I look out of it constantly and see the kids I write about. As long as they're out there I'll continue to write for them as I see them.

**JORDAN:** Is there ever a role or function for a stereotype in fiction? Perhaps to introduce the reader to a character or to expose the danger of such attitudes?

**WILLIAMS-GARCIA:** Yes. Sometimes length is an issue. You have to establish concrete figures immediately. The work may not allow this character to be more than a stock character. I consider Lydia in *Fast Talk* to be a stock character. She is the quintessential post-sorority deb, with a strong middle-class professional ethic. Her attitude and motions are all centered around this. She is a minor figure in *Fast Talk*, because she's only in a few scenes. However, she's an important figure because you understand Denzel's ability to play social chameleon is inherited from Lydia. Now, among us in the community, Denzel is a highly recognizable figure. We all know about young men who can trace themselves back to the divine. I would hardly call him a stereotype. Main characters cannot be stereotypes. A stereotype is committed in the mind of the reader as following a predetermined path. How boring that must be to have to read through such a character! Let alone write. I don't like those kinds of characters, although I've used them. Cindy and Jay Jay in *Blue Tights* are stereotypes. They're both nothing else but bitches. That's all. It serves a purpose, but as characters they're not fun to write because they're not real.

**JORDAN:** Was storytelling a part of your growing-up experience and, if so, how has it affected your writing?

**WILLIAMS-GARCIA:** I wish I could say it was, but that wasn't the case. Now, I would entertain myself and tell some stories . . . but you know, I was always hiding somewhere listening in on the grown folks talking. I remember full conversations they'd have after funerals, weddings, and other instances. I never understood what they were talking about. They spoke in codified grown talk. But every now and then I'll pull something out from memory and play it back to see if I'm yet grown enough to comprehend the world of adults. These snatches of hushed adult talk continue to find their way into my stories.

**JORDAN:** How would you describe Joyce's "love interest" with Sam versus Andre? Are they part and parcel of the same thing?

**WILLIAMS-GARCIA:** From Sam, Joyce gets that father figure. She wants to be Daddy's girl. She wants the love of someone who can protect her from the men on the street, someone who can make her feel like a little girl. This older male figure represents this to Joyce. He knows this and pushes all the right buttons. He asks her how her day was. She's more in need than she is naïve. She knows there's a price to pay for all of his concern and she's almost willing to pay it. Thank God a bell goes off in her head that says "Something's not right here. He don't love me like he loves his daughter." It's really when he mentions his daughter that things start to click. After all, she really wants a father figure.

Andre epitomizes the ideal of a lover. Her mother has already told her, "Well, it's not love unless he has green eyes." How many of us tell our kids some such nonsense? "Does she have nice hair?" We train our kids to look for superficiality. Well, Andre looks the part. Then later, she gains a better perspective and is able to see both Sam and Andre in the same light. It's not until she's able to see this that she can walk away.

**JORDAN:** But I see women in their thirties, nearly forty, maturing into middle age who are no more emotionally developed than Joyce.

**WILLIAMS-GARCIA:** Oh sure. We have inherited some really strange ideas about what makes a good mate. We also have strange ideas about fulfillment. You can no more get fulfillment from another person than we can get it out of a can. Little something my husband told me. It's true. I think what I'm saying to the Joyces out there is old, and goes for the Minnies [grown women]. The great hunt for love must start from within. Told you it was old.

**JORDAN:** For every Joyce who does not succumb to a Sam, there are so many more who do. Why do so many girls, later women, so quickly turn to such demeaning, self-destructive relationships?

**WILLIAMS-GARCIA:** You have to know you're worth something to want something better. Someone like Joyce lives on the words of others. Lives on the value that others assign to them. They cannot grasp anything of value because they don't start with a value of self. Your esteem demands a standard that you must uphold—I'm speaking morally and spiritually. That's kind of hard to do when you set your sights on black men in a rather limited pool. What about that generation of men who did not come back from the Vietnam War, or did not come back whole? And the next generation of men locked out of society by drugs, street life, and prison? The pickins are poor. So, what do you do? You compromise. You overlook. Or you look for other. You put up with too much shit. The stuff in the psychology books sounds good, but it don't exactly tickle your toes or warm you up on a cold winter night.

**JORDAN:** Joyce's father remains a shadow, at best lurking in the background of her life. But still Minnie, her mother, has some unresolved conflict concerning him. How would you describe this unresolved tension that's still there?

**WILLIAMS-GARCIA:** That's a very contrived portion of the story. What I'm saying to the Joyces out there is, one day you'll see the person whom you so easily traded away your girlhood to and you will not be a part of his life—even though you have his child. His life will not include or consider you in the least, but your life revolves around the life he gave you. Hopefully, you won't regret your children, but you always ponder your choices. Joyce's father was just one of Minnie's poor choices. I don't think she still loves him. I think it haunts her that he has no idea what he's taken from her. Or more accurately, what she's given up. It's all about choices. In many instances we can choose what happens to us.

**JORDAN:** Religion plays a central role in two characters' lives—J'had and Aunt Em. How would you describe their uses of religion?

**WILLIAMS-GARCIA:** Thank you for asking! Just as Sam and Andre shared an interchangeable role, Aunt Em and J'had are also interchangeable. Religion has saved them both; one from being a street thug and the other from an unforgivable act—unforgivable only to the character. The difference is J'had is more nurturing to Joyce. Em means to be nurturing, but cannot be truly giving because of her own tragedy. Instead of having compassion, she spouts religion. She is so filled with shame and guilt that she passes it on to Joyce. "Those men look at you because you're not a good girl.

Get down on your knees and pray." J'had says the same thing: "You say you want respect, but are you worthy? Sister, look at the way you are dressed. A man has but to look at you and see every secret of your body." When Joyce gets offended he tries another route: "Sister, your body is like a jewel. That is only for your husband's eyes." Same message, different melody. That's the one thing Aunt Em couldn't do. She couldn't say, "Come here, baby," and explain in a less judgmental tone what men are responding to. "Get on your knees and pray." Because Joyce's need for love and acceptance is so great, she is receptive to J'had. But both "ministers" tell Joyce to accept some responsibility in her moral behavior and her appearance. Both are saying make a change. Ironically, both ministers are in need of healing.

**JORDAN:** There's a passage when J'had walks Joyce home, and the mother is enraged. Later Joyce is able to tell Minnie about the failed "relationship" with J'had, and Minnie says, "I love you, baby." How would you characterize the relationship between Minnie and her daughter? In many ways, Minnie is one of those women who has missed childhood.

**WILLIAMS-GARCIA:** The first time Minnie slaps Joyce it is because she herself was being slapped by both premonition and reality. Her then twelve-year-old sanitary-wearing woman-child has forced her into a role she has not fully grown into—mother. I believe she is afraid that Joyce will be every bit as hardheaded and womanish as she was. She sees her daughter making every mistake she's made, and she wants to spare her from every pain. Of course it comes out wrong.

Joyce idolizes her mother. Since Aunt Em was Joyce's guardian while Minnie was absent, Joyce treasures every minute she has with her mother. But just as Joyce worships her mother, she is also resentful of Minnie. Joyce's well-being and self-worth are tied into Minnie who is never there. Unlike Minnie, Joyce does not have a ballet dancer's body. She doesn't have a boyfriend, so how can she get pregnant and prove herself a woman? How will she measure up to her mother?

Both mother and daughter are missing parts of each other. Unless they reach out to each other, they will never be whole, in the sense of having certain qualities to pass onto generations of daughters. Qualities that encourage self-fulfillment. We so much have our eye on womanhood we forget that we must be girls first. Many generations ago we had very little choice about our own development. In this day and age we actually have choice. Minnie wants her daughter to realize her choices, but like many parents who speak from hardheaded experience she cannot articulate this in a nurturing way.

**JORDAN:** Tamu tells Joyce that some of the female dancers are jealous. Do you think that jealousy tends to keep us apart as women, and how do we deal with it? How does the woman who has an unhealthy dose of jealousy get rid of it?

**WILLIAMS-GARCIA:** You know, my mentor told me jealousy zaps your youthful oils. I believe that. We would do better to take the energy we expend in cultivating envy and to focus that energy on ourselves. The same energy we expend stewing over a sister who dresses better, is more articulate, has too many male friends, has a longer job title, can be spent reevaluating our own approach. Trying something new. Looking up helpful, healing information. We really must be better sisters to one another. We need to seek each other out. This is at the core of *For Colored Girls*. Healthy relationships with our mates and children will not spring from unhealthy roots. We must heal personally, spiritually, and trust the sister in each other. I believe Hispanic women have sisterhood down pat. They all become surrogate mothers to each others' children. The roles of aunt and godmother are highly respected, especially by the child's mother. They respond to each others' needs as women almost intuitively. For black women it is very hard. We are conditioned to be competitive. We are suspicious of each other, of our sisters' good intentions, of our cheeriness. It is difficult to approach domestic relationships in fiction without acknowledging the unhealthy root. Reaching out must happen. Acknowledging and questioning certain behavior patterns must happen. Now, I don't mean making yourself crazy with perpetual self-analysis and getting tied to some psychological guru the way Jane does. You know, there's a white woman on my job who will make a statement, apologize for it, explain the history of her self-consciousness and then apologize for that! What I'm talking about is stopping, and questioning our behavior when patterns emerge. "Why do I behave this way to so-and-so? What do I gain by this behavior? What is really bothering me? What steps can I take with help or on my own?" We can start with little things. Smiling at each others' children. Practicing our spirituality. I mean, is there a religion out there that says "Every woman for herself"? "You're better than your sister—make sure you let her know this." Me? I'm amazed how many women out there look just like my sister, my mother, myself. "We could be related" I always say to myself. Fool. You are related.

**JORDAN:** By the end of the novel, Joyce is closer to being in control of her life, not at the mercy of her friends or men. What advice would you offer young women such as Joyce who may not have that "star" performance that makes a difference between popularity and obscurity? How do they gain control?

**WILLIAMS-GARCIA:** Find something about yourself that you like. Something that does not fade with time and fashion. Take some time to fine-tune it and keep it close to your heart.

**JORDAN:** Interestingly enough, chapters 15 and 16 focus on Andre and Gayle and highlight Joyce's triumph in understanding her womanliness and her sexuality. Did you juxtapose those two chapters to point out an emerging Joyce who has really come into her own?

**WILLIAMS-GARCIA:** Yes. There's a terrible danger of being in the God role with the pen. You don't want to leave things unresolved. I just get too heavy-handed sometimes. I needed to say a few things to Joyce. First, I wanted her to feel how heavy that baby was to carry and for her to say "Thank God, that's not me. He's cute and I'll babysit, but I got things to do." I wanted her to feel that weight and to be able to say that. She is a primary candidate for the big-belly syndrome. "Even if I can't have him, I'll have his child to parade and love."

She had to get over Andre because even though she had come a long way, he was still the ideal lover. That kind of ingraining is not so easily removed. She has to really see him with different eyes.

**JORDAN:** Is the white dance teacher really racist as Joyce claims she is?

**WILLIAMS-GARCIA:** Joyce has tunnel vision; she can only see what she thinks is there. Is her teacher really a racist? Probably not. All we know is that Joyce is hurt, angry, and feels excluded. But we're not there when the teacher says she can't be in the showcase. We have to take Joyce's word for what the teacher says. I hint to the reader that Joyce is not always a reliable source. Joyce is also a lot more sensitive than the other girls. She turns everything into a negative and aims it at herself.

**JORDAN:** What makes her comment about the teacher suspicious is the line from her mother who asks Joyce, "Well, can you dance or not because I don't want to go down there fussing at those people for nothing," but Joyce doesn't follow up.

**WILLIAMS-GARCIA:** Later in chapter 10 or so, Joyce watches Mrs. Sobol rehearsing Merryl and she is amazed at how hard Mrs. Sobol is on her star pupil. Joyce thinks the teacher favors Merryl because she is white and has no hips. It never occurred to Joyce that Mrs. Sobol could find fault with Merryl. Then another student watching Joyce says, "You're good. Aren't you in the show?" Joyce turns around and runs because she cannot handle the compliment. I'm telling the reader not to trust Joyce; she can dance ballet, her teacher does not hate her, Merryl is not out to show her up. Joyce is just so good at jumping into her negative bag. It's comforting in there. Joyce doesn't realize the teacher is hard on her because she sees so much there. Hassan is as hard on Joyce as the white teacher, if not harder, but Joyce will take it because he's a daddy figure, and she wants to please. But then she retreats into her bag: "Oh, he doesn't really want me to dance the queen." She is true to her inadequacies.

**JORDAN:** I just thought of Denzel when you mentioned that. He's able to take criticism from certain teachers but not from others.

**WILLIAMS-GARCIA:** We all went to school with Denzel. When you have been praised as the young Socrates of the black community, you can't be told anything, and that's Denzel's problem. He has been elevated so high his growth is stunted.

**JORDAN:** Only a school like Princeton would make him think twice about himself. I'm sure if he were attending a Hampton University, he would just think that all niggers are crazy.

**WILLIAMS-GARCIA:** I think he would be in for a rude awakening at Hampton, being around so much black royalty. Who would kiss his crown?

Unlike Joyce, he must fall from the sky and hit the dirt before it starts getting real to him. He's so busy slicking everyone, he slicks himself. Won't ask for help, won't focus on his special needs as a young black man, but will yelp "de white man, de white man" like a wounded pup when he goes down failing.

Of the kids who've previewed the book, they all like the scene where Denzel gets beat up. They applaud. He must be leveled. Where Joyce has zero self-esteem, Denzel is just out of control. Just as Joyce must accept that she can succeed, he has to accept that he can fail, and that the point of failure is a good place to start learning something.

**JORDAN:** The scene in which Wendy explodes is extremely powerful and complex. Are there elements of truth in her accusations that Denzel had in fact been given his position, or is she saying whatever will hurt him? How would you describe her? She is a devoted friend.

**WILLIAMS-GARCIA:** Wendy is too devoted a friend. Denzel does not deserve her friendship. He has a long history of shitting on Wendy, and she's been a good old guy about it. He was her first sexual experience. He shrugs, she's mute. He talks her into being his vice-president of the student body instead of running against him as president. He ruins her prom night with no consideration to her. Are her accusations true? Did they really give him valedictorian honors over her because he was black, the school was black, and she was the lone white girl? Well, their grade difference is an eighth of a point. Of course race was a consideration. But if you know Denzel, in addition to race, it was his slew of impressive titles, his overall appeal. "How can we deny this young black man the valedictorianship?"

Wendy was just overdue for an explosion. When she says "You owe me something," you know she is not just talking about the prom.

**JORDAN:** Is Vernon's problem with Denzel's relationship to Wendy that Denzel actually takes Wendy seriously as opposed to seeing her as a flirt? After all, he tells Denzel of his earlier episodes with a white woman.

**WILLIAMS-GARCIA:** Yes. It bothers Vernon that Denzel says "This is my friend." If Denzel had said, "Yes, this is just my little white fling," they'd be passing stories back and forth.

**JORDAN:** Would you ever consider writing a novel from a white female character's point of view?

**WILLIAMS-GARCIA:** Wendy is a minor but vital character. Could I do a whole novel from Wendy's point of view on interracial dating? It wouldn't even occur to me. That's a book for someone else to write. Wendy satisfied opportunities to set up Denzel's pattern of behavior. He is intrigued only by challenge, and she is both white and his academic rival. Although she is his friend, he treats her badly. He does not honor his relationships because he does not honor their value.

**JORDAN:** Denzel is clearly uncomfortable with entering Princeton, but he pretends he is not. He has reaped the benefits of his civil rights–era parents, but here is another opportunity that he does not value.

**WILLIAMS-GARCIA:** Can you imagine! "Me, go through the back door of Princeton?" Denzel is so insulted by the very prospect of entering Princeton through a remedial or special admittance program that he does not take advantage of the opportunities he's being given. He would not have been given that chance unless he truly was Princeton material. I believe he is. He's just never really challenged himself or placed value in his academic gifts. We need such programs for our young people. We tell our children and students that college is nothing like high school. Those words are not enough. They really have to be confronted with the collegiate experience on some introductory level. Especially our bright students. They are not ready to make that crawling, learning motion. Freshmen undergo tremendous change in one semester. For the first time they must rely on their home training, their esteem, their judgment, their faith, and have no one to fall back on. That's when they start to find out who they are. We as parents can only assure them of our support and take comfort in the knowledge that we raised them well.